SISTERS

Sam K. Rodriguez
Sisters

Published by BooxAi
ISBN: 978-965-578-279-0

SISTERS

SAM K. RODRIGUEZ

CONTENTS

1

———

JARED BROOKS CAME FROM MONEY, the kind that went back generations. Jared had been raised with the finest nannies, and educated in the finest schools. He had been given every opportunity for success. He spent a few years in college, and from the looks of it spends family money and more time with friends than in class.

He understood that his life was very comfortable and that the ones who came before him worked so that he could reap the benefits. Jared had a bone deep need to be a part of making a difference. His mother was all about the charities, but to Jared that wasn't enough, nowhere near in fact.

His father had wanted him to follow in the footsteps that lead to the family wealth, in one area or another. Again, it didn't spark him, he wanted to do more. Jared had a kind heart, and always thought of others first. His mother made no secret that she disliked and didn't understand why her son acted that way, thought that way.

One of Jared's saving graces was a childhood friend, Andrew Abbot. They had known each other for as long as either could remember, becoming as close as brothers.

Andrew was like Jared raised with money, and what brought the two together so strongly was their absolute dislike for it. They were raised with the idea that money made you better than everyone and that you were above everything. It was an idea that even at a young age didn't sit well with either of them.

Together Jared and Andrew decided before college that they wanted to make a change and make a difference. After spending two years on associate degrees in criminal law, they told their friends and families they were going to spend the summer traveling abroad. Instead, Jared and Andrew joined and graduate from the police academy.

There was only one person there to watch both boys as they made the passage, he stood in the shadows. Ross Brooks hadn't believed it when his son had sat at the dining room table three months before and informed them, his parents that he was going to travel all summer. It hadn't taken much for Ross to track Jared down, and in all honesty, Ross hadn't been surprised by where he found his son.

After pulling weekends, holidays, every grunt job, and then some. Jared and Andrew had both made the step up to detective and were partnered with each other. They were starting their fifth year in the major crime unite.

Jared was sitting at his desk, wrapping up the paperwork, and looking for the next lead on their latest case. It seemed the harder they worked to wrap up the ones they had open the more came across their desk. Jared had to go to court that day as well. He glanced at the clock; Andrew was running late again which could only mean one thing.

Andrew was a man about town. He was always sweet talking the pretty girls, always looking for a good time. Jared had slowed down some coming onto his 31st birthday. He seemed to be spending more time at the desk then bellied up to the bar with Andrew.

Jared shook his head as his friend and partner came walking into the squad room and made his way to his desk.

"Glad you could join us today," Jared said not looking up.

"It's not what you think." Andrew shot back. His tone had Jared looking up from his paperwork. Andrew's light brown hair was all over the place, and his brown eyes were lit up with excitement.

"Oh, and what could it be?" Jared asked.

"You got plans next weekend?" Andrew sat at his desk, and shifted to his computer, turning it on to run through the morning routine.

"No, but that doesn't mean anything." Jared waved at his desk.

"Good, you're coming with me," Andrew said being a way to focus on watching his computer come to life for the day.

"Where?" Jared watched his friend, not sure if he should be worried or not.

"I have to participate in a wedding," Andrew said still not making eye contact with Jared. Jared who was about to take a sip of coffee stopped.

"Yours?" He smiled; Andrew was known for having a very strong abjection to marriage. In that, he flat refused to ever do it. Jared could not miss an opportunity to tease and watch his friend straighten his back.

"Funny but no, my cousin Eddie is getting married. He asked a while ago I told him to keep me as a backup. As it turns out he called this morning and I'm needed." Andrew then turned to Jared, a plead in his eyes. Jared thought about it, and let Andrew wiggle on the hook for a minute.

"Alright, I'm down. We're going to have to check the schedule to make sure we don't have weekend duty" Jared said, then turned back to the case in front of him. The room kept the buzz of finding and tracking leads, by mid-morning Jared's phone was in use so much he would hang up and it would ring the next second, he was in his grove when he picked his phone up on the next ring.

"Brooks."

"Jared." Jared froze and shut his eyes as his mother's voice rang in his ears.

"Hello, mother." He opened his eyes when his computer signaled an incoming email. With a quick glance, he noted that it was from the district attorney's office. He opened it, scanning though.

"Sweetheart, do you have lunch plans?" Helen asked.

"No, I don't have lunch plans," Jared said not even half listening to his mother. He pulled his attention from the email when a hand slammed on the desk across from him. He looked at Andrew with a what the hell look.

"Oh wonderful, what time should I pick you up?" Helen asked now having Jared's full attention. He closed his eyes as what he had agreed to sink in, Andrew could hear Helen through the phone and was smiling as he too checked his email.

"Well mother, I have court today," Jared said reaching for something, anything.

"We'll make it an early lunch, I'm right around the corner why don't we go now? What was that noise?" She asked.

"Andrew just dropped something on my desk," Jared said with his head down on the desk.

"Well, you're on the phone he doesn't need to be so rude," Helen said, Jared picked up on her tone.

"I'll be right out mother." He hung up before he said or agreed to anything else.

"You have fun with that," Andrew said from his pile of paperwork.

Jared stood and pulled his gun from the top drawer of his desk. Slid it into his holder as he turned back to the email.

"No court today moved to tomorrow." He said putting his phone in his pocket, then turned and walked out.

It wasn't that he didn't like his mother, she was just pushy. Always wanting information about what was going on in his life. She also had an opinion about every aspect of his life as well, how Andrew should be a better friend. For years she had tried to break the two boys up, insisting that Andrew was no good for her son.

Helen also thought it was her duty to find her son a wife. She had started setting up blind dates for him. Ross had quickly put a stop to that, but she had slipped in a few over the years. Jared's favorite of her attempts to keep a firm hand on his life came when she found out that he had joined the police force. She had tried everything she could think of to get him off the force and into the job she thought he should have.

One of her attempts had his captain pulling Jared into his office. It had been an interesting talk. The captain had asked if Jared wanted to leave, after Jared reassured him, he wanted to stay the captain had informed Jared just how far his mother had gone. Calling in a favor, the CEO of the top accounting firm had called for references. Jared had put a stop it her fiddling, and after the outright fight they had, she hadn't talked to him for a few months.

It had been one of the few times he had dug his feet in when it came to his mother. It however hadn't stopped her from trying to control the other aspects of his life.

The town car was parked across the street, and Jared slid in smoothly.

"Hello, mother." He said leaning in to kiss the check she offered.

"Hello dear, what time is court?" She asked looking back at the phone in her hand.

"I have an hour, maybe sooner if I get called." Jared prayed that Andrew called.

They had a system, one that was put in place when they were boys. They always helped get the other one out of having to do or be somewhere they didn't want to be. This lunch was no different, and if Andrew wanted Jared as backup for the wedding, he better makes the call to get him out of this lunch.

"Wonderful. We need to make a stop first. Have you heard of that little bakery off 2nd? Daisy something?"

"Sure, Daisy's Cakes. It's been around for a while, family owned. Can't say I know the family, or that I know how well the cakes are, why?" Jared asked.

"Your father's birthday is coming up and I'm looking for a better place to have the cake done. The last place I went to was completely horrible and I will never go to them again. If I have my way, it will be out of business in a matter of months" Helen said looking out the window.

"Dad's birthday is still a month or more away mother. When are you planning the party?" Jared asked looking at his mother.

"Eight weeks from now. Do you think you could arrange to make it?" She asked looking at him.

"We'll have to see." Jared looked out the window to see them pulled up to a little shop, with Daisy's Cakes in a white cursive on a black backing with three daisies along the bottom.

The car stopped and Jared got out. Standing he took in his surroundings, a quiet but busy part of town. He had been all over it in his years working the street, but he hadn't been to this shop before.

He walked up to open the door and held it for his mother, the bell and smell hit his senses, chime and sugar. He took in the space, the room opened in front of him, the register was in the middle, long counters ran both ways. Glass cabinets under them to display the wonderfully fresh baked goods offered. On the left was a wall of high glass cabinet devoted to chocolates, the back wall held shelves and black boards to tell prices and special, the right wall was glass like the front.

Jared's attention was moved from the room to the woman who came from a doorway behind the register. His heart skipped, her dark brown hair was pulled back into a bun, making her blue green eyes sparked like they had a happy secret, and her oval face brightened as she gave him a smile with her full lips. As he took her in, he noticed that she had a light flush in her checks that he assumed was from the heat of the ovens.

"Welcome to Daisy's cakes, how may I help you?" She asked, Jared felt something catch in him.

"I want to make an appointment for a tasting," Helen said using a nice tone, but her eye's held something else. Like a promise that if this girl didn't step right Helen was going to have her for lunch

"How much time do you have right now?" The woman asked, still smiling. Jared wondered if this girl knew what she was doing. Helen looked down at her watch.

"Ten minutes." Helen batted her lashes then smiled sweetly, to her mind it was just enough time for the girl to not be able to come up with something on the fly.

"Please have a seat, I'll be just a moment." She said as she waved to the table and chairs placed to the right of the door. Jared followed Helen, and pulled out her chair for her.

"I'll give her five, then we are leaving," Helen said once she was settled and looked around the room like it was coved in dirt when it was pristine.

Jared thought about the woman who had greeted them, she was young, and she was hot. Jared thought about asking for her number, but he was with his mother. That alone killed it, he would come back another time. He pulled his phone out as it signaled.

"Oh, Jared put it away." Helen scuffed.

"I can't mother you know that." It was a message from Andrew.

Need a life saver yet?

Ten more minutes.

Jared put his phone away as the young woman made her way back though the doorway caring a tray. She set it down on the table. On it were eight different cakes with a variety of fillings and frostings on eight different little plates, with two forks.

"These are our basics; however, we can make any combination you like. Please help yourself." She spoke.

The young lady watched as Helen picked up the first cake, and gave a quick description of it. Then turned to Jared who had chosen one and gave the description as well. She turned back to Helen just in time to watch Helen close her eyes as she got the full taste. The young lady tried to hide her smile, but one side pulled free. Jared hadn't missed it, then he tasted his bite, and all things wiped from his mind.

The soft, sweet cake melted in his mouth, the filling added a surprising tang, and all came together as the sharpened sweet frosting hit the taste buds.

"Oh my" Helen said, she quickly moved to take bite after bite from all eight. Stopping only to savor and enjoy, when she was done, she looked at the young women. "I would like all eight flavors; I want them done in an eight-tear style. I want simple, and elegant. All white- Do you need to write this down?" Helen asked when she saw the young woman make no movement to do so.

"I'm waiting for a date, if it's too close I'll have to decline your business." Jared coughed out a laugh, nobody ever talked to his mother that way, and with such a sweet smile.

"Do you know who I am?" Helen asked sitting up a bit straighter

"I'm sorry ma'am I don't, only because you haven't introduced yourself," the young lady said. Jared liked this girl, before Helen could answer Jared's phone went off. Pulling it out he checked it.

"Brooks" He answered then stood up to walk away from the women.

"Time man, need me to come get you?" Andrew asked.

"No, I'll be there." Jared turned back to the woman when he ended the call.

"Mother, I need to get back," Jared said walking back, from the body language Jared knew his mother would get her cake.

"Yes, dear of course." Helen looked to her son, then back to the young lady. "Do you have a card?" They watched as she walked over to the counter, pulled one off the top of the pile, and handed it to Helen. I'll be calling to finalize the details and decoration."

"I'm looking forward to it." She smiled as they made their way to the door. Jared gave the young lady a quick glance over his shoulder then walked out of the shop.

2

———

"Sara!" Abigail Mathews called out. Abigail was the oldest of the four sisters that owned Daisy's cakes. Sara was the second oldest and had just walked into the back with the tray of half-eaten slices of cake. Abby was standing by one of the back counters tapping her foot.

"What?" Sara asked as she moved the slices to the garbage.

"How did the tasting go?" Kadence the baby of the family asked. Sara turned to her sisters; Abby had light brown hair that was almost like Sara's. It fell down her back in waves, her eyes were green and bright, highlighted by her flawless makeup. Kadie was leaning over a three-tier cake putting the finishing touches on it. Kadie had pixie short dark brown almost black hair that she held back with bandanas. Her eyes were the same blue green as Sara's.

"The tasting went fine; we got the order. Abby, I assume you're here to ask about your cake and to drive me crazy with all the last-minute details for your wedding." Sara moved the empty dishes to the sink.

"Eddie said I needed to come to check with you. I also remembered that Morgan flies in today but can't remember when." Abby walked over to the high drafting table they used for paperwork, orders, and keeping track of business. She started to move papers around, as if she was looking for something.

"Put your hands up and back away slowly," Kadie said as she stood straight then lend on the counter to take a drink from the bottle of water never far from her. Sara looked over her shoulder as she rinsed the dishes.

"I second that, the last time we let you near the books we almost lost the place," Sara said from the sink.

"You guys are being dramatic," Abby said but she moved away from the table.

"Takes drama to know drama," Kadie said, then turned to Sara. "What time does Morgan come in?"

"This evening, we'll have just enough time to close and make it to the airport before her plane lands." Sara walked over to the paperwork table. "When are you coming in to do Chocolates again?" She asked Abby.

"Next Thursday, to make sure you have enough to get through the two weeks I'll be gone. I checked the freezer, if sales keep going the way they seem to be going I'll double what I usually do for two weeks."

When the girls were young their grandmother, mother's mother. Would bring them in all together and one by one to work with them, teach them. Find what lit the spark in them and grow the flame. Abby had a way with the chocolates, Kadie was the decorator, Sara the baker, and Morgan before she left had a way of knowing what the customer wanted as soon as they were in the shop, it also helped that Morgan loved numbers.

"Sounds good to me, I'll make sure we're not here," Sara said

"How about the dresses? Did you ever get it all figured out?" Abby asked but looked away

"Yes," Sara said through her teeth. "I did."

Abby had picked out bridesmaid dresses six months before the wedding. What had been the difficult part was that she couldn't stick to how many attendants she wanted. She had flexed from four to twelve to seven. Finally, with only three months to go, Sara finally put her foot down and made Abby stick to a number. What nobody saw coming was that Morgan would call with news that she would not be making it.

Abby being the drama queen that she is threw a huge fit and demanded that Sara fix it, and now. Sara spent the better part of two months trying to get Morgan to the wedding and to figure out why the third in line would say she couldn't make it at all.

Finally with only three weeks to go, Morgan called and said that she would indeed be making it to the wedding and coming early to help.

"Yes, I have them all, they are at the house hanging in your closet. I talked to Eddie last week and found out that he is one man down, however he has assured me that he knows just the guy." Sara said moving to her workstation, then she looked at Abby, "Are you going to hang out till we go get Morgan or do you have other things to do?"

"I have a ton of things I need to go do." Abby grabbed her bag. "I can meet you here, or you could pick me up on your way?"

"We'll pick you up, only if you agree to be at the end of the driveway waiting for us. If you can't do that then no deal." Sara teased.

"Call when you're on your way." Abby waved over her shoulder and was gone. The chime on the door went off.

"Man, it sucks that Evie called out," Kadie said as Sara turned to go help the customer.

"Yes, it does." Sara agreed.

Evie was a childhood friend the sisters met when they

moved in with their grandmother. After their dad left, their mother decided to move home. Where she would get the help and support needed to raise four babies. At the time Abby was 6, Sara 5, Morgan 3, and Kadie did not quit 1. Evie was 4 and the five made for fast friends that lasted through the years.

When Sara took over the bakery, she asked Evie if she would be interested in a job. Just to help, working the counter, helping with the clean up after they closed. Evie had jumped at the chance, then she was married with a baby on the way and wasn't the reliable friend they once had. Sara had found it was easier in some ways to just work without her.

The rest of Sara and Kadie's day went by smoothly, Sara stayed up front with the steady stream of customers that came in for their afternoon shopping. At 6pm Sara flipped the sign and locked the door; Kadie came from the back.

"I've cleaned the whole kitchen, if you say you've already counted down, we're good to go," Kadie said as she leaned on the counter.

"Bag is under the counter; grab it and we can go." Sara smiled. They walked to the back, grabbed their bags, hit the light, and set the alarm as they walked out the door.

"Call Abby tell her we're on our way," Sara said as she got into the driver seat of her four door Jeep wrangler.

"Already on it," Kadie said as her finger flew over the keyboard of her phone. She hit the send bottom and climbed in.

"How long has it been since Morgan came home?" Kadie asked looking over at Sara. "I was thinking Christmas but that isn't right. Then I was thinking she hasn't been home since Eddie asked Abby to marry him. So, it must have been before that because of the dinner we had."

"Morgan hasn't been home for more than a year," Sara said matter of fact.

"That's too long," Kadie said shaking her head and looking out the window.

"I agree. I'm curious to see how long she is going to stay. Every time I asked her, she pulled one of her change the subjects on me and then had to go before I get back to asking again." Sara said as she navigated her way to Abby's house.

"She's good, if she can dodge your questions, you're worst then a cop sometimes." Kadie teased.

"And how would you know how bad a cop is?" Sara teased back. "Oh, Abby must be excited too, look she really is waiting at the end of the driveway."

"God bless her, I want to be there already," Kadie said when Sara pulled over to let Abby in.

"I'm not even going to say anything about the front seat," Abby said as she opened the back door and got in. "Let's go, Sara." She added when she bounced in her seat.

"Alright." Sara put the car in gear, and they headed to the airport.

As expected, the airport was busy, they worked their way to baggage claim. Sara had agreed to meet Morgan there. They couldn't keep still, the four had been too close growing up. With life being what life could be like, it only concreted the bonds that were already unbreakable. They took turns pacing back and forth with the occasional sit down that never lasted long. Kadie was the one to spot Morgan first and stopped in her tracts.

"There she is." She said and took off like a shot. Abby and Sara watched as Morgan dropped her bags to catch their baby sister.

"She's crying," Abby said standing next to Sara, watching the sisters hug.

"They both are, but yeah I'll figure that out," Sara said.

"You always do." Abby started walking towards the two that were heading over. Kadie moved out of the way so that Abby could get in a good hug. Pulling away she too had to wipe at tears. Sara walked up; Morgan met her halfway. Sara pulled her into a hug and held on.

Morgan fell apart when she was wrapped into Sara's arms, all she had to do was get home. That is what she had told herself for the last three months, and now she was home. She stayed longest in Sara's embrace, so warm and motherly.

What people outside their close cycle didn't know was that Sara was the head of the family, she was the one they counted on to fix all the problems, get them out of a jam, and the one they didn't want to let down.

"Too long Morgan, too long," Sara said in her ear as she started to sway with Morgan. The sisters were just about the same height at 5'4. Sara pushed Morgan back to look into her bluer than green eyes. Morgan had let her naturally curly dark brown hair loose, with it hitting her shoulders, and framed her face beautifully.

"Let's get you home," Sara said.

"I need to eat first; those peanuts did nothing for me," Morgan said.

They went to get her bags, then headed out for dinner. Sara noticed for all the talk Morgan made about how hungry she was she didn't eat very much. They laughed and joked, they filled Morgan in on the details of the wedding and what still needed to be done.

"You need to try your dress on," Abby said as they walked out of the restaurant.

"Shot gun!" Kadie yelled.

"Not fair you had it on the way to the airport then Morgan had it here," Abby whined.

"You are nearly 30, when are you going to stop whining?" Kadie said as she put her hand on the front door.

"When I get the front seat," Abby said with a teasing smile.

"Fine only because you are getting dropped off and I can

move to the front. I'll sit with Morgan." Kadie smiled over at Morgan.

"Oh, thanks sweetie." Morgan put her arm around Kadie's shoulders.

"Alright everyone gets in I need to get to bed," Sara said making sure the car was unlocked. They laughed more on the way to drop Abby off, with the promise of seeing them the next day Abby got out and headed to her waiting fiancé.

True to her word, Kadie who was the smallest climbed over to sit in the front seat. The conversation rolled till they pulled into their driveway. Together they carried bags inside, and up to Morgan's room. Seeing Morgan wanted some time to settle in Sara and Kadie went to bed leaving her to do just that.

Morgan readied for bed, setting an alarm to get up and go into the bakery tomorrow. She needed to get back into the bakery, and all that came with it. She told herself as her eyes closed, this time she would never leave it again.

3

———

"WHAT ARE YOU DOING?" Sara asked as she came down the stairs that lead into the kitchen. She was in her usual jeans, t-shirt, and running shoes. Her hair was pulled back into a braided bun that sat low on her neck. Morgan sat at the counter with a glass of water in front of her, she too was wearing her work cloths.

"I'm going in with you today," Morgan said trying and failing to sound confident in her decision, at four fifteen in the morning it was hard to sound confident in anything.

"Sweetie, you look really pale, are you ok?" Sara moved to the coffee marker, happy to find a full pot ready and waiting for her.

"Yeah, I'm good," Morgan said as she thought how her day started. She wasn't ready to share with Sara that she had already spent twenty minutes in the bathroom getting sick.

They both turned as they heard a groan on the stairs. "Still not a morning person, is she?" Morgan smiled at Sara who smiled back

"No, she isn't, she can't really talk till after the first cup of coffee. I wouldn't be so happy about our baby sister having such an addiction, but we wouldn't make it without her." Sara cut off when Kadie entered the kitchen and headed to the coffee pot. With her cup full she moved to sit next to Morgan. After the first few sips, she turned to look at her sister.

"Hi sweetie," Morgan said as she watched Kadie, watch her.

"I'm glad your home, we will be with you every step of the way. You need to tell her, and now so she can work through it." Kadie said giving Morgan one last look and then going back to her coffee. Morgan looked over at Sara with surprise on her face, who had the same look for Kadie.

"What are you talking about?" Morgan asked looking at Kadie

"You want me to tell her? You have been gone a while, but you are still my sister." Kadie said this time giving Morgan a stair down. It wasn't until Sara stepped in did it end.

"I don't have time for this, what's going on?" She asked then watched as finally Morgan let out a breath.

"I'm pregnant and I moved home." Morgan gave a *are you satisfied* look at Kadie then turned to Sara. "If I can have my room back."

"Of course, you can. Wait what about Mark?" Sara asked

"We're getting a divorce. We have to go; I'll fill you in on the way." Morgan moved slowly off the stool knowing fast movements only made the nausea worst.

"Alright," Sara said and almost like she was on auto pilot she finished the morning routine and the three of them headed to the bakery.

Jared would have gone back to the bakery, but his world had picked up speed. Opening, and closing case after case. Late nights, early mornings, some nights not even getting home because of the job. But she was never far from his thoughts, her oval face, bright eyes, he found himself wondering how long her hair really was, the bun had given nothing away.

He was working on a report when Andrew came into the squad room. Dressed for a night on the town.

"Well, don't you look pretty." Jared teased.

"Why yes, I do," he said straightening his tie. "I have the rehearsal, and dinner tonight. Remember the wedding you're coming to with me tomorrow." Andrew said sitting down and checking his computer one last time before shutting it down.

"That's right, hey how did today go?" They talked about a lead they had gotten, it seemed to be providing the answers they needed. They had long ago made a deal to never talk about work outside of work, sometimes however it was unavoidable.

"Shit, I got to go," Andrew said after his eye caught the time on his phone. "The dinner after is at the steak house in The Sharron, if you want come by for a drink or bite to eat." Andrew slid his phone into his pocket, and his gun in the holder on his side. Then he waved as he walked out.

Jared spent the next two hours on paperwork and theories. He looked up when his phone signaled an incoming text.

Andrew: "Stop working and come eat."

Andrew always had his back. Jared leaned back and rubbed his eyes. It was Friday night, but he had the kind of job that didn't stop for weekends or holidays.

Jared: "Yeah, on my way."

Jared followed the same routine, shutting down his computer, pocketed his cell phone, and holstered his gun. He would get a bite to eat and plan his next move with the case and the bakery girl.

The week that followed was as crazy as Sara could handle, between Morgan coming home, and Abby's wedding. By Friday night Sara was ready to call it, grab a case of wine and go into hiding. It wasn't like she didn't expect it, the small fires that would come up. What had thrown her was when they started Tuesday and just kept coming, when she had ten out, she would turn around and need to put out ten more. Eddie, bless him, worked to keep a handle on Abby, and in the end, she had become too much for him. It wasn't until Morgan snapped at Abby, chewing her out for calling in the middle of the night, did Abby simmer down to manageable.

4

____

Sara didn't take a deep breath till they were in the steak house for dinner. The rehearsal had gone better than expected, even with the late groom's man. Abby had informed Sara that he was Eddie's cousin and a cop. It was a miracle that he had made it at all.

The Sharron was turning out to be a wonder to work with. They had known of each other for a while because Daisy's cake had delivered more than their share of wedding cakes, and other treats for other events. It was nice they were able to have the rehearsal, dinner, wedding, and reception all in one place. Sara had blocked out most of a floor for out-of-town friends and family, and the cherry on top was being able to reserve two bridal suits for the night before and the following day so the men and women could party and get ready the next day.

"Hey you, ok?" Kadie had come over to stand with Sara who was watching the room.

"Yep, you?" Sara looked her sister over. They had planned a toast for Kadie to give at the start of dinner.

"I'm ready. Hey, have you seen Morgan, she looked like shit the last time I saw her?" Kadie was scanning the room.

"Morgan said one of the groom's men is wearing a cologne that was turning her stomach. I hope she can manage to come out sometime tonight." Sara looked around the room then back at Kadie "She doesn't want to tell Abby till after the wedding, but I have to say it will be a lot harder to keep that under wraps if she throws up all night." Sara said taking a deep breath. She decided to get this show on the road.

"Let's go sit so you can give your speech and we can eat," Sara said moving away to find their seats. Morgan joined them right before Kadie stood to give her speech.

"Nice timing" Kadie whispered standing with her wine glass and butter knife. She began tapping it to get everyone's attention.

"Good evening, friends and family," Kadie said when the room was quiet. "I want to take the time to thank you for coming tonight," she stopped to clear her throat

"As the youngest sister I can tell you that I know all the embracing stories. It even crossed my mind to share a few, but instead, I decided on something much more special." Kadie pulled a folded letter from her bag and turned to her sister, and began to read.

"My darling girl, tonight on the eve of your wedding you will be surrounded by friends and family who love you." Sara had asked Abby about the letter their mother had written, and if it was ok to share. Abby hadn't read it, and even with the first sentence, her eyes began to fill.

"At your side will be a man who thinks the world of you, and would walk through fire for you. That is all I have ever wanted for you, well aside from good grades, a clean room, and manners." Kadie took a breath, as she smiled, heard a few giggles come from her sisters. "I wanted you to find your sun, the one who could keep you grounded as well as give you the freedom we both know you need. To my first baby girl, congratulations on finding your love."

Kadie looked up happy to have been able to get through the whole thing, she raised her glass "To Eddison, and Abigail" without thinking she knocked back what little wine she had in hopes of keeping the tears away.

"Well done" Sara said when Kadie sat down.

"Yeah, good job, I have enough trouble not crying as it is, and you just had to throw that in." Morgan wiped at her nose and gave a watery giggle.

The night moved on, and after dinner, people began to mingle. Sara went to the bar and ordered a glass of wine. She sat alone, and even though the room was buzzing with noise and activity she felt a calm come over her.

"Is someone sitting here?" A male voice pulled her from the quiet place she had found.

"No, go right ahead," Sara said then turned to see who she had let sit next to her. She met his warm brown eyes and felt a jaunt to her heart. She couldn't have looked away if she wanted to and she hadn't. It hit her brain that there had been one other man to make her feel like she was hanging upside down. He had come into the bakery a week or so back, but had made no move to introduce himself, they had shared small looks giving her stomach and heart flutters.

"Are you sure?" He asked smiling. Sara couldn't help returning the smile, *hot damn!* She thought to herself.

"Sorry," Sara looked away "Yes, I'm sure." Sara took a sip of her wine, hoping it would help her very dry mouth. When she was sure she could talk and not make a fool out of herself, she looked back at him. Only to find he hadn't taken his eyes off her.

"It's very long." He said softly.

"I'm sorry?" Sara looked at him with confusion.

"Your hair, it was tied back the last time I saw it," Jared said trying to put her and himself at ease. He knew how to talk to women; he felt his nerves creeping in. She made him nervous the thought made him smile.

Jared had made it in time to sit and eat with Andrew, who had gone off to flirt with the bridesmaids, in fact, he saw Andrew sitting with one now. She had dark curly hair and light eyes; in the light, she looked a bit pale. Jared had been looking around the room thinking about getting a drink, but the phone could go off any minute and he was on call.

Then he spotted her, she stopped his heart, in the dark green dress Her dark brown hair was long, it fell down her back almost touching the seat of her chair. He hadn't known he was moving toward her till he was standing next to her just watching as she sat there with a wine glass on the bar in front of her as her eyes closed.

"Yes, it was, and yes, it is," Sara said taking another sip of her wine. "I put it up every day, so I don't realize how long it is till I leave it down like I did tonight." Sara watched him take the seat next to her.

"Would you like a drink?" She asked him.

"No, thank you." He said turning his body to her. He watched as she did the same.

"So, are you part of this evening's event?" He asked looking into her eyes, so dark and deep. He felt himself wanting to get lost in them.

"Yes, I'm Abby's little sister, well oldest little sister. I'm Sara Mathews." Sara held her hand out, he took it his grasp soft, and firm at the same time. Sara felt just this small touch move through her body, sending a tingling sensation all over.

"I'm-" Jared was cut off by his phone ringing, as he dug it out Sara got a look at his gun. "Brooks," he said into the phone. "Yep, alright be right there." He ended the call, replaced the phone then looked at Sara.

"Next time," he said then he turned and was gone.

Sara sat there dumb founded for a moment, she felt like she

had just got hit by a bus and didn't know what the buss' name was. Sara took a moment and a few sips of her wine. She looked down at her watch, it was just about time for them to wrap this part of the evening up. Sara started to look for her sisters, she found Kadie first as she was just down the bar flirting it up.

"Hey, it's time, I need your help," Sara said when she stood next to her sister. Kadie bid her goodbye to the guy she had been talking to and together they moved into and around the room. Sara and Kadie had talked about making sure they moved the people who needed to be moved out. Kadie was to take one side and Sara took care of the other.

Sara felt relief when she ran into Morgan on her way to find Abby.

"Hey, are you ok? You are not looking so hot." Sara said moving to her.

"No, and I know. Can we go home yet?" Morgan asked close to tears.

"Yes sweetie, we are rounding everyone up now, go sit by the door I'll be right there." Sara waited and watched as Morgan made her way to the door, then continued her search so that she could get Morgan home. She let out a breath when she spotted Abby and Eddie in a back corner booth.

"Hey," she said as she approached them.

"Hey Sara, what's up?" Abby smiled up at her sister, just so happy and in love.

"It's time to go and I need to go get Morgan home she isn't feeling well." Sara waited for Abby to make her way out of the booth, before giving her a hug. "I love you and I'll see you in the morning, don't overdo it tonight ok," Sara said pulling out of the hug.

"Not to worry my dear sister, I'm going up and to bed," Abby said, and Sara had no doubt she would do just that.

"Alright then," Sara said and turned to Eddie "I'll see you

tomorrow too, oh and your tee time is at ten. Have fun tomorrow" Sara waved and went to get Morgan to take her home. She was surprised to see Kadie sitting with her, Morgan had her head resting on Kadie's shoulder with her eyes closed.

"Alright babe let's get you home," Sara said softly as she got to her sisters. When Kadie made it like she was going with them Sara stopped. "I thought you were going to stay?"

"No, I want my own bed, and to know who the hottie was that you were talking to" Kadie raised a brow waiting for Sara.

"Nobody." Was all she gave her sisters.

5

JARED WOKE up on his couch, after looking at his watch he saw that it was almost noon. The phone call he had received, while at the bar with Sara took him, and Andrew into the early morning hours. He crashed as the sun came up. He looked around, and he found Andrew had crashed into the recliner. Jared had a light memory of Andrew saying he just needed to sit down for a minute.

"Hey," Jared threw one of the old newspapers at Andrew to wake him up. Had the satisfaction of watching Andrew just about throwing himself out of the chair.

"Shit, what time is it?"

"Noon. What time-" Jared watched as Andrew settled back.

"I've got time. Hey, are we on call tonight?"

"No, we swapped because of the wedding," Jared said then made his way to his wonderful life-giving coffee pot.

"We do need to go in today just to make sure we got everything covered. What time do you have to be there?" Jared asked coming back with two cups when Andrew hadn't answered.

"Three the latest, wedding is at five," Andrew said after taking the first sip.

"Alright, I'm going to go in and make sure our report is in order, then I'm going to hit the gym. Meet up with you later." Jared said still standing, he drank his coffee, thinking the next best thing was a shower.

"I'm down for that, but I want food first," Andrew said rubbing his eyes.

"Ya, I'm going to go shower then we'll head out," Jared said and started out of the room.

"So, who was the very attractive woman you had at the bar lastnight," Andrew asked, Jared stopped just as Andrew knew he would. Andrew knew it was Sara, as they had met at the rehearsal, he just wants to see how Jared would react.

"Who was the darks curls?" Jared shot back.

"Just somebody," Andrew said quickly.

"Same" Jared shot back. Both knew the girls where anything but, they just weren't ready to admit it to themselves or each other.

Sara, Kadie, and Morgan were all up by the time Jared and Andrew crashed. They had dressed, eaten, had coffee and tea in travel mugs as they made their way to the hotel to get ready for the day. Sara made a detour to the bakery where they carefully loaded the cakes into the back of her jeep.

"Kadie, I have to say the cake is so beautiful," Morgan said from the front seat.

"Thank you, I asked her to trust me to know how she wanted it, but you know how she can be. We spent weeks talking about the design she wanted, in the end, I had drawn one up and she loved it, she even went as far as to say that I was right, and she should have just left it to me." Kadie said sounding a bit full of herself and smiled as she looked out the window.

"That is big" Morgan agreed, "I'm glad the dress fit when I tried it on, it is loose enough for my growing belly," Morgan said laying a hand on the small bump that was forming.

"I still can't believe that I did notice it when I hugged you in the airport. Now whenever I hug you, I can feel your belly." Sara said as she navigated through the early morning traffic.

"I felt it." Kadie said proudly "But I didn't want to be wrong and hurt your feelings"

"Thanks for that, instead you called me on it the next day" Morgan looking at Kadie.

"When were you planning on telling us, if Kadie hadn't steeped in?" Sara looked over at Morgan watching to see if she would try to lie.

"After the wedding, maybe after I had gone to the doctor to make sure everything was in order."

"Why wouldn't things be in order, wait you have gone to see a doctor?" Sara looked over at Morgan.

"Well, I took the test and came home to find my husband doing some chick on my kitchen table. After that, I decided to get a divorce and come home. I wasn't going to let anything stop me from that. If I had told Mark about the baby, I would have had to stay and share custody."

"I'm not sure that's the way it works, I think you should talk to Eddie about that. He is the family lawyer after all." Kadie said from the back seat. They had pulled up to the hotel, the valet had come over to Sara's door.

"Hi, we are here for the Mathews/ Bennet Wedding. The wedding cake is in the back and needs to get to Sue in the kitchen." Sara said to the young man, he handed her a ticket, and she handed him a tip.

Morgan and Kadie where both waiting for her on the side-walk. Together they made it through the lobby, and to the elevators.

"So, what did you do when you found them on the kitchen table?" Kadie asked as they rode up.

"Grabbed my camera." Morgan smiled wickedly.

"What?" Sara asked surprised.

"I needed to have hard proof that he was cheating, if I didn't, I couldn't get the divorce. That is what it stated in our prenuptial agreement" Morgan started out of the elevator first.

"What does the agreement state?" Kadie asked following her.

"A hundred grand for every act I can prove." Morgan had to stop because her sisters had "What?" she asked turning to them.

"You got a hundred grand because you came home early and grabbed the camera?" Sara asked slightly dumb founded.

"Well, I'll get four, he really didn't know how to keep it in his pants. Come on its Abby's day and she's waiting for us. We can talk about all that tomorrow or something." Morgan turned to start walking to the room.

"Wait" Sara grabbed Morgan's arm to stop her. "Are you ok?"

"I wasn't but I'm home now so yes I am." They hugged each other quickly, the girls put it away as they walked to Abby's room. Once the door opened, they were ready to dive into getting ready for the wedding.

The hours flew by, they spent time at the hotel spa. Getting their manies, and pedies. Going back to the room after a lunch for their hair and make-up. All seven women were ready an hour before they had to head downstairs, pictures were taken as the sisters helped Abby get ready. Abby handed Sara her vale, with tears in both of their eyes Sara fastened it to Abby.

"Alright ladies, let's do this!" Abby said so excited, and happy it flowed around her.

"You did good here," Kadie whispered to Sara.

"Thanks, kid so did you," Sara said wrapping an arm around Kadie's waist.

The last year's hard work was coming to an end, all the planning, all the craziness was coming to a happy close. They all fell in line as Abby started her way out and down to the wedding. They had help from cousins to make sure people were seated, and ready for when the girls came down. Once settled in the line, the music started, and one by one went down the aisle.

6

SARA COULDN'T HELP SCANNING the room for her Mystery Brooks. Would he be at the wedding? She couldn't help asking herself, even as she scanned the two hundred or so faces looking at her. She took a deep breath as all eyes went to the back as the music changed again to let the room know the bride was coming. Sara looked over to watch Eddie as Abby came into view. He loved her and would take care of her. Sara felt relieved as she saw it all over him.

They exchanged promises and rings, Sara carefully wiped a tear as they kissed, and were announced husband and wife. When she made it back down the aisle both Abby and Eddie were waiting for her. They brought her up into a hug and thanked her over and over.

The parties moved to pictures as the guests moved to pre-dinner cocktails. Everyone was smiling and laughing as the photographer took many pictures. It was during a time that the photographer was busy with just the bride and groom. The men and maids where milling around waiting to be called up for more pictures. That Sara noticed Morgan standing next to a side door. She was with Eddie's cousin the cop, Andrew. They had been introduced yesterday.

He was talking to her and rubbing her back. Sara could tell by how pale Morgan was she was very close to getting sick. Sara watched, as if he felt her body, muscles tighten. Sara watched Andrew take Morgan though the door so that she could get sick out of the room.

Without thinking Sara moved, going out of the room and to the bar in the ball room, she slipped back to the hall and made her way quickly over to Morgan and Andrew. Morgan was bent over the trash can and Andrew had his hand on her back. Sara went wide to catch his eye, not wanting to seem like she was sneaking up on him. He turned to her, opened his mouth to say something then smiled as Sara handed him a bottle of water and left them.

"There you are." Abby walked over to Sara just as she came back into the room.

"Sorry bathroom break, what do you need?" Sara started walking away from the door that separated the room from a sick Morgan.

"I think we got all the pictures, we're ready to go to the ball room. Do you know where Morgan and Andrew are?"

"Andrew, he is the cousin cop, right?" Sara asked stalling. She might need to throw Andrew under the bus in order to keep Morgan's news under wraps.

"Yes, he didn't get a call, did he?" Abby asked, Sara turned so that Abby's back was to the door and Sara could watch for Morgan and Andrew to come back into the room.

"I might have seen him in the hall on my way back in, how long has he been a cop?" Sara asked, watching over Abby's shoulder.

"He's a detective actually, he joined the force when he was twenty-one." Abby said as she turned to scan the room, "Oh I hope he doesn't have to leave, what should we do if he does." Abby asked turning back to Sara.

"We'll have one guy walk in two girls, not to worry," Sara said, and with a sign of relief, she watched over Abby's shoulder Morgan and Andrew coming back into the room.

Morgan's color was better, and she had the bottle of water in hand. Sara couldn't help the little smile as she watched Morgan walk over to them and Andrew's hand never leaving her lower back.

"Sorry, Abby I needed to get some air," Morgan said as she came to stand with them.

"Oh, sweetie you don't look very well, do you think you have an hour left in you? The dinner and dance?" Abby asked, worried that the hour was going to be too much.

"I'm better now let's do this" Morgan smiled at Abby with reassurance.

"Alright," Abby walked away and raised her voice. "Everyone line up, we are going to the ball room."

"Are you sure?" Andrew asked Morgan before Sara could. Sara watched as this man she didn't know look at her sister as if she was the most important thing ever. Sara didn't like it, didn't trust it.

"Yes, I'm sure. This is her day and I'm not going to ruin it" Morgan said looking into Andrew's eyes.

It was at that moment Sara saw Morgan thought the same of Andrew, he was important. It had Sara wondering what the hell had she missed in the hall, or maybe it was last night.

"Alright then, let's go," Sara said and walked away to join the best man. Sara noticed that even now the guy swayed a bit. He turned and looked down at her, his eyes were glossy. *Drunk* Sara thought *Great.* They could hear the DJ start to introduce them, as they made their way in.

Dinner was wonderful, then came the cake and toast. Sara had practiced and written down what she thought she wanted to say. In the end, she spoke from the heart, giving a much better speech then she could have ever pre-planned.

Sara watched from close by with two warm towels just in case, when the bride and groom went to feed each other a bite of cake. The room wasn't disappointed, Eddie came out of it with most of it on his face then in his mouth, and Abby had some in her hair and down her neck. Eddie happily spun his back to the room and dipped Abby just enough to clean off her himself.

They took the warm towels and headed to the dance floor for their first dance. Sara knew the wedding party dance would take place after that. She stood by and watched her sister and Eddie have their first dance, he spun her, and she laughed. Sara felt her heart soar for them, so happy.

Sara saw the wedding party had gathered knowing their dance was next, Sara scanned faces looking for the best man, with no luck. The song ended and everyone swept to the floor, ready with their partner when the music started. Sara stood a little back from the floor not wanting to draw attention to herself. She felt a tap on her shoulder, she tried to hold back the flare in her temper, before she bit off someone's head.

"Yes?" she turned at the same time the word came out through clenched teeth. Her eyes meeting warm brown.

"May I have this dance?" He asked calmly, not bothered by the flame she knew she had in her eyes. It took her brain a moment too long to realize what was going on, she had placed her hand in his and warmth traveled over her whole body.

As he led her to the dance floor, she tried to keep the blush she felt from head to toe from showing. He swung her into the dance picking up on the beat of the Life house's You and Me. He held her close for the dance yet kept a respectful amount of space between them. She was taken aback by how much this handsome stranger could affect her. When she looked up and into his eyes, she felt a huge smile spread across her face.

"You have a beautiful smile," Jared said meeting her eyes.

"You dance very well; a girl could hardly keep a straight face when she is spun so wonderfully around the dance floor," Sara said continuing her smile.

"Thank you. You also gave a wonderful speech, very from the heart." Jared said looking down at her, feeling his own smile come.

Jared had watched from the back as Abby and Eddie exchange their vows, then moved to the ball room and waited. He had started to feel stupid just watching and waiting for his moment with her. Then he saw her on the sidelines while all the other attendants started to dance and knew this was his chance.

"It was, I had one all typed up and everything but when it came to it, I felt it was better to just wing it," Sara said.

"Do you wing it often?" Jared eyed her as he asked.

"More then I'll ever admit to." Sara had Jared smiling at that.

"Your sister looks very happy" He tilled his head to where Abby was kissing Eddie.

"Oh, she is," Sara looked up at him. "How do you know them?"

"Andrew, he's, my partner." Jared saw something move into her eyes, question, disappointment, even a touch of sadness. "I'm a detective, he's, my partner." Jared smiled as Sara's checks turned a bit pink.

"He is Eddie's cousin; I was told it was wonderful luck that he was able to be part of their day." Sara talked fast after her quick judgment.

"He is, Andrew and I also grew up together, our mothers are friends"

"I'm sorry," Sara said it without thinking. Then as she realized what she said her eyes grew, she took the hand she had on his shoulder and covered her mouth "That was so rude, I'm sorry"

"No, it's ok. I am sorry too. If I could have Andrew as a best friend but not have to deal with his family I would. He feels the same way about me and mine so we're even" Jared gave her a reassuring smile.

"So, what is your plan after the wedding?" He asked changing the subject.

"Let's see tomorrow is Sunday, I'm going to sleep." Sara closed her eyes as if just the thought was too good.

"Rough week?" Jared asked, watching her open her eyes again.

"Rough year, we have been going at this wedding planning for a year. I'm so glad they're together, but it had its hard times. About six months in Kadie had to pull the mom card to get me back on track."

"Mom card?" Jared asked and noticed the song ended. The next was swinging into a quicker beat, but he wasn't done talking to her. He smoothly moved them off the dance floor and to the bar.

"Would you like anything?" he asked when they had reached the long slightly busy bar.

"I'll have a shock top, orange wedge please." Sara smiled at the bar tender, then turned to Jared so that he could order.

"Same" Jared turned to Sara "I figured you a wine girl."

"It depends on my mood." Sara took her bottle and tapped his "Thanks for the dance" She took a sip.

"So, mom card?" Jared asked after he took a sip. He was moving the conversation back. He wanted to find out more about her, he also tried not to sound like a cop. He knew with a decade under his belt he didn't know how to ask questions without sounding like one.

"I'm the fixer in the family, Morgan nick named me glue once because I kept the family together. About seven years ago we lost our mother to cancer." Sara had to take a breath, that was never easy to say. Jared moved to take her hand in his.

"I was in my first year of college, Abby in her second. Morgan was a junior in high school, and Kadie was a freshman. Abby and I came back, I stayed" she said with almost a shrug like it wasn't a big deal to put her whole life on hold for her sisters, and her mom.

"What were you 18-19? That's a lot to take on." Jared said thinking about what she would have faced at that age. At a time in her life when it should have been about parties and finals, she had taken on so many responsibilities.

"There wasn't a choice, I came home and did what needed to be done. I wouldn't change it for the world." Sara smiled and took a drink then turned to look around the room. She saw Kadie heading to her with a worried look on her face.

"Next time." She turned and smiled at Jared then walked away to meet Kadie halfway to find out what had gone wrong.

"I'm sorry, you looked like you were having a good time, and we would handle this without you, but we can't. Who's the guy?" Kadie turned and started to head back the way she had come Sara followed.

"Nice try, and I still haven't gotten his name. What's going on?" Sara looked at her sister trying to get a clue. They were in the bathroom when Kadie stopped spun and put her butt on the door.

"It will be easier to show you." Kadie took a step back and opened the door to the women's bathroom. Morgan was leaning against the wall.

"Oh, are you alright?" Sara rushed to her sister.

"Yes, I'm fine. But I don't think he is" Morgan pointed to the last stall with her thumb.

"What? He?" Sara walked to the last stall, and when she opened it, she found the missing best man passed out drunk, using the wall to slump against. "Well, that's just great.

Do either of you have an idea how to get this guy out of here?" She looked back at her sisters.

"Yes, I figured out what to do I just couldn't figure out how to execute," Kadie said happily.

"Alright let's hear it." Sara walked over to stand with her sisters.

"We get him a room; he pays for it, and we dump him in it. The part I couldn't figure out was how to get him out of here." Kadie said her shoulders slumping a bit.

"Ok, so we need someone or a few to help get this guy out of here." Sara looked at her sisters as she thought about it

"Oh, I know" Morgan pushed off the wall. "I'll go fast." She started to walk to the door when it swung open, and Abby came in.

7

———

"WHAT IS GOING ON?" Abby asked worriedly

"Nothing," All three of them said together. Then they started laughing.

"I'm pregnant, and I didn't want to make a big deal about it till after your wedding because it's your day and your time." Morgan smiled "I have been getting sick on and off all night and they" She turned to look at Sara and Kadie "have been helping me."

"You're pregnant?" Abby asked with tears in her eyes and a smile on her face.

"Yes," Morgan said smiling back, but with slight hesitation.

"That's wonderful news," Abby said and threw her arms around Morgan, then stepped back "Oh I can feel your belly. Well, if that's all, I'm going back to my husband we will celebrate better when I get back, wait, are you still going to be here?"

"Yes, I'll still be here, I moved home," Morgan said.

"What?" Abby looked from Morgan to Sara and Kadie. Trying to see if it was true.

"It doesn't matter now, go back to your wonderful husband

and we'll talk when you get back. Go enjoy your night." Morgan said and pushed Abby out of the bathroom as she left too.

"Well, you have to admire her timing," Kadie said as she turned to the mirror and gave her hair a little fluffing.

"I was wondering when she would tell her, and now not only has she pulled Abby into the loop, but she saved a friendship." Sara moved to stand next to Kadie, checking the make-up she rarely wore.

"You ready to talk about your bar friend?" Kadie asked watching Sara in the mirror.

"Nope," Sara shook her head.

"You will eventually" Kadie smiled knowing her sister.

"May-be if I ever get his name. I know he is partners with Andrew." Sara said not meeting Kadie's eye.

"Which one is Andrew?" Kadie asked watching her sister.

"Eddie's cop cousin," Sara said looking at Kadie now.

"Oh, the one that has had Morgan's eye for the last couple of nights," Kadie said then stopped. "Do you think we need to worry about him?"

"Maybe, I know she can handle herself, but I believe as her sisters we should watch out for her. We didn't spend a lot of time with Mark, and it seems he failed her." Sara stopped talking as the bathroom door opened. Two men walked in.

"Um gentlemen, I believe you have the wrong door," Kadie said smiling, she looked at Sara who had locked eyes with the one with dark brown hair and warm brown eyes.

"Morgan sent us," Andrew said, watching how Sara's eyes had locked on to Jared.

"This is Jared Brooks" Jared reached for Sara's after he shook Kadie's and together, they just held for a moment. Just like last time Sara felt the zings spread through her body.

"Jared, it's nice to meet you," Sara said a small smile pulling at her lips.

"We were told you had a problem, interesting, I was under the impression you fixed all the problems" Jared smiled at Sara

"This one is a bit out of my range." Sara moved to put a hand on Kadie who was getting her hackle's up, not understanding Jared was teasing.

"Please go have a look for yourself, the last stall." Sara and Kadie watched as the guys moved into the back of the bathroom.

"What was that?" Kadie whispered, slightly pissed.

"He was teasing, don't worry. I wonder where Morgan went off to," Sara whisper back.

"Hey, where's Morgan" Kadie called out to the men who were standing in the doorway of the stall, as they were thinking of what to do.

"She ran into an aunt or something" Andrew called back to them.

"What do you think?" Andrew asked Jared quietly.

"Well, we have to get him out of here, I say get him into one of the rooms and call it a night. We don't have to take him in." Jared said then moved to the sleeping guy to dig for his wallet. He had it when he walked back to Andrew, "You know a Gavin Mitchell?"

"Yeah, he's the best man," Andrew said then looked at the guy again.

"That explains why I found Sara on the sidelines, anyways you want to get him the room or do you want me to?" Jared said going through to find a card to use.

"I'll stay here, you go, and get those girls out of here. They deserve to go enjoy the party." Andrew said.

"Agreed" Jared said and moved to Sara and Kadie. "Alright we got this, you girls go and enjoy all your hard work." Jared opened the door for them.

"Thank you," she said walking past him, to wait for Sara.

"But-" Sara was stopped because Jared had stepped up to her, and the door closed.

"I'll find you later. Go, you worked hard on this, have a dance with your sisters, and have another drink. I'll take care of this." Jared watched Sara battle with herself.

She was always doing the fixing and even though Morgan had gone and gotten the guys; Sara still wanted to make sure it was taken care of. At that moment he was asking her to trust him. Asking her to take a step she hadn't taken since before her mom was sick. Jared moved even closer, tilted her chine up with his fingers. Tingles traveled all over her body, here was a hot guy so close to her. His touch sparked something in her, heat and need.

"Trust me to do this Sara," He said locking eyes with her. "I'll come and find you when it's done." He watched as she conceded, she let her breath out.

"Alright, you can take care of this one." She smiled but Jared could tell her heart wasn't in it. She stepped away and walked out to join Kadie.

"What was that about?" Kadie asked as they moved back to the party.

"He's taking care of it; I'm letting him take it from here," Sara said and moved to slide an arm round Kadie's waist. "Come on let's rescue Morgan, get Abby, and dance," Sara said smiling at Kadie, trying to relax.

"Alright," Kadie said as she looked back and saw Jared watching them, he gave her a nod. Kadie turned back to the room looking for her sisters so they could have that dance.

8

____

SARA RELAXED as the beats of the songs worked through her body, soon she was laughing with her sisters. The dance floor was alive, and Sara moved with it. When the music slowed, and people coupled up Eddie came to claim his wife. Kadie, Morgan, and Sara moved to the bar for a refresher then back out to the dance floor when the beat picked back up, Sara danced with her sisters and the few guys that asked her.

Jared and Andrew got the drunken best man into a room, they were walking back into the reception and stopped at the door. Andrew watched as Jared did a scan, watched as Jared's whole-body language changed when his eyes stopped. Andrew followed his sight line to see Sara dancing with another man. Andrew looked at his friend.

"You've got it bad, and you just met her. Don't you think you should slow it down just a bit," he said then Jared looked at him.

"Tell me something first?" he asked.

"What?" Andrew asked with confidence.

"Without looking at the room, where's Morgan?" Jared waited a beat then raised his brow. "I'd say we both have it bad.

Now we need to figure out what to do with it." Jared started to move to the dance floor.

"Let's get a drink first, that guy was dead weight and I'm thirsty," Andrew said getting Jared's attention and moved them to the bar.

Sara was dancing when she felt a chill work up her spine, she carefully looked around the room. Then she saw Jared standing with his back to the dance floor ordering a drink, Andrew was standing next to him but was facing out. She watched as she danced the two moved almost mirroring each other. Sara figured it was so that they were always watching the other's back. Sara signaled to her dance partner that she needed a drink and moved off the floor to head to the bar. Before she could get there, she was approached by one of the servers.

"Miss Mathews, we need you to come to the kitchen for a moment." The young girl said, "Yes, of course, I'll be right there," Sara said then started to move to the bar again. Jared still had his back on the dance floor, so Andrew watched her walk up. She stood between them.

"Everything ok? Everything works out?" She looked at Andrew, turning her back on Jared.

"Everything went fine," Jared said, he had leaned down to her ear. He smiled as he watched the shiver work through her body. Sara moved away enough to turn around.

"Thank you for taking care of that." She said trying to catch her breath. She hoped it would come off as being winded from the dance floor.

"Here you look thirsty" Jared pushed his beer to her.

"Thank you, again." She took a pull from the beer, then turned to look around the room. Her eye caught the young lady standing by the kitchen door. "Shit" she set the beer down and took off to the kitchen.

"Where is she off to?" Both Jared and Andrew turned to see Kadie standing behind Jared.

"The kitchen." Jared answered, "what can I get you?"

"Just water, I'm getting us home tonight. Morgan was going to do it, but she will most likely fall asleep in the car." Kadie went and stood between the two men like Sara had. She took the water Jared ordered for her.

"Morgan?" Andrew asked.

"Sitting down, I need to take her a water too," Kadie said after taking a big drink of water.

"I'll do it if you could point the way," Andrew said then turned to order a water, Kadie pointed the way, and he took off.

"What do you want with Sara?" Kadie asked, surprising Jared.

"To get to know her." He answered watching her.

"And then?" Kadie put her hand up "Let me get this out first as I suspect whatever had her rushing to the kitchen is just about handled. Sara isn't one to just hand something over for someone else to handle especially when it comes to her family. If you get your foot in the door you better be prepared to walk the rest of the way in. As her sister and what I saw tonight, it wouldn't take you much to get the foot in." Kadie said watching him. "The other side of that is us, one for all kind of thing," Kadie said then took a sip and watched Jared take a pull from his beer.

"That's some heavy stuff Kadie. What-" He was cut off.

"I saw the way you looked at her when you got back, and she was dancing with Kenny. I'd say your barley have your feet under you. Tread lightly is all." Kadie smiled at him, then turned to go sit with Morgan and Andrew. Minutes later Sara came up behind him.

"You're still here." She sounded slightly surprised

"I was waiting for you" He turned to see her smile at him.

"Come dance with me." He held his hand out and when she took it, he pulled her to the dance floor.

Abby came and sat down with her sisters and Andrew. "That's nice to see. Nobody has ever put that look on her." Abby said and took Kadie's water and drank deep.

"Nobody has ever put that look on him," Andrew said as he had his arm draped over the back of Morgan's chair. Abby turned to Kadie

"What's that about?" She mouthed.

"Later" Kadie mouthed back.

"Anything we need to worry about?" Abby turned to Andrew.

"His mother." Andrew smiled at Abby.

"She can handle her own, if that's all there is to worry about, he gets my vote. Anyone who can get her to relax and put that look on her is worth keeping around just to see what happens. Kadie we are leaving in about ten minutes there are things that need to get done and I don't want to bother her." Abby said standing.

"Sure" Kadie stood to follow Abby. Leaving Andrew and Morgan at the table.

"Is that all?" Andrew asked.

"What?" Morgan asked looking an Andrew. He was so heart stopping handsome, she found herself wanting to kiss those lips.

"Her blessing, she hasn't even talked to Jared, and she has given him her green light," Andrew said watching Morgan.

"Would you rather we grilled him for hours?" Morgan smiled "You know just as much we do, what you share with us, what we share with you." She said with a shrug.

"That's true. So, you want to go out some time?" He asked the question had Morgan laughing.

She had told him she was married, but heading to divorce, and was with child last night. They had been having a wonderful time, and Morgan had been surprised by the easiness they had. She hadn't wanted him to run but she wanted him to have all the facts. His phone had called him away in the nick of time. She dropped the bomb and he had to go.

Andrew had waited to corner her, the timing had come during the photos, and he had thought about it. He had decided to be with her in anyway he could have her. He wanted to be a part of her life. Then it was her turn to duck the bomb. He had felt her muscles bunch and got her to the trash can just in time.

"Yes, I'll let you know when," Morgan said smiling, Andrew reached for her hand and kissed it. Morgan's heart soared, she was falling fast for this man. She had spent the last five years with a man who didn't believe in such a sweet jester, he had been about himself and that was all.

"I hope it's soon," Andrew said then they were joined by Kadie.

"Everything is ready, now we just need to send them off. DJ is going to announce the last song then we are all going to line up and send them off." Kadie said sitting down.

"Where are they going?" Andrew asked.

"Upstairs for tonight, then they fly out tomorrow for two weeks in London," Morgan said. "We are going to have a brunch for them tomorrow, they'll open presents then be off."

"Where is it going to be?" He asked.

"You ask a lot of questions," Kadie said with a scowl towards Andrew.

"Only because I don't know if I'm supposed to attend," Andrew said keeping his cool.

"You don't have to, from what Abby said they were just grateful you could make the rehearsal and wedding," Kadie said looking at him, then the song ended. "This should be good." They looked back at the dance floor where Sara and Jared were still dancing.

They watched as Jared and Sara stopped as the song did, then the look on Sara's face as the DJ called for the last dance. She tried to pull away from Jared, but he held her, the three watched as he talked to her, then watched as she looked over at them. Kadie held a thump up, Jared let Sara move away just enough then spun her back to him. The heat from the move had the onlookers watching no more.

"Well, it seems he's going to be better for her then I thought," Kadie said.

"Did you doubt her?" Morgan asked but had a knowing look in her eye.

"No, I didn't." Kadie smiled.

$$9$$

EVERYONE MOVED to make a hallway for the couple to walk through as they bid goodbye. Jared had moved behind Sara. He kept one hand on her hip and a cup of water in the other. Kadie, Morgan, and Andrew moved to stand with them.

Jared lends down to whisper into Sara's ear .

"Will you go out with me?" He asked smiling as the shiver worked over her body again.

"Like on a date?" she whispers back over her shoulder.

"Yes," Jared smiled as Sara turned her head to look at him. He watched as her eye traveled down to his lips, she licked hers and the thought move through her eyes. He didn't back up when she inched her way in, he closed the last little bit when she hesitated.

When his lips touched hers, the earth moved, the air left his lungs, and sparks went off. He felt his hand tighten on her hip, hoping that would keep him steady. He felt the cup leave his hand, he moved his hand under her chin to keep her there while he dove deeper into her, into her heat, into her taste.

A throat clearing brought him back, he finished the kiss softly and sweetly.

"Is that a, yes?" He asked looking into her eyes when she opened them.

"Yes," Sara said trying to catch her breath, meeting his eyes. The heat and want in them had her wanting to kiss him again. The cheers of the crowd had her turning back to the couple, just as Abby and Eddie walked by. Jared kept his hands on Sara's hips. Sara lends back, her body relaxed. The wedding was over a year of planning over.

"Holy F," Kadie said, it had Sara jerking to attention.

"What?" She said looking at her sister.

"We did it, we got Abby married." Kadie and Sara smiled as they shared a look.

"Yes, we did," Sara said smiling.

The five of them spent the rest of the time cleaning up, making sure people moved out, it wasn't hard as most of them did after the bride and groom departed. Morgan helped the best she could, but she was beaten. Kadie buzzed around the room, giving good-byes as people made their way out. Sara did the same. The guys helped the hotel staff start the tear down of the room.

"What does your week look like?" Jared asked as he stood with Sara in front of the hotel waiting for the valet to bring her car around. Kadie was talking with Andrew who happily had an arm wrapped around a half sleeping Morgan.

"Full, like I imagine yours is, we could do lunch anytime this week. Just come by" Sara said with a smile.

"I'll do just that." Jared couldn't help the pull he had on this woman, and now that he had a taste of her it was a demand. He needed to touch her, be near her get another taste of her.

Slowly he moved to kiss her, and their lips met. He worked to keep it light. Sara did as well, the fact that they were on the street with company played in the back of both their minds. Sara had her hands on his ribs on the inside of his jacket, she fisted his shirt in hopes it would keep her grounded, she felt Jared slide a hand to the back of her neck.

The light brushes were turning into something deeper and faster than either was ready for. Sara moved without thinking and pressed her body against Jared's finding it well toned.

"Sara, Jared" Kadie's voice cut through their hot haze.

"Damn it" Jared whispered against Sara's lips "I would say sorry, but I'm not." He smiled as he rested his forehead against hers waiting to find his footing.

"I wouldn't accept your apology anyways," Sara said and let a light giggle out, she pulled away. "Till next time."

She walked to the passenger seat of her jeep and got in. Andrew had already helped Morgan get into the back seat and Kadie was ready in the driver seat. Kadie took off when Sara had her seat belt on.

"You ready to talk about it yet?" Kadie asked.

"Nope but wow I did not see that coming." Sara settled into the seat and closed her eyes, suddenly very tired.

"I don't think any of us did." Kadie waited for a beat. "Sara?"

"Yeah," she said with her eyes closed.

"He matters, whether you're ready to admit it yet or not. It's all over you and him." Kadie said looking at Sara briefly.

"Are you telling me to be careful?" Sara opened her eyes to look at Kadie.

"I'm telling you that you will try to make it seem like it isn't a big deal, play it off. But it is, so yeah, I guess I am, be careful." Kadie took her eyes off the road for a quick minute to share a look with Sara.

Sara thought about it all the way home. She fell into her bed thinking of what Kadie said and replaying the night. Being in Jared's arms spinning around the dance floor was when she drifted off dreaming of other ways of being in his arms.

10

———

Sara woke up laying on her side. Morgan was laying facing her.

"Still the easiest way to wake you up. Just stare at you" Morgan smiled.

"How long have you been here?" Sara asked trying to get her bearings.

"Maybe five minutes, I need to talk to you," Morgan said.

"Alright," Sara said adjusting her pillow, facing her sister and any problem that may come at her.

"I'm having feelings for Andrew, the kind that flips my stomach, in a good way. Trust me I know all the bad ways. I keep waiting for the guilt to come over me, but it isn't. I feel like Andrew is where I should be." Morgan had a worried look in her eyes.

"Sweetie, love is a tricky thing. When is your divorce final?" Sara asked watching her sister, Morgan hadn't held back, it was one hell of an issue to start the day with.

"Any day now, Mark was served the papers the day I flew home, he hasn't made any attempted to contact me so I'm sure it will just be done," Morgan said letting her breath out and looking at the ceiling.

"Could he prolong it?" Sara asked.

"Yes, he could not sign them. I'm sure his dad will deal with that." Morgan stopped as a noise at the door caught their attention.

"So, this is where the party is" Kadie moved to the other side of Sara's bed, Sara moved to the middle making room for Kadie to climb in.

Sara closed her eyes as Kadie cuddled up to her. Kadie had done this for as long as either could remember. Sara's bed had always been the one everyone came to. Their mother could always find her girls in Sara's bed. The three just lay there, letting the minutes tick by. Finally, Morgan started to move.

"We have a brunch in two hours, I'm taking a shower first," Morgan said but stayed where she was.

"I'd say I'll race you to the bathroom, but I really like where I am," Kadie said sleepily. "It has been too long since we just laid in bed.

"I told Jared this was exactly what I planned to do this morning, but at that point, it was wishful thinking." Sara stared at her ceiling. "He matters." Sara turned to Kadie "I get it now." Sara took a deep breath.

"Alright I'm going to take the first shower then go down, start the coffee and water for tea, you two can fight over the second shower." Sara got up and headed to her bathroom. When she was dressed, she braided her hair as she walked down the stairs. Sara stopped short as she found Morgan crying and Kaide working to comfort her.

"What happen?" Sara asked as she bee-lined to Morgan.

"Mark called while we were lying in bed this morning. He left a voice mail." Kadie said then pointed to the phone on the table. Sara picked it up to play the message.

"You stupid slut," Mark sounded pissed, his voice made

Sara feel uneasy. "You think you can play like that? Well, I've got news for you. I'll give you 24 hours to get it taken care of before I step in and take care of it myself. I'd say that it isn't mine, but I know how lacking you are in the sack. Oh, and be sure you thank that dumb shit of a sister, if it hadn't been for her friendly little phone call, I would have never known just how much of a backstabbing bitch you really are."

Sara pulled the phone away and looked at Morgan, who was a wreck.

"Did you listen to it?" Sara asked Kadie.

"No, I had come down with her but watched as she played the message. Then you came down, is it bad?" Kadie was still holding onto Morgan

"Yes, it is," Sara said and moved to sit and talk to Morgan.

"Sweetie, how long has he been like that? Has he ever hit you?" Morgan started to cry more, and Kadie had to change where her arms were as Morgan seemed to be slipping. Sara moved in to help Kadie.

"Let's get her upstairs," Sara said, with Kadie they helped a hiccupping Morgan to bed. Sara had left Morgan's phone downstairs, and took the wireless house phone out of the room with her as they left a sleeping Morgan.

"What the hell?" Kadie quietly spats out, her eyes flashed with anger. They had stopped just before going back down to the kitchen.

"It is much worst than I thought, we need to get through the brunch and then we'll deal with Mark." Sara said grabbing a hold of Kadie's shoulders "Go take your shower, then come down and help me cook. We both need coffee." Sara waited till Kadie was heading up to her third story attic bedroom.

Sara went downstairs and thought about how to fix the situation. She was deep in thought and had her second cup of coffee when Kadie joined her. The two worked on the breakfast, twenty or so people would be there in a matter of minutes to watch the couple open gifts, then send them off. They were wrapping up the final touches when the back door opened and in walked Eddie and Abby.

"Good morning!" Abby said bouncing into the kitchen to give her sisters hugs.

"Good morning," Kadie said then moved away before Abby could hug her. Sara watched Abby's face fall.

"Eddie, we haven't had time to move the gifts in if you could start, we'll be out in a minute," Sara said but didn't take her eyes off Abby.

"Sure" Being a man who wasn't stupid and had spent his fair share with them. He knew when an opportunity arouses to get out of the line of fire, he took it.

"What?" Abby asked when the door shut. Sara didn't say anything instead she walked over to the table picked up Morgan's phone walked back to Abby, pressed play, and handed it to her. Both Sara and Kadie watched as all the blood drained from Abby's face. When the message was done, she handed the phone back to Sara

"Oh god, what did I do?" Abby said weakly.

"You lit a shit storm that we didn't even know about. What the hell were you thinking when you called him?" Kadie yelled from the other side of the large counter.

"I was calling to say congratulations, and to say it was a bummer that he hadn't made the wedding but happy that they were moving home," Abby yelled back.

"When have you ever called him, why would you call him now?" Kadie shot back.

"Get off my ass this isn't my fault" Abby fired at Kadie.

"Well, I can get mad at you for calling him, you shouldn't have done that," Kadie said as she swung an arm through the air.

"I was trying to be friendly and supportive; I didn't know it would backfire like this." Abby turned to Sara. "What do we do?"

"I'm not sure yet. I think we need to call the cops because he is threatening her, I think we should call his father because he's the one handling the divorce. But I don't know how much Morgan wants me to handle, of all of us Morgan is the one who likes to handle it on her own. I'm not saying that you two can't stand on your own two feet, when it comes down to it you know we have each other's back."

"Morgan knows that too," Kadie said calmer now.

"But she has been gone too long and has it in her head she has to do it all on her own," Sara added.

"She came home, that's a start," Abby said sadly. "Do you think she'll ever forgive me?" Abby looked at Sara.

"Yes, I'll forgive you" Morgan walked into the kitchen from the living room. She would have found it irritating to find her sisters talking about her, but she had heard enough for it not to. She walked in weakly "Sara handles it all, I'm so tired of all of it. I'm going to go back to bed, I'm not going to make good company. I just came down to give you a hug and tell you to have a great time." Morgan said walking over to Abby.

"But we need to fix this," Abby said her eyes big, and dramatic.

"Sara will," Morgan said. "I have been trying to hold it all on my own for so long. I just want to hand it over for a while, I'm just going to focus on growing this baby and working at the shop. We'll need to bring Eddie in on this, he'll know what to do." Morgan said then turned to go back upstairs. The sisters watched her go, then turned to each other.

"Let's get through the brunch, and send you guys off. Everything will be fine." Sara said taking a breath, everything had to be fine.

11

———

It had been three days since Jared had last laid eyes on Sara, he was excited and a little nervous as he walked into the bakery. Again, he was hit with the sugar that seem to hang in the air, fresh and warm. He went and stood at the counter waiting for Sara to come bouncing up, but he was met with Morgan.

"Welcome to Daisy's cakes, how can I help you?" Morgan smiled; Jared noticed it didn't touch her eyes. His brain started to think of all the why's.

"Sara, I'm here for Sara." He said quickly, surprising himself by the lack of smoothness.

"Oh, that's right lunch, three days not bad." Morgan nodded then moved around the counter to the door, she locked and flipped the sign.

Jared waited for his body alarms to go off, but when Morgan looked back at him, he was calm. There was something in her face, that reassured him.

"So how is work? Can you talk about it? Maybe I shouldn't have asked." Morgan asked and Jared watched as Morgan's checks tinted a light pink.

"Work is fine, you can ask. I won't tell what I'm not allowed to." He said giving her a reassuring smile.

"Ok good," Morgan turned and walked to the back, without a word Jared followed. He was led down a short hallway with pictures and calendars on either side of the walls. He walked into a room that opened to take up most of the back of the building. It was sectioned off with long stainless-steel counters, ovens ran along one wall, and the opposite was what looked like a decorating station. He noted the pan rack full of cupcakes some frosted, others waiting. Music played around them; he saw Kadie sway with the beat as she frosted a tray of cupcakes. He looked around the room and found her, Sara was bent over a drafting table writing fast and flipping through papers.

"Morgan, I hope whoever it was you told them that we're closed and to come back in an hour," Sara said then wrote another note. Jared walked over and stood by the desk. Whatever she was working on had her full attention.

"So now I'm just whoever?" He watched her pencil stop as his voice cut through her concentration. She looked up at him, he couldn't help the smile of just being with her brought. He had spent most of the last three days thinking of her, none of his memories did her justice.

"Lunch?" He asked and watched as Sara opened her mouth to give what he thought might be an excuse when Kadie piped up.

"Oh yes, I'm starving, how about you Morgan?" Kaide looked over at Morgan.

"Oh, I'm so hungry this kid is taking all I've got and more," Morgan said smiling.

Jared almost laughed at the look Sara shot at both her sisters. Morgan moved quickly to help Kadie put things up for them to leave.

What nobody knew was that Andrew had sent a text to Morgan giving her a heads up that Jared was on his way. Otherwise, he would have met a locked door, and wouldn't have known that Sara was planning to work through lunch. Morgan gave Jared a wink, as she walked by him to the back door.

"We'll meet you in the car," Kadie said quickly following Morgan out the door. Sara looked at Jared, "It's a standard lock if you want to go the other way." Sara found herself holding her breath waiting for the letdown. She couldn't believe her sisters, and what they were doing.

"Have a little more faith in me. I picked up on the tightness of your family at the wedding. If taking your sisters out to lunch with us is the only way I get to see you, get to know you, I'll do it." Jared said as he held his hand out.

"Come on Sara, I'm on call and don't know how long I have." That hit Sara like nothing else could. He was an officer of the law; he would never know how much time he had.

"Alright, do you need to take your own car then?" She asked standing up.

"No, I'll have someone pick me up if I have to," Jared said with a shrug.

"We won't go far then" Sara took his hand, and she started to follow him out when he stopped and turned to her.

"Wait," he said moving into her.

"What?" Sara asked looking up at him in surprise. He had his lips on hers and she was lost. It was soft and slow like the other kisses, then it was hot and demanding. She hadn't given it a second thought; she gave all he demanded in those quick moments.

"Hi," he said breathlessly finally ending the kiss and pulling back.

"Hi," Sara opened her eyes to find him smiling at her.

"Now we can go." He said giving her a smile.

They chose a little sandwich shop that was close to the bakery because it was such a nice day they ate outside. Morgan and Kadie quizzed him down. Both were good for his mind, getting him to answer questions, at the same time keeping him relaxed. They laughed and joked, Jared becoming accustomed to the teasing that came naturally for the girls. As expected, Jared's phone went off, it was Andrew calling him back to the station. Jared ordered a sandwich to go. Once he had it and had paid for lunch they walked back to the bakery.

"So, when can I see you again?" Jared asked when Sara walked him to his car.

"Whenever you like. You know where I am." Sara looked up at Jared when he pulled her into him. She met him as he kissed her, enjoying the fall that came with every meeting. He pulled away before either could go too far under.

"Till next time" He smiled and left her.

Jared walked to his desk and tossed the sandwich to Andrew who had the phone cradled to his ear, he stopped typing just in time to catch the sandwich. Jared had taken his light jacket off, put his gun on his desk, and without sitting picked up his ringing phone.

"Brooks," he said waking his computer up.

"You sound so different on the phone or maybe it's a cop thing," Sara said with a giggle. Jared's heart stopped, he had left her fifteen minutes ago and at the sound of her voice realized he had started missing her the moment he drove off.

"What can I do for you, Miss Mathews?" Jared smiled and then stopped when Andrew looked over at him.

"Two things, well three but we'll get to that later," Sara said in his ear. Jared had to take a breath; this woman was his undoing. "First I need to know if you're free tomorrow night, and second I need to know if you could help me with a problem I have." She said and Jared could hear a touch of shyness in her tone.

"I can get off at 5, and I'm not on call what do you have in mind?" he asked.

"Dinner with me," she said softly.

"I can do that, what's the problem?" Jared asked he heard his email ping at him. He opened it and started to scan over it waiting for Sara.

"Morgan is being harassed." Sara sounded hesitant. Jared couldn't help looking at Andrew, who thankfully wasn't looking at him.

"Alright, is this an official complaint or is it between you and me?" Jared got a note pad out to take notes, whichever Sara said Jared would take note.

"Does it have to be either or?" It was almost as if he could see the worry on her face, it came through her voice loud and clear.

"No, sweetheart it doesn't" At that moment Jared made the decision that he could be there for her. She needed him to stay objective, that was how he was going to be there for her. A safe, trusted place for her to come to. "Do you want to come in, or do you want me to come to you? The sooner the better."

"Can you come to the bakery, tonight after six?" Jared could hear the relief in her voice.

"Yes," he said, "we'll come to the back door."

"We?" She asked.

"Andrew is my partner, and he is going to want to know what's going on with Morgan" Jared shut his eyes he knew Andrew was looking at him across the desks.

"Can he stay objective too?" Sara asked. Jared smiled; he had nailed it.

"I don't know, he is going to have to work that out himself," Jared said.

"Well, he has till six to figure it out." Sara was sounding more like her usual self. "I have to go; my ovens need me. See you later" she said then was gone.

Jared hung up and faced his friend.

"What am I going to have to work out?" Andrew said almost glaring at Jared.

"If you can be objective when it comes to Morgan?" Jared turned back to his email. "we're needed downstairs." Jared stood up, and turned to Andrew "You have till six to figure it out." Jared knew his friend would take four hours and eleven minutes to do just that.

12

———

SARA, Kadie, and Morgan had come to the decision quickly to involve Jared and maybe Andrew after they listened to the recent message left by Mark. At six they closed the shop, Kadie had gone just before closing and took the jeep to get Morgan Chinese takeout. By the time Kadie came through the back door, Sara was just finishing the clean-up and laughed because she had just jumped a foot out of her skin. Morgan came back with a tray of goodies that were on their way out.

"Fronts all locked up," Morgan said setting the tray down.

"Might as well enjoy them," Kadie said, then they moved stools around one of the counters to set up for dinner and the guys.

"So" Morgan started as she sat down "I was thinking about the specials, and I ran into your new recipes. I think we could try one out next week. I also want to know when you're planning the popcorn." Morgan stopped when she saw Kadie shake her head "What?" Morgan asked reaching for a set of chop sticks.

"She doesn't want to hear about it, talk about it, think about it till November 1st, and come January 2nd it's back to the silent treatment," Kadie said sitting down and grabbing the closest white contrary; she opened it looked in and passed it to Morgan.

"Why, I love that popcorn." Morgan gave Sara a sad face when Sara moved to sit with her sisters.

"You and half the city, the demand is so high for those two months it's all I make. We never fail to end in the black those months." Sara grabbed a carton checked it then got a set of sticks.

"You have ended in the black every month for the last four years," Morgan said digging into the carton Kadie past her. Then she looked up at Sara. "Sorry, I was going over the calendar for specials and saw a few numbers."

"It's fine, but whatever you do don't tell Abby, if she knew we would be in the red for sure," Sara said before she popped a piece of sweet and sour chicken into her mouth.

"So, if I ask really nicely, would you make my popcorn?" Morgan gave Sara her puppy dog look, but Sara didn't look.

"Put that look away, I mean it, Morgan. No." Sara got up and walked to the walk-in for bottles of water.

"Don't waste your time Morgan, I spend all year begging." Kadie set one box down and moved to find the fried rice. Then the back door opened, and Jared and Andrew walked in. "Sorry, we didn't wait for you," Kadie said as she found the right box, and dug in.

Andrew moved to the empty seat next to Morgan. "Take off your coats and stay awhile." She smiled at him, then looked at Jared.

They both did and with that, their guns were in full view. Sara was walking back, as the men sat down. Her eyes going straight to the guns.

"Do they make you nervous?" Jared asked when he caught her eye.

"No, I don't think so. The opposite actually." Sara sat down next to him. She passed water around to everyone.

"I think we could do the cranberry- apple muffins next week," Sara said taking one more bit of the sweet and sour, then passing it to Jared, and reaching for the fried rice Kadie had. Kadie passed it and went on the hunt for another container.

"Popcorn," Morgan said setting the container down, she handed a set of sticks to Andrew and kissed his cheek. Then handed him a container.

"Forget it, you won't win this. I just got the smell of Carmel out of my closet. No, and that is my final answer." Sara said then smiled at Jared who had gotten into the rhythm of eating and reached for her water.

"You know, when she put her foot down it was only me asking, Abby gave up too easily. But now that your home" Kadie raised a brow at Morgan. "The three of us could work her down." Sara watched as her little sisters turned their puppy dog eyes on her.

"Wait, wait, no stop! Oh, come on." Sara set her water bottle down and shut her eyes. She took a deep breath "We're taking about one week, right?"

"Well, I want a batch, and I think Kadie wants a batch." Morgan looked at Kadie "Is that right?"

"Yes." Kadie agreed bouncing on her seat with the excitement that she may get Sara's Special Carmel Popcorn before Halloween.

"Would you both back off if I just made you each a batch, and not run it as a special." Sara opened her eyes to watch her sisters, who by now were so happy thinking they had won.

"Yes!" they said at the same time.

"Alright, I'm new to this. What is so special about popcorn, it's just popcorn." Andrew asked as he moved to another container.

"I'm with him on this," Jared said taking a drink from his water bottle.

"You guys just need to try some, and you'll understand. We got her to agree, now we just need her to do it." Kadie said as she put her sticks down, she was done, Morgan followed soon after.

Sara took one more bit of the noodles and then passed them the Jared. The guys kept eating while the girls talked more about the weekly specials. When Andrew who was the last, set his sticks down Sara got up and started clearing the counter. She touched Morgan's shoulder, as she walked by.

"Alright, so about 3 months ago I came home early to find my soon to be ex-husband having sex with some blond on my kitchen table. I went and got my camera and took pictures; he was too into it to notice. I left, went to a park down the street, and thought about what the next steps should be. I decided to come home early for a week and ended up taking pictures of him with three other women." Morgan took a breath ask she looked at Jared and Andrew "I took the pictures to our lawyer the one who had drawn up our pre-nuptial agreement. It is stated that I have to have proof of any affairs, I can't just have hunches."

"A week after I caught him, I filed for divorce, three weeks after that I sold my car, two weeks after that I sold my condo. I decided to have everything sold in that place the day after I came home for the wedding. I was told that he would be served the same day I left. I hadn't heard from him till Sunday after the wedding, in the form of a voice mail."

Morgan had gotten her phone out, after putting hit the speaker on she hit play, Marks's voice cut through the quiet. Kadie grabbed Morgan's hand, and Sara moved behind Morgan putting a hand on her shoulder.

Jared watched Andrew; he was keeping his anger well in

check. When the message was over, they all seemed to take a deep breath.

"Why didn't you tell him about the baby before you left?" Jared asked using his soft tone.

"I had taken a pregnancy test at work and had come home early, to find him on the kitchen table. I didn't think he needed or wanted to know" Morgan answered.

"So why the call today and not on Sunday?" Andrew asked looking at the three sisters. Jared already knew, they had planned to handle it themselves.

"He left this" Morgan said and hit play on the next message.

"Morgan, you stupid bitch. You can run but you can't hide. I'm coming for you, and that bastard child you thought you could have, I'm going to make you sorry-" the message ended.

Jared looked up and saw Morgan's eyes fill, Andrew turned pulling Morgan into his arms. Then Jared looked at Sara who was staring at him. Jared nodded his head; he would take care of this. After Morgan stopped crying Andrew let her go.

"So now we have to figure out what to do," Morgan said wiping tears as she giggled weakly. Jared had noticed Sara did that too when she was nervous.

"Well first we need to take your phone in as evidence, then you need to file official charges. Do you have any idea what caused the change?" Jared asked.

"Abby was the one who called him, congratulated him on the baby, and said she was sad that he hadn't made the wedding, but happy that he was moving here. She didn't know, and just assumed." Morgan took a sip of water.

"So, he hasn't gotten the papers yet?" Andrew asked keeping a hand on Morgan.

"He has to have them, he would also notice the people going in taking everything, the locks being changed." Morgan looked at Andrew. "In the agreement, I get a hundred grand for every act I prove."

"That's a lot of money," Jared said thinking there was another reason for Mark.

"I didn't think he would get this upset. I don't know why he's so upset about the baby, I'm gone, it's not his responsibility." They watched as the dots connected, and the light went off above her head.

"Oh god that's it, money. All of this is going to come down to money. He would owe me eighteen years of child support on top of alimony." Morgan put her face in her hands, her body started to shake. Before anyone could comfort her, she sat up laughing. "He could end up in jail because he's being stupid over money." Morgan looked at Jared, he smiled back at her.

"He doesn't know you intend to not put him on the birth certificate," Sara said running a hand down her back.

"I could let his father know," Morgan said.

"Why his father?" Andrew asked

"His father is our lawyer," Morgan said with a shrug.

"That explains a lot," Jared said grabbing for his water.

"What do you mean?" Sara asked moving to sit next to him.

"Daddy doesn't think his boy is stupid enough to get caught, that's why I'm assuming he put the whole prove it in the prenup," Jared said watching Morgan.

"File your complaint and get in touch with his father as soon as you can. Let them know you just want out, and the baby is yours." Jared said giving Morgan a nod.

"I can do that." She said letting her breath out, nodding back at him. Then she looked around the room, her family and the two new would stand with her, have her back. That above all everything had her relaxing.

"Alright, well now that is somewhat settled. Who wants dessert?" Sara asked as she moved to a set of cabinets behind the drafting table.

"I'm still too full, from dinner," Kadie said as she stood and stretched. "And we have this lovely tray of leftovers."

"Oh well if that's the case I won't share with you" Sara walked back to the table with a stack of tins 6in wide and 6in deep. "Jared, would you like some?" Sara winked at him

"Sure" He took a tin, popping the lid he was hit with the smell of Carmel, salt, and butter. He opened the lid and found a full can of popcorn.

"You, sneaky witch," Kadie said reaching forward to grab a tin. Andrew reached for one and had it snatched out of his hand by Morgan, who quickly popped the top and took a bite. Andrew watched her close her eye as she savored the first bit. Then he dove in for a handful.

"Oh my god, you make this?" Jared said as he finished chewing

"Yep, but only for two months a year, I knew we were going to be hitting some bumpy road and it's their favorite," Sara said as she watched her sisters laugh and eat the popcorn.

"Jared it's the same." Andrew's eyes were big with excitement

"I know," Jared said going back for another handful

"What?" Sara asked looking at them.

"A few years ago, someone brought in a tin of this into the station, it was gone in a matter of minutes. We have been trying to track it down ever since." Jared said smiling at her.

"Wait till they find out; we'll be the winners" Andrew smiled and ate another handful.

"Winners?" Morgan asked.

"After everyone ate it, but nobody knew where to get more a competition was born. Whoever could find the popcorn again wins a hundred bucks" Andrew winked at Sara "Thanks babe."

"Hey, watch it," Jared said and moved an arm around Sara's waist. Sara smiled and rested into Jared.

13

———

OVER THE NEXT WEEK, Sara and Jared spent every minute they could together, lunches, dinners, even a few movies. It was tricky with Sara working so early and Jared being called away. They made it work, Sara was enjoying her time with him, enjoying getting to know him. She drove home after a dinner cut short thinking about what Kadie had said, he mattered, and it was growing.

Jared walked into the squad room on a warm spring Monday morning, Andrew was already sitting at his desk.

"Well, this is a switch," Jared said going through the routine of undoing all he would have to do when they left. He turned his computer on and settled at this desk. When he looked at Andrew, he found his friend staring at Morgan's cell phone. Still in the evidence bag.

"Anything new?" Jared asked.

"No, though I can tell you the lawyer's dad isn't happy about the baby news either. He said he will be having a chat with his son and so far, the calls have stopped. I called Morgan last night to make sure he hasn't been calling the house or the bakery so far, nothing."

"No news is good news?" Jared asked knowing his friend and partner.

"I would agree but my gut tells me this isn't just going to go away. From what Morgan has shared he's a piece of work. I would really like to get him for more than just harassment." Andrew said sitting back.

"Do you think he'll show up?" Jared turned to the email notification

"Yeah, I do, before this is done, he's going to show his ugly face." Andrew put the phone away, changing gears and cases. He filled Jared in on what he got before Jared came in. They were both elbow deep when Jared's phone rang.

"Brooks."

"Jared sweetheart." Helen's voice shirked through the phone. Andrew laughed.

"Hello mother, what can I do for you," Jared said not paying attention.

"Lunch with me today, eleven o'clock. Can you do it?" Helen asked

"No, sorry mother I have a full day. I'm not stopping for lunch today." Jared cradled the phone between his ear and shoulder. So that he could type a response back. While his mother just talked in his ear.

"Jared, are you even listening to me?" She asked, sounding short.

"Yes, you want me to go to lunch with you and dad because we haven't shared a meal for a month." He said going back to the email. What Helen didn't know was that Jared and his dad got together almost every week.

"Mother I can't do it today." He said as he started looking for a specific note.

"So, I have to wait another month before I see you, Jared I'm your mother," Helen said by her tone she couldn't decide if she wanted to be forceful or whiny, so it had come out both. Jared rolled his eyes, knowing she would keep pushing, and if not today then she would just call again tomorrow. The longest he had ever been able to hold her off was a week when she really worked on him. Jared closed his eye knowing where this was Meg's leading.

"Lunch at eleven? I may be able to do it, but it can't be an all-day thing mother. I have a job that needs my attention." He said closing his eyes, he really didn't want to. The thought of how the lunch would keep her away for a while was his goal.

"Well, you have a family that needs your attention as well. We'll pick you up, goodbye dear." Helen hung up before Jared could say anything else.

"Well, you have fun with that," Andrew said not looking up

"What are you doing for lunch?" Jared asked, leaning back in his chair, covering his eyes with his hands.

"Not a chance in hell am I going with you, I'm not sure yet," Andrew said smiling.

They got back to work till Jared's phone rang again. It was his mother telling him they were out front.

"Call if you need anything," Andrew said as Jared loaded up.

"Yep thanks" Jared walked out.

Jared found himself sitting at a table at the country club his parents had been a part of for as long as he could remember. He wasn't as surprised as he should have been when he found out his dad wasn't going to join them. His mother was always pulling stunts like this.

A beautiful, blond southern bell sat across from him. Her name was Meg Emerson, she was his lunch date. Not only had his mother pushed him out of working through his lunch but had also set him up on a blind date.

He kept his cool, was polite, and watched the minutes tick by. His mother left the table, and he could feel a foot creeping up his leg. That was his last straw he shifted back when Meg's toes made it to his knees. It was at that moment he decided he was done, with the lunch and his mother's attempts at fixing him up.

"Meg, I'm not sure what my mother has told you, first I'm not like that. I prefer to know a woman for longer than a lunch before I take her to bed, and I'm seeing someone." He said it moving further away from her.

Had I known my mother was setting me up, I would have put a stop to it." Jared scooted back and stood up. "Have a nice afternoon." He finished and turned to leave.

"You be sure to call if you change your mind," Meg said then straightened as Helen made her way back to them.

"Jared, what are you doing?" She looked at Meg who had quickly replaced the look of wanting to one of sadness at being left in the middle of lunch.

"I'm leaving, I have work to do and I'm seeing someone," Jared said firmly as he watched his mother's eye heat then frost, he had embarrassed her. She pulled him away from the table, and shot a smile at Meg over her shoulder.

"How dare you speak to me that way. You just embarrassed me in front of Miss Emerson. Now you go back and finish your date with the lovely young woman. You have been too long without a date and it's time for you to settle down." Helen's eyes didn't let up. Jared let out a breath.

"I'm seeing someone," he said watching her. Nothing changed for her, as if he hadn't said anything.

"Goodbye mother, it was nice seeing you." Jared turned without a backward glance and left. When he was outside, he pulled the phone from his pocket and called Andrew.

"Hey come get me," Jared said without waiting for a hello from Andrew.

"Sure, where are you." Sara's voice was light and soft. Jared pulled the phone from his ear to make sure he called the right number.

"Where is Andrew?" He asked wondering why Sara had answered.

"Next to me, do you need to talk to him?" Her tone had changed from light to slightly serious.

"No, I just need a ride." He closed his eyes and took a breath.

"Ok, where are you?" She asked, Jared told her then he heard her relay the information to Andrew. "It will be a few minutes." She said coming back to him.

"I'm going to start walking," Jared told her then got off the phone. He had already started the walk; he hadn't wanted his mother to come out and try to drag him back in.

That got his mind working, what the hell was his mother thinking? Setting him up wasn't something she had done for a while, as she was always trying to have a firm hand in his life. It had gotten easier to tell her no, and take a stand for himself the older he got. He was about seventeen when he put his foot down for the first time, it was amazing. It also helped his dad always have his back, and it was on that occasion that it was proven beyond a shadow of a doubt.

Jared saw Andrew's car heading his way, he felt his heart fall a bit. He had hoped Sara would have come to his rescue. Of course, he had just left a lunch date with another woman, that didn't sit right in his stomach. They would have to talk about it, he wouldn't lie or keep things from her. The car pulled up; Jared opened the door.

"Hey, handsome need a ride?" Sara asked with a big, beautiful smile Jared's heart stopped, and his blood heating and traveling south. Without a word, he got in the car, reached for her face, and took her mouth.

Sara didn't know how she had kept the car from rolling. The moment that Jared's lips touched hers she was lost. The heat rushed over her skin; her blood was pumping in her ears. She couldn't contain the gasp and moan when his hand moved under her shirt to find her soft skin. He took her mouth over and over, never able to satisfy his need for her. He held onto the last bit of sanity, he used it to pull them out of the heated haze he took them to. They were in a car, pulled over on the side of the street.

"I missed you too," Sara said trying to get her breath back.

"I don't know how much longer I can keep my hands off of you." He said when he pulled her back for one more sweet kiss.

"I vote for not much longer, but not in the car. Yet." Sara giggled; she took a breath. She flipped a U-turn and headed back to where the others were.

"So how is your day going? Jared asked not taking his eyes off her.

"Fine, we're closed on Mondays so the three of us went in to clean, and plan. We have a box of goodies for you and Andrew, that had been Morgan's idea." Sara kept her eyes on the road as she spoke to him.

Jared's mind ran over his day. He landed on the lunch he had just left. He would tell her the truth even if it ended things, he hoped that it wouldn't. It wouldn't be the first relationship he had that ended due to complications with his mother.

"Sara, I need to tell you something." He said looking at her.

"Does it have to do with the lunch I just picked you up from?" She kept her voice even.

"Yes."

"Alright, let's hear it." Sara was surprised that she had manganese to keep her voice so even when her stomach and heart felt like she was hanging upside down.

"I went to lunch with my mother, I was under the impression that my father would join us. I would have held her off if I knew that he wasn't joining but still I went. She had me meet a young woman at this lunch. Then she left us, I was set up on a lunch date. It wasn't my idea, and I left as soon as I could." He said watching her, she stayed relaxed, so he continued.

"I also told both the woman and my mother that I was seeing someone and not interested in anymore setups." Jared waited, he knew he had thrown it all at her, and now the ball was in her court.

Sara was quiet until they pulled up to the little sandwich shop, the one they had gone to on their first date. Jared could see Andrew sitting with Morgan and Kadie outside at a table covered with an umbrella. Jared watched his friend smiling and laughing with Morgan. He could see the fall in his eyes. Jared couldn't help but smile.

"They look happy, don't they?" Sara asked then added, "I haven't seen that light in Morgan's eyes for a while, her husband never put it there." Jared turned back to Sara and waited. He could see something in her eyes too.

"So, you're not interested in anymore set ups?" Sara asked looking at Jared.

"Just with you." Jared smiled; he lends to her. Sara found herself leaning into him.

"Just me?" Sara couldn't help the little smile that pulled at her lips. He was making a stand for them. She was all for it.

"Perhaps I should have asked you before, will you be my girlfriend?" Jared asked moving a hand to the back of her neck, pulling her face slowly to him.

"Yes," Sara said looking into the heat of Jared's eyes, then his lips met hers. Heat and want to be moved through her as he is slowing took her mouth, his hand softly holding her to him.

At that moment she didn't want to question it. She questioned everything, second guessed everything and everyone. Her sisters were the only people she trusted, but with Jared in his embrace she just let it all go, he had a way of doing that to her. She would start rethinking it when they were apart again. The high he gave her always seem to dwindle the longer they were apart.

Sara's stomach gave a loud growl, that made her jump, her hand flying to cover it up.

"You haven't eaten?" Jared asked concern in his eyes.

"No, I came and got you instead. Then we had this little talk." Sara smiled at him.

'Let's get you fed. Stay there." He added quickly. He got out and Sara watched him move around the car to the driver's door. She looked up at him brightly as he opened the door for her. She grabbed the hand he held out for her, pulling her from the car. He followed her to the table to join the rest of their family.

14

———————

JARED AND ANDREW were only with the girls for fifteen minutes when they were called away. Sara put her head down and ate after they left knowing her sisters were going to jump all over her. She didn't doubt that they had seen her making out with Jared in the parking lot, she would have had something to say.

"So, I was thinking we should do a movie tonight, what do you think Morgan?" Kadie asked sipping on her Iced tea.

"I think that would be a great idea. Andrew didn't have anything new on Mark." Morgan sat back and stretched. Her belly was growing, and quickly.

They were planning on hitting a bookstore after lunch. The internet was full of information, Morgan knew that if she wasn't careful what she found was just going to freak her out. That and she was a book worm at heart. She found comfort in the way a book felt in her hands, felt the weight shift as she moved through it.

"Sara, you don't need to eat so fast. We have the rest of the day," Kadie said.

"Oh, and I made a doctor's appointment today." Morgan sounded proud of herself.

"Good, when is it?" Sara asked as she reached for her soda.

"Friday, I made it for the lunch break. We seem to have a steady flow increase."

"That's because you're home," Kadie said, looking at her phone. "We have always done better when you were home. We would have a good few days or weeks, however long you were home. Then it always died down after you were gone." Kadie finished her soda and looked at Sara to see if she was done.

"You're kidding." Morgan smiled at Sara waiting for the confirmation that Kadie was pulling her leg. Then frowned when Sara just looked at her.

"She's right, we have always done better when you were home. We can carry our own and have been. I'm a little worried actually."

"Why?" Kadie asked.

"We were doing good; you and I could handle most days. Evie has been coming in less and less. Not that we don't need her, but we can manage without her. Now that Morgan's home I have a gut feeling we are going to be in over our heads soon." Sara pushed her plate away and sat back. "We need to plan for that and the time she is going to take off when she has the baby."

"We could offer Evie full time work?" Kadie offered but Sara could hear the hesitation in her voice because Sara felt it too.

"Why doesn't Abby work?" Morgan asked, as she stood up. One of the guys had taken care of lunch before they left.

"Sara and Abby can't work in the same area day after day. Abby doesn't like running the front end." Kadie stood too, followed by Sara.

They made their way to Sara's jeep. "For as much as you bring business up when you're in the front, Abby brings it down." Kadie finished from the back seat.

They drove to the bookstore, spending more time than they planned. Kadie heading to the cake decorating books, Morgan to the parenting books, and Sara to the baking. In the end, all three of them walked out with a bag each filled with books. What had been planned as dinner and movie night turning into dinner and books night.

Kadie looked up from her book, she had a pen in hand. She liked marking her books, making notes in the margins. She found Sara in one of the big chairs, knees pulled up with notebook in reach as she too liked to take notes of recipes that she could make hers later. Morgan was stretched out on the couch, asleep with her book laid open over her belly.

"It is really nice to have her home," Kadie said softly, Sara looked up.

"Yeah, it is. I want to go with her to the doctor, but she said it was going to be a run of the mill appointment. She said I could go with her another time, but I think Andrew is going to start going with her."

"That's quick," Kadie said, she too had the question everything twice. Her life had conditioned her to do so.

"Well, he makes her happy. Why do you want to question that?" Sara watched her baby sister.

"Because we know what happens when it's too good to be true." Kadie looked back at Sara.

They had been through too much not to have that idea stuck in their head. Their dad had walked out, raising four girls had been too much for him. One day he was there, the next he went to work and never came home. After that, they moved in with their grandmother, who had left them as well. Only this time it was for heaven. The hardest blow had been when their mother had lost her brief but very hard battle with cancer.

Kadie looked over at Morgan who was off in dream land. They had understood why she had left, understood her need to go and live her life. Neither Sara nor Kadie had left, though Kadie had quietly waited for Sara to shut down the shop so she could leave too.

"You're happy too," Kadie said looking back at Sara.

"I am, but that doesn't mean I'm leaving," Sara said reassuringly. Sara and Kadie were close, increasingly so after their mother had died.

Sara had woken up often with Kadie in bed with her. Sara knew Kadie had worried that she would wake up one day and Sara would be gone. It wasn't until the middle of her junior year did Kadie stop coming to Sara's bed every night.

"Ok, I'm going to bed. Who knows what tomorrow will bring us?" Kadie stood up, taking her books with her she headed upstairs. Sara just sat going over it all in her head.

"I have never envied her for being the baby," Morgan said sitting up. Sara turned and pulled out of her thinking.

"Me either," Sara said. "I'm going to head to bed. You can either come with us or take Kadie's car in the morning." Sara stood, and she put her books in a pile.

"I'll come with you," Morgan said it took her a bit more effort and quick thinking to get off the couch. "Man, I am getting big." She said when she was upright.

"You are so beautiful," Sara said smiling at her sister. "May I?" She asked as she held a handout to Morgan's belly

"Yes, and you're my sister you have to say that." Morgan watched as Sara moved her hands over her belly

"As your sister, I'm not allowed to lie to you." Sara smiled as she felt a nudge against her hand.

"And it's awake," Morgan said with a sigh.

"It? Really?" Sara said raising an eyebrow.

"Well, I can't say she or he as I don't know yet," Morgan said looking down at her belly, putting a hand on the other side.

"Nugget, let's call it Nugget," Sara said smiling.

"That works," Morgan said with a smile. The two made their way up to their rooms.

Sara set her books on the window seat before she changed

into her t-shirt and boxer shorts. She was brushing her teeth when her cell phone signaled an incoming text.

"Are you still awake?"

Sara smiled it was from Jared. She walked to the bathroom finished her teeth then went back to her phone.

"Yes, just finished getting ready for bed. What are you doing?"

She asked then started to braid her hair. With it being so long, she found it safer to braid it before bed.

"Waiting for you to come downstairs and let me in."

Sara's heart stopped. Then she had the feeling of hanging upside down again. She quietly made her way downstairs, using the set that would bring her down into the living room. She walked over to the front door, unlocked and opened it.

There he was standing in the dark with the streetlights on behind him. He moved quickly after he took her all in, from her fresh face to the boxer shorts and bare feet. Stepping in and to her, he grabbed her, bringing her to him, kissing her, devouring her. He shut the door quietly, then pushed her against it.

He couldn't tell her why he was there, to check on her he had told himself. After lunch the rest of the day he had faced he just wanted to lose himself in her.

"Hi," she said breathlessly when Jared moved away. His body still had her pinned to the door, his forehead on hers.

"Hi," Jared said just as breathless. Sara moved her hands from his shoulders to the inside of his jacket, down his sides she felt his gun on his hip and stopped. He looked into her eyes.

"Bad day?" She asked.

"Ya, it all went to shit after we left." Now that he was with her, he almost felt stupid for coming. He felt better +9yes but she needed to sleep. "I should go-"

Sara stopped him when her lips moved over his, her hands moving up his back.

"I think you should come with me." She pushed him away and grabbed his hand. He was led through a living room, to an eat in kitchen.

It was big and beautiful, with glass front cabinets, a large counter that had bar stools, and a big round table set in the larger bay window. It was clean and set to rights in the soft glow of the light above the strove.

"Have a seat, tell me what you can." Sara led him to a stool. He sat down and watched as she moved around the kitchen. She filled a tea kettle, taking it back to the stove to turn the heat on under it. She reached into a cupboard and looked over her shoulder when he didn't say anything.

"You're so beautiful." He said admiring the view and was rewarded with a small smile.

"Thank you," Sara said putting the tea on the counter and making her way over to stand in front of him, keeping the counter between them.

Sara could have been taken the moment he put her against the door, she was sure if he moved on her here, she would go with him happily.

"It was just a bad day with bad guys, Homicide isn't for the weak. Andrew and I called it, having hit a wall, and knowing tomorrow could be just as bad. He went home and I came here."

"How did you know where we lived?" Sara asked with a smirk

"I looked it up from the report Morgan filed." Jared smiled back. The hot water started to whistle, and Sara moved fast. Making two cups of tea, she hadn't needed one, but he did, and she would join him.

"Do you like it sweet?" She asked over her shoulder. She started to turn around when he hadn't answered but stopped when she felt his body press against her back. He moved her braid and bending down kissed her behind her ear and down her neck till he ran into her shirt. She felt zings and zips move up and down her spine, her body moving against his. He moved back up to her ear.

"Yes, please." He whispered, smiling she added the honey. She moved away from him taking both cups she went to the French doors that led to the back yard, and the large deck with table and chairs. He followed without a word.

"Sara?" He asked when they were sitting in the dark, a table between them.

"Yes?" She knew what was coming and was glad for the darkness

"How many guys have you been with?" Jared asked, not wanting to push too much too fast. Then waited for Sara.

"One, we dated our senior year and went to the same college. When mom got sick, and I came home it ended things." Sara picked her cup up and took a cautious sip.

"He didn't understand why I was choosing to come home; all he saw was me not choosing him," Sara said quietly sipping her tea in the spring evening. Acting like it hadn't ripped her heart out. Jared knew better.

"You haven't dated for seven years?" Jared made sure to add the teasing note to the question. Sara giggled.

"I've had dates, but they didn't go that far. Once they caught on that I'm the fixer, that my plate is full most of the time with my family and the bakery. Realizing they wouldn't be my one and only priority they don't stick around." Sara shrugged it off.

"They never wanted to help, maybe even fix what they could for you?" Jared asked realizing he was sitting with one strong woman, and as he got to know her, he liked and respected her more.

"Nope," Sara said taking a sip and thinking about Kadie. "My family is worth a lot to me, I don't just let anyone help, or take over. That and no one has managed to get by Kadie. She has an interesting ability to call a guy out and then laugh when they run. So far one guy has made it through" She looked at him.

"Eddie" Jared said.

"Yep," Sara closed her eyes as a warm breeze moved over her skin. Jared watched her; he could have told her that Kadie had called him out already. Another time. They sat in the quiet a little longer, Jared noticed Sara hasn't opened her eyes again.

"I need to let you sleep." Jared stood, startling Sara, who had drifted off while she enjoyed the breeze.

"What?" She said her eyes not quite opening.

He moved over to her, setting her cup down on the table. He bent over and picked her up from the chair. Cradled in his arms Sara rested her head on his shoulders as he made his way into the house.

"Upstairs, light open with the door on," Sara said half asleep. He almost went to the living room to go up the stairs but then saw a set going up from the kitchen.

At the top of the stairs, he saw the other set, the one leading to the front of the house. As he looked around, he saw a set of French doors, and six open doors but only one had a light on. He walked to it, and going in he was bathed in soft light, surrounded by soft colors. He noted that she had the same bay window as the kitchen, hers held a window seat. He walked to her bed and carefully pulled the blankets back, laying her down he bent over to kiss her forehead. He stood, looking down at her for a moment. He wasn't surprised when the feeling of climbing in with her slammed against him. Not to push, just to hold.

"Next time," he said quietly, then he turned to let himself out. First stopping out back to collect the teacups, and putting them in the sink he locked the door behind him as he left.

He was just getting into his truck when his phone rang.

"Brooks," he said leaning back, not wanting to deal with whatever was on the other end.

"Jared, It's Meg Emerson." Jared sat up like a bucket of ice water had just dumped on him.

"Why and how did you get this number?" He didn't bother to cover his tone of anger and frustration.

"Your mother gave it to me; you didn't leave it after our lunch," Meg said sweetly. Jared pulled the phone away from his ear, shut his eyes, and counted to 10.

"I didn't leave it because I had no reason to." Jared put his seat belt on but didn't turn the car on.

"But how am I to get in touch with you? I really felt a connection at lunch I know we would be great together." Meg sounded so hopeful.

"Meg, we are not going to get together, I am seeing someone else," Jared said firmly.

"But your mother said I was perfect for you. We really should give this a shot." She said starting to sound like she was losing patients as well.

"Well, we aren't. Goodbye," Jared said then hung up.

He tossed his phone to the passenger seat. His heart almost stopped when it rang. He didn't have the ability to just not answer it, he took note. To never give his mother the number again.

"Brooks," he said, then let out his breath as it was dispatched. He turned his truck on and headed back to work. Feeling tired but recharged at the same time.

15

SARA STOOD LOOKING at her work board the next morning, holding her third cup of coffee. She was feeling the late night with Jared, but she smiled knowing she wouldn't take it back for anything. Sara turned back to her worktable and settled in, mixing, kneading.

The music they turned on gave her good beats to work to. She was swaying as she took cake pans out of the oven, when she turned around, she was met with Kadie and Morgan both standing with their arms crossed, watching her.

"What?" Sara asked, then smiled.

"Nothing." They said together, then turned and went back to their day.

Sara tried to not let it bother her that she hadn't heard from Jared all day, after all, he was a detective. He didn't work banker's hours; he was called all the time. She would wait, it was fine. Morgan closed the front, and Sara and Kadie cleaned up the back.

They had done dinner and a movie. Sara was getting ready for bed and was watching her phone. Then she was laying in her bed staring at her ceiling, trying not to think about it. She drifted off going over the night before, and Jared.

Sara swung her arm out to turn off the alarm, when she rolled back, she felt weight and heat in her bed. Instantly she put her arm around Kadie, she almost went back to sleep.

"You're too hot," Kadie said sleepily,

"I know." Sara snuggled her closer. Sara couldn't remember the last time she woke up with Kadie in her bed. It had been a while.

"Shower time." She said moving to get out of bed.

"Sara?" Kadie's voice was still sleepy.

"Yes?" She said stopping and waiting for Kadie to say what she needed.

"Do you think Jared is going to shoot me if I come in here in the middle of the night?" Kadie asked and Sara couldn't help but laugh.

"If Jared is here, are you going to want to come in here in the middle of the night?" Sara asked and saw Kadie look over at her.

"Good point," Kadie said, "Do you think Andrew is going to want to have coffee before he goes?" Kadie asked moving from the bed

"Goes?" Sara asked looking at Kadie.

"He was sleeping with Morgan last night." Kadie tossed the blankets and got out of bed, Sara did the same. They stood looking at each other for a beat, then both grabbed a corner and made the bed.

"We'll make him a to go cup if he wants one," Sara said shooting Kadie a smile as she walked to the shower. Her mind wondered because that's what your mind does when you're in the shower she thought to herself.

She was dressed and, in the kitchen, fixing to go cups of coffee and tea when she heard footsteps on the stairs.

"Do you like sugar and or cream in your coffee?" Sara asked then turned when she didn't get an answer. Andrew almost looked guilty.

"Sugar, one please." He said, then moved to stand at the counter with her.

Andrew wasn't a stupid man. He knew who the head of the family was, he was looking at her. And knowing the shit storm Morgan was in, he was going to have to make one hell of a case. Sara took her cup and turned to look at him. She may have been leaning against the counter like they were old friends, it was anything but. She was watching him, waiting for him.

"I stayed the night." he started.

"I'm not stupid." She gave him a *do better than that* look.

"I'm not going anywhere." He said, firmly, straight forward.

"Unfortunately, that is something that takes time to prove. Morgan's a big girl, she can make her own choices. Right now, she needs family and support. She needs "not going anywhere", and all that comes with that. So, we 'll just have to wait and see." Sara said handing him his coffee.

"But you can bet your ass I'll be watching you. Kadie came into the kitchen for hers. Sara handed Kadie her coffee without taking her eyes off Andrew.

"He's still standing," Kadie said after the first few sips of coffee. She gave Andrew an assessing look "Make a good enough case?" She looked at Sara.

"Come on we got to go," Sara said to Kadie, grabbing her purse. "You can bring Morgan." She said turning back to Andrew.

Andrew watched them leave, then he let his breath out. He hadn't realized he was holding it. He stood in the kitchen drinking some damn good coffee. His mind traveled over last night. The touching, the heat, the need. Spending the night with Morgan had been everything. She was his, he made sure of that last night. Now he needed to see the papers, not that he didn't trust her. It would mean she was really his. He was pulled from his thoughts when he heard her on the stairs.

"Hey," she said smiling. She walked over to him, he set his cup down to take her in his arms.

"Hey," He kissed her, intending to be light. Taking what she offered, giving back as well.

It deepened with newfound heat, more so when he felt her hands move under his shirt to his skin. Fire rushed through them, he had to have her one more time. Morgan pulled him, through the living room, to a bedroom that was back under the stairs. All without breaking the kiss.

"Shit," Andrew said, waking up with Morgan in his arms. The sun was up, and his phone was ringing.

"Abbot, yeah I'll be right there." He hit the end button and moved to kiss Morgan.

"Mmmm," she said smiling, moving her body against his. God help him he thought.

"Sweetheart we have to go." He rubbed his hand down her back.

"Ok, what time is it?" She asked more awake. Andrew looked at his phone.

"Almost eight." He put it back down and moved to kiss her shoulders.

"Well, crap we really do need to go." She opened her eyes to look at him, smiling. Then moved to get her clothes.

When she stood, her hair was a crazy dark curly mess, her skin soft with a light flush. Andrew's eyes settled on her growing belly. He didn't see some other man's kid when he looked at her, he saw hers, and his heart soared when he felt the baby move. He had been slightly worried he would hurt her, but she had evaporated those thoughts and fears when she touched him and asked him for more. They dressed, he made her a light breakfast, then he took her to the bakery.

"Call me if you need me." He said holding her face as he gave her one last kiss.

"I will," Morgan said getting out of his car, she waved a hand and walked into the bakery.

16

"Well, well. Look who has decided to join us this fine morning." David from the coroner's office said as Andrew walked up to the coroner's truck with a coffee in his hand. As Jared stood next to the body on the gurney.

"What have we got?" Andrew asked about taking a sip when his cup was taken from him. Jared stood next to him, taking a drink.

"Thanks sweetheart. Damn, that's good coffee where did you get it?" Jared asked thinking he would have to go get some of his own.

"Mathew's café," Andrew said watching Jared.

"You're still alive and you got coffee. Lucky bastard." Jared said. The two dive into the case in front of them.

After a day of teasing, Morgan sat on a stool in the back. Watched as her sisters finished cleaning. She was tired, but very happy about it.

"God, she can't stop smiling, Sara makes her stop smiling," Kadie said as she wiped her counter for the last time.

"I don't make you stop smiling after you've had a good night," Sara said as she flipped through some paperwork.

"So, what do you want to do tonight?" Morgan asked.

"Eat and sleep, I had to double our bread this morning. You sold the last of it an hour before we closed." Sara said still not looking up.

"What do our orders look like for the rest of the week?" Kadie said walking over to look over Sara's shoulder. "Holy F-" Kadie reached for the stack of orders they had.

"Do you think we can do this?" Kadie started flipping though.

"Yep, I would have canceled them if I didn't think we could handle it," Sara said making notes. "Alright," She put her pencil down. "Let go." Sara stood and stretched her back. "Hey, have you heard anything from Mark?" Sara looked at Morgan.

"Nope. I'm hoping that he'll just sign the papers and be done with me."

"We're all hoping that," Kadie said, putting the orders back, going to get her bag, and head out the back door. Sara and Morgan followed.

Sara spent her evening elbow deep in dirt and plants, she weeded and watered. She worked her body harder, knowing she would crash when she hit her pillow. After a taco dinner thanks to Morgan who was still on her good night high, Sara bid her sisters goodnight and went to shower her sore muscles. She put her t-shirt and shorts on, grabbed one of her baking books but was asleep before she cracked it open.

She was laying on her side when she opened her eyes. Her lamp was off but there was a soft light coming from her bathroom. She always kept a little light on in the bathroom. She had walked sinto too many walls when she was younger.

"Morgan told me it would work, but I have to say I had my doubts." Jared smiled at her. Sara's heart stopped then started again going twice as fast. He was here, he couldn't call or text for two days, but he could just show up being all cute and hot.

"You don't call, you don't write," Sara said with a straight face.

"I can make up for that, and it will never happen again," Jared said moving closer to her. Sara put a hand out to stop him but found a naked chest. Her hand heated as it lay against his hot skin.

"You think you can just come jump into my bed, seduce me into forgiving you?" Sara said but knew her voice wasn't as hard as she had intended it. The heat of his skin under her hand was distracting.

"Well, I was going to beg for forgiveness, in hopes of getting coffee in the morning and leaving it at that. But now that I'm here I'm not sure I can stay here, in bed with you, and not touch you." He moved slowly, running his hand down her side, grabbing her hip, pulling her into him.

Sara allowed herself to be pulled into him, and his heat. Jared moved his hand up her back to the nape of her neck, pulling her into a kiss.

Heat rushed through her, and she dove into it, her hand moving over his ribs and up his back to hold him to her. She had missed him, a lot. She would have been worried he had been hurt but Andrew would have said something.

"Two days was too long." Jared said breathlessly "I missed you," he said trailing kisses down the side of her neck.

"Why, two days?" she questioned moving to allow him all the access he wanted.

"I was thinking I would slow things down; I didn't want to rush you." Jared moved to her lips again, taking them both under again.

"It was too long, I missed you. I wouldn't let you rush me." Sara said breathlessly.

"Ok, then let me know when to stop," Jared whisper against her skin. He moved over her, laying on her, settling between her legs. He devoured her mouth, losing himself in the heat of her. Her hands moved over his back; her hips moved under him.

When he couldn't take it anymore, he sat up on his knees pulling her up to pull her shirt off, she fell back breathing hard. He watched as she filled her lungs with gulps of air. He moved to kiss her, stared at her lips, and moved down. He took care to go slow, knowing that if she needed to, he would stop.

Taking his time kissing and sucking her breasts. He moved lower, taking her shorts and underwear with him as he went. He stroked, kissed, and sucked till she was wet with need. He moved back up her body.

"Baby, your sisters are going to come." he smiled down at her. She licked her lips, then nodded her head.

He moved down her body again, learning more. He started licking and sucking her again, taking his time, enjoying all of her. She was his, and there would be no doubt when he was done with her. She bucked under him screaming into a pillow. He worked his way back up her body, taking his sweet time.

"Do you want to stop?" He asked, praying she said no.

"No, I need you" She wiggled under him. He carefully moved so that he was at the entrance to her body, his heart hammered in his ears. Sara reached up with both hands and held his face.

"Please." She begged not breaking eye contact. She sucked in the air, and he pushed into her. Sara watched as Jared's eyes went soft. She moved her hands to his back and moved her hips bringing him in deeper. She felt full, she didn't know if she wanted him out, or to move, or not to move.

"No, baby just relax, let me." His voice was horse, but she listened. He kissed her, adding more to the fire that she already had burning for him. She pulled her knees up more so that he was burned to the hilt in her. So full, so wanted, so everything.

Sara never wanted to let go. Jared barred his head into her shoulder, he pulled out slowly, then dove into her again. Hitting a sweet spot every time he drove into her, again and again. Sara felt herself building again feeling wound tight.

Jared moved faster as he felt her quicken again. He moved to kiss her again, taking her screams as he felt her already tight body tighten more as the orgasm took her over.

He couldn't have held it off more if he tried, he found his release in the last of her spasms. Staying in her, he rolled them to their sides so that he wouldn't crush her. He held her as she drifted off to sleep, Jared looked over at the clock, it was late. But she needed to soak a little or she was going to be sore tomorrow. He very carefully moved out of her; she opened her eyes.

"Baby, you need to soak a little, I'm going to go run you a bath." Jared watched Sara close her eyes again and smiled.

"There are salts under the sink, come get me when it's ready. I'll be right here." She smiled when he started a trail of kisses from her shoulder down to her butt. Then he was gone. Sara could hear the water running, she could hear him moving around in her room. He turned on the side lamp for extra light. Then he was back, kissing her back. She rolled to him.

"You need to open your eyes before I put you in a tub of water." Sara did just that and found Jared smiling over her, he had put his shorts on.

"Hi," she said.

"Hi," he smiled back. Then picking her up he carried her to the tub. He set her down carefully, she closed her eyes to the burning and stinging. Opened them then it stopped.

"Are you ok?" He asked, Sara looked up and found concern all over his face.

"Yes." She said with a smile.

He left her to go find a new t-shirt and boxer shorts. Coming back in time to hand her a towel as she stood up. She dried off and dressed, they moved to bed. Then Sara froze.

"What?" Jared said moving to her, pulling her into his arms

"Birth control?" Sara looked up at him. He lends down and kissed her.

"Condom. You miss a lot when your face is in a pillow." He said smiling at her. She went to push him away, but he caught her head, both smiling while they kissed.

"Let's get you to bed." He said moving away from her.

"Are you staying?" Sara asked as she climbed in.

"That was my plan, unless." He said watching her.

"No, I want you to, it's just" she paused for just a second, but it was enough for Jared to catch. "don't shoot Kadie if she comes in."

Jared turned the lamp off and crawled in with Sara.

"Why would I shoot her?" Jared thought about that for a minute. "Ok, why would she come in here?"

"Sometimes she has really bad nightmares. Really bad, you might hear her scream. She usually comes crawling into my bed when they are really bad." Sara said facing Jared. He couldn't help but think it was another test. Not that she didn't want him, but too many had left without dealing with what was.

"Alright," he said letting out his breath "so no going to bed naked which is a bummer and are you sure we'll all fit?" Jared felt the instant relief in Sara's body, she fully relaxed and melted in his arms. "Do you know what causes them?" Jared asked stroking Sara's face

"Not really, we think they are tied to everyone leaving." Sara closed her eyes and shrugged her shoulder.

"Sleep baby." Jared kissed her forehead letting it go for the night, and with that settling thought drifted to sleep.

17

———

JARED WANTED to curse when he heard an alarm going off, then rejoiced when it stopped. He felt the bed shift and heard whispered giggles.

"You're too hot" Kadie whispered.

"I know" Sara whispered back.

"So, Jared and Andrew stayed the night, should we make them to go cups?" Kadie asked.

"Yes," Jared said and smiled when he felt the bed jolt and both women jumped.

"Well at least you didn't shoot me, should have put a heart attack on the list though," Kadie said as Jared felt the bed shift again. "I'm going to go shower, see you downstairs," Kadie said as she slipped out of the room.

Jared moved and wrapped his arm around Sara before she could jump out of bed.

"When is the coffee going to be done." He asked burring his face into her neck.

"It's done, I set it the night before because I can't think straight enough in the morning. I'm going to go shower." Sara moved out of his arms and left the warmth of the bed. He heard the shower go on, thought for two seconds, and went to join her.

"You didn't scream as loud that time, not as good as the first time?" Jared said when he could talk again. Sara had her legs and arms wrapped around him; he was tightly barred in her heat.

"Better, I was just more mind full of that part of this adventure." Sara winced as he pulled out of her, she moved to stand under the hot water.

"I'm an adventure?" Jared asked taking the condom off. He grabbed her body wash, put some in his hands, and began rubbing soap all over her back and going around her stomach.

"Of a lifetime," Sara said turning around, going on her toes she kissed him. When she was rinsed off, she got out.

Sara and Jared got ready with the flow and motion of two people who had been doing it for years. They made their way down to find Morgan, Kadie, and Andrew in the kitchen with coffee and tea.

"So, Sara?" Andrew started once she had taken her first sip of the wonder that was her coffee.

"Yes?" she answered eyeing him over her coffee.

"I was just wondering." he paused "when the next batch of popcorn was coming?" Andrew smiled, by the way, he turned it on, Sara didn't doubt it was the smile he used when he wanted something. Sara turned and looked at Morgan then at Kadie, they both had puppy dog begging looks. Sara shut her eyes.

"No," then she thought about the last one. She opened one eye and looked at Jared. He was hitting her with his best smile. "Damn it, you, guys. I haven't even finished my coffee." Sara took a deep breath and closed her eyes.

"Told you we should have waited," Morgan said to Kadie.

"It wasn't my idea." Kadie pointed to Andrew.

"No, she is your sister, you both should have stopped me."

Sara tried to hide the smile. Then Jared was behind her. He lends down to whisper in her ear.

"That's mean." He whispered. She opened her eyes, turned to look over her shoulder, and caught his look. He knew she was playing. The others had bought it, her own sisters bought it, but Jared hadn't. They smiled at each other.

She walked out of his arms to the pantry. Pulling four cans, two larger than the rest. She walked over to Jared, kissed his cheek, and handed him a large tin. She moved to Kadie gave her a smaller tin, Andrew the larger one, and Morgan the smaller.

"What? Why do they get bigger ones?" Kadie fronded at Sara.

"Because they have to take them to work." Sara smiled as she walked back to her coffee.

"What, wait, I didn't agree to that," Andrew said looking grief stricken.

"We got to go," Sara looked at the clock "Are you riding with us?" She asked Morgan.

"Yes." Morgan slid off the stool. Kissing Andrew on her way by.

"Stay, hang out just lock up when you leave." Sara kissed Jared goodbye. The guys watched as the three sisters walked out. They shared a look.

"Well, this is going to be interesting," Andrew said sipping his coffee

"Already is." Jared filled his cup then added the lid. "Ready?"

"Ya, do you think she'll know if we don't take it to work," Andrew said moving to the door, cup in one hand, then under his arm.

"Yes, she will," Jared's mind thought about Sara, memories moved to the shower they shared this morning.

"Can't wait till the weekend, can you?" Andrew stepped out of the house.

"Nope." Jared locked it and together they walked to Jared's truck.

Jared and Andrew got a head start on the day due to their early morning. They set one tin in the middle of their desks, they put the other in the kitchen area of the squad room.

"That in itself is a crime," Andrew said looking longingly over at it.

"It isn't even your tin," Jared said with his head down writing in one of the case files that needed his attention. He kept his head down, checked emails, and took phone calls. He looked up when someone called his name. Both Andrew and Jared looked up, Meg Emerson made her way over to Jared's desk.

"Hi honey, I got tired of waiting. So, I brought you lunch." Meg came and set the basket on his desk.

Jared shared a look with Andrew. Andrew typed an email to dispatch. Minutes later their phone rang. Jared picked it up

"Brooks"

"Hey Jared, Andy just sent word that you have a problem?" Lynn asked.

"Ya," Jared said giving Andrew a quick smile.

"You need me to call you out?" She asked.

"We'll be right there," Jared said.

"What do I get for this call?" Lynn asked.

"We can work something out," Jared responded then dropped his eyes to the tin in the middle of the desk. When he looked back at Andrew as his shoulders slumped, picking up on what was going on.

"Right, we'll be right there," Jared said hanging up as he stood. Grabbed his cell phone, gun, and jacket.

"Meg," He looked right at her. "I don't want to go out with you, I am seeing someone, she is special and as long as she wants me, I'm going to stay with her. I don't want you to call, I don't want you to come by here, I don't want to see you again." Jared said looking at her, then he looked at Andrew, Andrew grabbed the tin off the desk. Jared walked over to Meg, "I'll walk you out." Together they left the squad room.

"What the hell was that about?" Andrew asked as Jared walked up to him. Andrew had gone downstairs but waited in the lobby as Jared all but pushed Meg out of the building.

"My mother set us up. This is the fourth time I have told her no," Jared said shaking his head.

"The country cub?" Andrew asked.

"Yep, now I need to make sure she can't get by the front door again, I'm sure my mother will call, and yours might," Jared said making his way to Lynn's desk.

"Thank you," he said to her handing her the tin. "I need to see the captain."

"He's right there, coming in," Lynn said nodding in the direction of the doors with her head.

Jared spent the next half an hour getting Meg more or less barred from the building, two minutes after Jared was back at his desk, his phone rang. Andrew eyed him then eyed the phone.

"Brooks" Jared said almost holding his breath.

"Jared" His mother's voice was ice.

"No," He said firmly, "I told you I was seeing someone. I don't want Meg or anyone else you try to set me up with. Now I'm working leave me alone." Jared hung the phone up. After sharing a look with Andrew, they dove into work. A little after four his mind was on Sara. He grabbed his phone to text her.

"Hey beautiful, how are you doing?"

He set his phone down, she was still at work. He wondered how her day was going.

"Slammed."

One word. She was slammed and it was almost time to close. He looked up at Andrew.

"Hey, you talk to Morgan today?" Jared asked, shuffling papers.

"Ya, they are really busy today. Why?" Andrew was shutting down his computer, the early in had given them room to leave early. Jared just shook his head as he texts Sara back.

"Dinner?"

Jared kept his phone in hand, while he too shut his computer down.

"Fast and easy, don't know when we are going to be done here."

"Let me know when you are home, we'll bring food."

Jared stood up putting his phone in his pocket, his gun on. He looked at Andrew.

"Dinner is on us when they get home," Jared said.

"Take me to my house I need a few things for tonight," Andrew said starting to follow Jared then stopped, he went to get the tin off the table. He opened the lid and found it empty.

"So, you going to tell Sara about your visitor?" Andrew asked as they made their way out of the squad room.

"Yep, I'm not going to lie or hide anything from her. Too many have pulled that on her." Jared said as they got into the elevator going down.

"Ya, I got that too" They bid good night to the front desk and headed out for the night. As they approached Jared's truck, Andrew's phone rang.

"Abbot" Andrew winced and held the phone away from his ear. His mother was yelling at him. Andrew looked at it and hit the send button.

"I think it's time to change our numbers," Jared said climbing in, then they set off.

"Have a good night enjoy," Morgan said to the last customer as she shut the door. She turned the lock and headed behind the counter. She counted down the drawer and made the deposit. Then she moved to wrap up what needed to go into the half off basket, as she went, she thought to herself it wouldn't be much.

When she was done, wiping up, putting things to right she headed to the back of the shop. Kadie was still bent over a cake due the next day; Sara was doing the frosting and fondue on a two-tier princess cake also due the next day.

"Morgan, I swear if you bring back one more order, I may have to kill you," Kadie said without looking up. The detailed work she was doing was fantastic but needed close attention.

"I don't know what you're talking about. I finished up front, what do you want me to work on?" Morgan moved over to the paperwork table, adding the three orders they received since the last time she had come to the back.

"We have three dozen cupcakes due tomorrow that need the frosting." Sara tilted her head to the rack that still had cupcakes, and other cakes in need of frosting.

"What happened?" Morgan asked as she took in the hours of work still ahead of them.

"Well between the bread, cakes, and cupcakes you pushed out the door today what we baked today went right out the door, so now," Sara said as she moved the tier she had just finished to the rack for Kadie, moved on to the second. "We need to play hard catch up."

With the music on, and the girls concentrating on their work as the minutes moved by them. Morgan worked on clean up, she would box and put away as either Sara or Kadie finished what they were working on. She organized the orders due in the next week, and because they had so many, she rearranged the specials they were going to run for the next three weeks.

Morgan looked up and saw Sara standing drinking her water. The dozen cupcakes for a last-minute order were done on her counter. Morgan grabbed a box and went over as Sara headed to the bathroom. Morgan was able to wipe the counter and start the last of her dishes by the time she returned.

"Thank you," Sara said coming back to a clean workspace. Then she went to help Kadie.

"What can I do?" Sara asked as she walked up to Kadie's workstation.

"Food."

"We have dinner coming as soon as I let him know we are on our way home," Sara said.

"Nice, so when do we get to go home?" Kadie asked as she took a step, standing up and stretching her back.

"Are you done?" Morgan asked coming over with boxes for the three-tier cake.

"Yes," Kadie looked around the kitchen drinking her water. It was all clean and put to the right, looking at her area. It only had a few dishes and needed a wipe down.

"Thank you" Kadie looked at Morgan. "Be right back." While Kadie took her bathroom break Sara and Morgan finished the cleanup. Morgan had the bank deposit in her bag and stood by the back door. Sara texted Jared that they were on their way home. The three walked out the back, Sara setting the alarm.

"What is he bringing for dinner?" Kadie asked when she was slumped in the back seat with her eyes closed.

"I don't know, all I said was fast and easy," Sara said driving them home. Sara investigated the rearview mirror when Kadie started laughing. "What?"

"You told the guy you're seeing that you want fast and easy." Kadie started to laugh harder, and Morgan started to laugh too. Sara smiled; she could handle being the butt of the joke.

"I'm changing the subject." Sara looked in her mirror. "Are you going out this weekend?"

"I don't know yet. When does Abby and Eddie get back? I

know we were going to have a welcome home dinner." Kadie said sitting up more.

"They get home tonight; we were going to have dinner tomorrow," Sara said pulling up in the driveway. They got out, heading into the house.

"I don't go out on Friday night anyways; it makes Saturday hurt way more," Kadie said pulling her keys out and unlocking the door. "I'm going to go change." Kadie tossed her keys on the little side table by the back kitchen door and headed upstairs.

"Here." Morgan dug into her purse to pull out the deposit.

"How did we do?" Sara asked taking the bag from her.

"Black." Morgan said, "Oh I'm going to go sit down for a bit." They both moved to the living room, Morgan sat down on the couch, settling in she closed her eyes. Sara moved to the study on the other side of the front door. She moved to the wall safe, and after locking the deposit away she headed over to the answering machine.

They kept the house phone for the bakery. For security, it was the same number their grandmother had had. Sara noticed the light was blinking, walking over she hit play.

"Your stupid bitch-" Sara recognized Marks's voice at once. She hit the stop button just as fast. She looked around the doorway to see if Morgan and heard. Morgan was now laying on the couch, with her eyes closed. No sign that she had heard anything.

"After dinner" She whispered to herself. Her head jerked up as she heard male voices coming from the kitchen. Heading that way, she smiled as she heard Jared and Andrew talking.

"Hey," she said walking in she knew she said it too quickly and a little breathy, both guys looked over at her. They were pulling white boxes from bags and putting them on the table. "What would you like to drink?" she turned when she saw Jared look at her trying to get a read on her.

"Do you have beer?" Andrew asked.

"We have shock top, orange?" Sara asked as she moved to get three from the fridge.

"Please." Both Jared and Andrew said together. Sara readied the beers and went to hand them to the guys. She met Jared's eyes and knew they couldn't continue the evening with the message hanging over her head.

"We have a problem," Sara said and felt herself hold her breath.

"Alright?" Jared said questioning.

"Mark left a message on the house phone," Sara said then took a sip from her beer. She watched both men deal, she watched them think about what to do next.

"We'll listen to it later, how did Morgan take it?" Andrew asked moving towards the stairs Sara could see the concern wash over him.

"She doesn't know, I pressed the stop button as soon as I heard his voice," Sara said quickly as she heard someone approaching the kitchen. Kadie came in from the living room.

"Morgan is out on the couch. Do you think we should wake her or let her sleep?" Kadie asked going to the fridge to get her own drink.

"I'll go wake her; she needs to eat then pass out," Andrew said walking out of the kitchen to the living room.

"What's up with him?" Kadie asked walking over to the table grabbing a carton, opening it, and setting it down to reach for another. Happy with this box she grabbed a set of chop sticks and dug in.

"Do you want to get plates?" Sara said looking from Kadie to Jared.

"Isn't this how you eat it, right out of the boxes?" Jared asked

"Yes, but-" Sara said and stopped.

"No, we don't need plates, let's eat." Jared smiled and pulled a chair out for Sara. "So, ladies how was your day?"

They ate and talked about their days. Jared knew he would talk to Sara about the Meg thing when it was just the two of them. Morgan and Andrew joined them though Morgan was no more than half a wake. When she had finished, Andrew took her to bed, came down, and joined the rest to finish eating.

"Holy F," Kadie said around a mouthful of noodles when she found out that Mark had called the house. "What are we going to do about it?" she asked looking at the three of them.

"We'll handle it," Andrew said after setting a carton down and reaching for another.

"Just like that. Are you going to keep us informed, in the loop?" Kadie said sending a look at Andrew that had him stopping.

"Why would you ask me that? No matter how ugly this gets, I will always keep you in the loop." Andrew gave Kadie a stern look in return.

"Just making sure." She said pacified for now and went back to her noodles.

They finished their dinner, and together they made their way to the den.

"Ready?" Sara looked at them. With collected nods, she hit the play button. Mark's voice filled the room.

"You stupid bitch, you think you can have someone tell me to stay away from you. You are mine. You will get rid of that bustard of a child you think you love. You don't love anything but me. I'll be seeing you real soon, you'll be damn sure of that." The room stayed silent as Sara saved the message and then took the USB card out to hand it over to Andrew.

"This guy is stupid. He thinks because he is keeping the messages short that we can't trace them. He isn't even thinking about what he is providing by leaving the message." Andrew said as he put the card in the evidence bag, which he always kept in the inside pocket of his jacket.

"He is stupid." They all turned and found Morgan sitting on

the stairs. Andrew walked over to her and helped her stand up. "Dinner didn't sit well." She said looking at him.

"Let's get you some water," Andrew said pulling her into his arms

"Stay with me tonight." Morgan looked up at him, close to tears. He could see fear, trust, and sadness. Without a word, he lends down and kissed her. Then he led her to the kitchen.

"Well," Kadie said then turned to Jared. "Are you staying too?" He nodded at her. "Good, I'm going up, we are going to be slammed again tomorrow." She turned and went up the stairs.

"I'm going to go clean up the kitchen," Sara said sounding more tired than Jared could have imagined.

"Do you want me to go?" He asked, the question stopped Sara, she turned and looked at him.

"No. I very much want you to stay." She said smiling, and he followed her to the kitchen. After everything was clean and put away Jared took her upstairs when she was yawing every few minutes.

"Did you bring clothes for tomorrow, or do you need me to wash those for you?" Sara asked when she pulled a night shirt on.

"I have clothes for tomorrow, and I send my clothes to a dry cleaner," Jared answered pulling the blanket down. Sara sat on her bed and looked at Jared.

"Do you think he'll show up?" She asked, Jared could hear the worry in her voice.

"Yes, I think it is only a matter of time. You call the moment he steps into the bakery." Jared sat next to her and reached out to hold her hand.

"I need to tell you something," Jared took a breath. "Meg Emerson showed up at the office today. She brought me lunch." Sara just stared at him, waiting for him to continue. "I told her I didn't want anything to do with her, and then I talked to my captain and now have it so she can't come to my office. If she has a problem, she has to go somewhere else." Jared held his breath, waiting for Sara to say or do something, anything.

"Ok," Sara just looked at him.

They had only known each other for two weeks. In what world could that be enough time to know someone, she felt the questions creep in. Did she trust him, know without a doubt that he wouldn't lie, or leave? She met his eye and stopped, he could have said nothing, he could have kept it from her. Instead, he was being upfront knowing she had trouble with trusting. Sara moved to her knees, then she moved to straddle him. Taking his face in her hands,

"Are you mine?" she asked settling on his lap, looking into his eyes.

"Yes, I am," Jared said with his hands on her hips.

They felt the moment, to hell with time. They knew they had something special, and if anything, they wanted to find out where it would lead them. Jared moved his hand up her back grabbing the back of her neck, binging her lips against his. He felt the moment she let falling into him.

She heard him grow when her hips moved against him. Raised her arms to the ceiling he broke the kiss to pull her shirt off. They were lost in each other, she wrapped her arms around his neck, as she felt his hand move her underwear away from her. She felt his fingers move into her, making her blood light on fire.

Sara gasped, tilting her head back, as Jared kissed and sucked lightly on her neck. The hand he had on her back kept her close, then he flipped them putting her on her back, he slid quickly down her body taking panties with him.

He found her wet for him, he tasted, kissed, licked, sucked, and teased. When he heard her scream into a pillow he smiled. After discarding his own bottoms, he flipped them again and pulled her onto him. He held her hips, her hands on his chest as he felt her slide down onto him.

Sara tipped her head back when heat flashed through her body as he entered her, pulling her back to him she was kissing him again, her hips moving to their own beat, and he let her take the lead. She felt her power and his surrender. He held her closer as her orgasm overtook her, he followed, as her body pulsed around him.

"You are who I want." He said looking up at her. He reached up to cup her face. Sara smiled and turned her face to kiss his palm.

"You are who I want too." She said so tired, she began to drift. He pulled her down to lay on his chest, he moved slowly rolling them to lay side by side. Jared went to the bathroom, coming back he was struck by how just looking at her stopped his heart. She was so beautiful and she was becoming important to him; he was surprised by just how much. He wanted to be with her, it was worth all the bumps they could or would have to endure.

Jared moved quickly, once he them both redressed. Not knowing if Kadie was going to have to come in. He claimed into bed, curled around Sara, and drifted to sleep.

18

Jared sat down at his desk, for the first time all day. The job demanded that they start early, the phone call coming in before the alarm when off. He remembered how he kissed Sara's sleeping head and he went down to meet Andrew in the kitchen.

"Damn, we won't get coffee this morning." Andrew had said grumpily as they walked out the back door.

After Jared put his gun in his drawer, he turned his computer on, he lends back closing his eyes. Andrew had been called to the DA's office. It was rare they didn't have to go together, but it happened. His phone rang pulling him from his thoughts. Sitting up he reached and picked it up.

"Brooks."

"Hey," Sara's voice was a bit strained but happy.

"Hey, what's up?" Jared couldn't keep the smile off his face

"I was wondering if you could by chance swing by and get Morgan from the doctor, she would have taken Kadie's car but the tires were sliced this morning, and I need mine to drop off an order, because Kadie has the van, and is going to the other side of town, and because we are damn near drowning in cake today, I can't go get her after as we have to drop her off during our joke of a lunch." He kept his smile as she spoke fast, then she took a breath.

"Yes," Jared said without thinking.

"Yes?" Sara questioned.

"Yes, tell her to call my cell when she's done, and I'll go get her." He said thinking about Sara, imagining her standing by her drafting table, jeans, and a t-shirt. Her long hair pulled back.

"Thank you so much," Sara said relief laced her voice, pulling him from his thoughts of her.

"You can thank me later." Jared smiled again when he heard Sara laugh.

"Deal, got to go, Bye" She was gone before Jared could say anything. He turned to his computer to open his Email, then stopping as what Sara said ran through his head. Kadie's tires had been sliced.

"Shit." He picked up his phone and called the bakery.

"Daisy's cakes" Morgan's voice came on over the line.

"Kadie's tires were slashed?" Jared closed his eyes as he waited to be answered.

"Damn, and she thought you hadn't caught on to that. Yes, they were." Morgan said sounding disappointed they hadn't been sly enough.

"Did you call anyone? When did you notice it?" He asked grabbing a note pad.

"We had to come to the shop, but we did call it into the police station close to us, we know some of the guys, they come in regularly. Jared, I have to go, see you later." Morgan hung up before he could get anything else out.

Jared made a note to call the officer who had been assigned to the case and share what they had. He turned back to the computer, looked at the email he had just received throwing him back into his work. He was elbow deep when his cell rang next to him.

"Brooks."

"Hey Jared, I'm done. I'm at the hospital on the east end, off 14th and Center." Morgan's voice had surprised him, the day was going much faster than he realized.

"Sure, be right there." Jared stood up, got his stuff together, and left.

He saw Morgan sitting on a bench waiting for him. Her usual crazy hair was pulled back and out of her face. She was staring off into space, rubbing her belly. Morgan looked up when Jared pulled up to her. Her smile was bright, too bright. He got out to help her up into his truck.

"Hey, how did it go?" Jared asked waiting for Morgan to take his reached hand. She signed.

"Fine, good," she said then let out a weak giggle. Jared knew it wasn't good and wasn't fine, just being around the girls he had picked up on their settled way they showed stress.

"Andrew or the bakery?" Jared asked opening the door and helping her into his truck.

"Andrew if you can," Morgan said getting her seat belt on, taking a breath.

"Alright," Jared walked around the truck, pulling his phone out to text Andrew.

"House, now."

"What?"

"Morgan, not Mark. Heading there now."

Jared got in when he didn't get anything back from Andrew. Morgan stayed quiet all the way to the station.

"Morgan?" Jared asked when he had parked.

"It will be ok, even if it's too much for him. I've got my sisters; I'll be ok." Morgan nodded her head then gave Jared the fake happy smile. Jared nodded and went to help her out of his truck.

Morgan followed him into the station. He stopped at a desk, let the ladies know he was there, and got any messages that were waiting for him, he turned to Morgan.

"This way." He said and made his way to the elevators; they went up to the fourth floor.

When the doors opened Jared stepped into a large hall with windows and doors, he led her down one hall and then turned the other way into a big room with desks and people. Morgan took it all in, one corner housed a kitchen like area, desks pair up all around the room. Jared walked to a set on the far end of the room next to a set of windows. He motioned for her to sit at the desk across from the one he stood at. Morgan watch as he pulled his phone out, put his gun in a desk drawer, and sat down to go through the messages he had. Then he turned to his computer.

"Hey Jared, who is this?" A tall blond walked over, she had her hair pulled back, and she wore a white button shirt with gray dress pants. Morgan looked from her to Jared and found Jared was looking at her, letting Morgan take the lead.

"I'm Morgan Mathews, I'm waiting for Andrew." Morgan sat a little straighter, her belly becoming more pronounced. She watched the blonde's eyes widen, then the fake smile moved over her face.

"Oh well that's nice, I'll talk to you later Jared." Then she turned and walked away.

"How long did they date?" Morgan asked Jared when the blond was out of ear shot.

"Too long for him, not long enough for her. A few years back, as I think that would be your next question." Jared said then picked up the ringing phone. "Brooks."

"Who the hell is she?" It was the blonde. Jared shut his eyes, what the hell was this?

"Not your concern, goodbye" Jared hung up, and Morgan

laughed. Then stopped when she saw Andrew walking towards her.

Somewhere in the back of her mind, she wondered how he would handle just having her here. Would he seem distant, or would he let the room know? He walked up to her and held a handout for her. Pulling her to her feet he wrapped his arms around her and kissed her. Heart stopping, blood heating kiss. Well, that answered that.

"Are you ok?" Andrew asked quietly when he pulled back.

"Yes." She said dreamily, then her mind shifted into gear. "May-be, we need to talk." Andrew looked down at her, watched her go from relaxed to not.

"Ok," he said then moved out of their embrace. He put his phone down, gun on the desk, took her hand, and lead her to one of the back rooms.

"What's going on?" Andrew asked when they were sitting on a bench facing each other.

"First, I want you to know, you are more than I ever expected. I had it in my mind that I would do this by myself, then you came along." Morgan sat straight, her fingers twisting as her nerves began to show.

"When you told me, you wanted to be there for me, be with me. It was wonderful to hear, I thought well that's nice but when it gets to be too much he won't stay. He's here now, and I'll enjoy it for as long as it lasts." Morgan smiled and watched Andrew try to say something, but she stopped him.

She had once believed she had loved Mark; she had married him hadn't she? She often wondered what it said about her, moving on so fast from her marriage. It was different with Andrew, it was so easy, so comfortable, so everything she had ever thought she wanted.

"I thought you weren't going to stick around after Mark started doing his thing, but you stayed." Morgan nodded her head, her hands still nervously twisting, now or never she told herself.

"I don't know how you're going to handle this next step." Morgan took a deep breath and then took a picture out of her purse. She handed it to Andrew and held her breath as she watched him study it.

"Two," he whispered.

"Two." Morgan watched concern, move to surprise, move to joy. When he looked at her, she saw the aw in his eyes.

"Girls, boys, one of each?" Andrew looked from Morgan to the picture he held in his hand.

"Boys, I've got two boys," Morgan said and looked at the picture in his hand.

"We, we have two boys." He said then he frowned, "If you'll have me?"

Morgan just looked at him, in wonder. He hadn't run, hadn't said this is too much I'm out. She reached out for him, he moved into her at the same time. Their lips met; heat surged. It took Andrew all he had to stop, remember where he was.

"Later." He whispered against her lips.

"Later," she said smiling at him. "I need to get back to the bakery, do you think you could give me a ride?" Morgan asked as she stood up. Andrew caught her hips, bringing her to face him. With a hand on each side of her, he looked at her growing belly, he lends in and kissed her belly. Morgan's heart melted, yeah, she was in love with him, and right now didn't care if it seemed too soon.

"Yeah," he said after a minute. "I need to talk to Jared really quick then we can go." He said standing and taking her hand in his. Andrew led her back to his desk and had her sit down in his chair as he talked things over with Jared. Morgan sent a text to Sara letting her know she was on her way back. She looked up when she felt Andrew move closer to her.

"What's the plan for tonight?" Andrew asked looking down

at her. She looked up at him and saw Jared looking at her as well.

"Tonight, we are having a dinner for Abby and Eddie, they're back. Do you guys think you'll be able to join us?" Morgan asked as she stood up taking Andrew's offered hand.

"I don't know," Jared asked grabbing the phone to make a call.

"We'll see," Andrew said placing a hand on her lower back to lead her to the elevators. Once the doors shut Morgan turned to him.

"Will you come to stay with me tonight?" She asked moving closer to him.

"Absolutely," he said and dipped down for a quick kiss.

Morgan walked into the bakery using the back door and was instantly thrown into the crazy. She rushed up front to relieve Sara who needed to get back to the ovens. The sisters didn't speak just high fived each other in passing.

When Morgan had taken a moment to check what they had left for the day she found they wouldn't quite make it through. She made a list of what she would need to bring from the back, when she was at the chocolate wall she stopped. They were out, Sara had sold the last of it while Morgan was gone. Abby would need to come in and make more chocolates for next day.

When she found a minute between customers, she called Abby.

"Hey sister, glad you're back. We are out of chocolates. Call me back as soon as you can." Morgan ended the call as the bell on the door chimed letting her know to get back to it. "Welcome to Daisy's cakes, what can I get for you." She said getting back into the swing.

At three Abby came walking in, Morgan was happy to see she was in her work clothes. Abby stopped at the wall of chocolates and turned big eyes to Morgan. A silent what the hell happened? She stopped by quickly to hug and kiss Morgan who was taking an order over the phone.

"What the hell?" Abby asked as she walked into the crazy back room.

"Morgan came home. I am blaming her for all of this." Kadie said as she worked a delicate design into the side of a large sheet cake.

"What are you doing here?" Kadie asked not taking her eyes off the cake.

"Morgan called and said we were out of chocolates; I saw the wall. We are defiantly out of chocolates. So, I'm here to make more." Abby walked over to her workstation, set her bag on the stool, and got to work.

Abby roasted, shelled, grounded. The sisters all worked in their own groves, Sara mixing, and baking. Kadie frosting, decorating. Morgan running the front end, coming back to retrieve what was needed to restock the front, or stopped to box an order for Kadie putting them in the walk in as she took one out. Even in the crazy, there was a calm that settled over them, as the four of them worked together.

Abby was working the chocolate into molds when the back door banged open. She looked up in time to see three men, walk in all talking to one another. With them came the scent of warm garlic, over the sweet, and warm sugar. She looked at her sisters who too had stopped working to see who was walking in, as the smell hit them, she could see hunger move over the determination in their eyes.

"Oh, my god." Morgan had said from the paperwork table. She was working on the books after she locked up for the day. Abby looked at the clock that hung on the wall and was surprised to see that it was close to seven.

"What are you doing here?" Sara said surprised when she laid eyes on Jared. Confirming that she too had lost track of time.

"Well, you said dinner. When we hadn't heard from you, we called Eddie, he informed us that Abby told him she was coming in to give you a hand." He walked over to her, kissed her lightly "After we finished and still hadn't heard from you, we deiced to bring you food." Jared said holding up a big bag, Sara noticed was from their favorite Italian restaurant. "How much longer do you have?"

Sara looked at what she had been working on, frosting a cake for Kadie. After that, she would be able to clean up. When she looked at the mess around her, she found none. Morgan had cleaned up behind her again. She looked over at Morgan and smiled.

"Ten more minutes?" Sara was asking Kadie and Abby.

"Ya, that works for me," Abby said smiling at her husband.

"Alright, where do we set this down at?" Andrew asked.

"On Sara's counter, it's the biggest, she can move over to Kadie's space so I can wipe it down," Morgan said getting off the stool, getting a rag she went to do just that.

Morgan smiled at Andrew who after setting the bags down, took her in his arms to kiss her.

"Have you told them?" He whispered in her ear.

"Too busy." She whispered back.

Morgan helped set the counter and collected stools for everyone. Eddie opened the wine, and Andrew had grape juice for Morgan. After everything was all set, cleaned up, and put away. Abby, Kadie, and Sara joined the rest.

When the girls were halfway through their dinner Sara looked up, as if for the first time.

"Hi." She smiled at Jared.

"Hey, beautiful." He said smiling back, giving her leg a squeeze.

"Alright, so fill me in. The bakery is crazy busy, I see you two are together," Abby said looking at Sara and Jared. "And you two," she added looking at Morgan and Andrew. "Last holdout." Abby put her arm around Kadie's shoulders.

"One of us has to be," Kadie said before taking another bit of her lasagna. After she swallowed, she took a sip of her wine, turning her attention to Morgan.

"How was the doctor's appointment?" Kadie asked and had Morgan chocking on her juice then looked at Andrew. "Well, that's good," Kadie said with a smile.

"It went fine, I got a firm talking to about the problems that could have come up with not going to the doctor sooner, they took blood and did an ultrasound." Morgan stopped to take a bit.

"What? Oh, don't do that." Sara said giving a *oh come on* look at Morgan who had timely filled her mouth with food so she couldn't talk.

"She did that on purpose," Abby said taking a drink of wine.

"Ok," Morgan said taking a drink of her juice. "It turns out I'm 20 weeks along, halfway done. I have to go back in two weeks to do another ultrasound, the doctor said the boys are too small for his liking and wants me to beef them up as best I can." Morgan took another bite, to prove she needed to eat. Then sat back as the news sank in.

"Holy F-" Kadie said then jumped up, rushing to Morgan. Morgan stood up to catch her, they laughed as they hugged. Abby was up next, Kadie spun Morgan out of her arms to Abby.

Jared ran a hand down Sara's back, she let out a breath she didn't know she was holding. Then she stood and moved to Morgan. Causing her to come to a halt in front of her. The sisters looked at each other for a moment, Sara pulled Morgan into a hug, and the room watched as whatever Sara said had Morgan relaxing into her sister's arms. They pulled apart, both with tears in their eyes.

The girls sat down again and spent the rest of the dinner

talking about babies. The decision was made to move the nursery into Abby's old room as it shared a Jack and Jill bathroom with Morgan.

Years before they put French doors between Abby's room and the sitting room on the second floor, they would make that part of the nursery. It was almost eight by the time they cleaned up, locked up, and bid their good-byes.

The guys hadn't had any of the wine so that they could drive the girls home. Sara handed the keys to her jeep to Andrew and got into Jared's truck. They talked all the way home. When they pulled up Sara looked over at Jared.

"Are you staying tonight?" she asked looking at him.

"Do you want me to?" he asked looking at her and smiling.

"Yes," Sara smiled back.

"Then I will." Jared got out and walked around to open her door. Sara slid out of the truck into Jared's body.

"Let's get to bed," Jared said before he took her mouth.

19
____

MORGAN SAT at the front counter; she was writing up an order she had just received over the phone. When she finished the order, she was going to lock the door for lunch. She couldn't help the smile she got when her mind drifted over Andrew and the nights that he had spent with her. It had been a week since they found out about the boys, and together she and Andrew were making plans.

He knew she had come home to be with her sisters, he respected that. They talked about when she would move in with him, Morgan wanted to, but she just wasn't sure when. He knew part of her hesitation was that she was still waiting to see if he would walk away. Time would be the only way to make it right, so he would give her what she needed, time and her family.

Morgan was smiling when she looked up at the customer who had just walked in.

"Welcome to" She stopped short, her heart dropped, and an ice chill ran up her spine as Mark stood in front of her.

"Hello Morgan, how's it going?" Mark smiled at her.

The smile she had once thought charming, one that had

flipped her stomach, and now she knew it wasn't a good flip. She squared her shoulders.

"What are you doing here Mark?" Morgan gave him a stern look.

"Why honey I'm here to take care of that problem you seem too stupid to take of yourself." Mark looked around the bakery. Morgan was quick, she sent a text to Andrew.

"911-mark bakery.

She hit send and shut her eyes thinking about Sara and Kadie in the back, she wouldn't call for them. She didn't know what Mark would do to them.

"Why don't you just sign the papers and leave," Morgan said as Mark turned his attention back to her.

"You would like that, wouldn't you? I always knew you were a whore looking for a buck. I'm not signing those papers; I'm not giving you four hundred grand. Forget it." He said walking up to the counter taking the divorce papers from the inside pocket of his jacket, tossed them on the counter.

"On top of that, you think you can come at me for child support, you're dumber than I thought," Mark said glaring at her.

"I didn't put anything in the papers about child support, I don't want you to have anything to do with these babies," Morgan said then swore in her head.

"Babies ha, you really are a bitch, having a litter." He stopped for a minute just to look at her as if settling something in his head first.

"Alright let's go, you're coming with me." Mark started to come around the counter.

"How about this, I'll sign the denial papers. I'll decline the money, and you sign your rights away." Morgan said quickly as she stepped back; realizing too late he had her cornered. "That way I don't get a dime, either way." Morgan hoped it would be enough to stop him from coming at her.

"No," he said shaking his head and moving slowly towards her, as if he was hunting her "Let's just go for a ride," Mark said the calmness of his tone sending uncomfortable shivers up her spine. She watched him coming closer something just not right in his eyes, everything about him making Morgan's skin crawl.

Their eyes were locked as he reached for her, his hands inches away from her arms. Morgan's mind raced, she questioned herself why she didn't fight, why she didn't make a move. She was too scared to, what if he hit her, what if he went for her sisters, what if.

"Touch her and I'll shoot you." Andrew's voice rang out through the bakery, he had come from the back. Jared moved around to the middle of the shop with his gun drawn on Mark. Mark smiled at Morgan then held his hands up and turned to Andrew.

"Just having a talk with my wife," Mark said, and Morgan watched Andrew holster his gun and walk over to Mark.

"Well, why don't you come with me first, we need to have a chat too, you're under arrest," Andrew said as he put cuffs on Mark.

Morgan watched the whole thing unravel. Andrew is so sure of his every move, his face stone. She tried to catch his eye but didn't. He was acting like she wasn't there at all. She waited, even when Sara came from the back, moved to hug Morgan, but Morgan stepped away. Morgan watched Andrew turn and walk Mark out of the Bakery, not sparing her a glance.

Morgan turned her attention to Jared; it took a moment to register he had said her name a few times.

"Call Eddie, now," Jared said nodding, he looked at Sara then was gone.

Kadie locked the door and turned the sign for lunch, they called Eddie and filled him in. Morgan didn't eat much of her lunch, she was too worried, and thinking about Andrew. His almost cold demeanor towards her, she felt uneasy. Between the visit from Mark, and then watching Andrew she honestly just wanted to go home and go to bed.

The rest of the day seemed to go by in a blur of cakes, bread, and customers. Morgan had waited for her cell phone to signal anything from Andrew with no luck. By the end of the day, she wasn't sure what she felt, tired, relieved, sad. Her emotions were everywhere, by the time they closed Morgan was nothing but relieved.

After the sisters got home, Sara made dinner, they sat at the bar talking and eating. Sara ran a hand down Morgan's back, it almost had Morgan in tears. Her emotions were still everywhere, it was talking all she had not to lose it. She had hoped by being home would help make her feel better.

"I'm going to go read on the couch." Morgan slid off the stool as Kadie was heading up to get ready for her night out. Sara stood in her way; Morgan was about to say something when Sara wrapped her arms around Morgan. Morgan wrapped her arms around Sara, rested her head on Sara's shoulder.

Sara didn't know how long they stayed that way; she had started to sway the way their mother had when they were little. Sara knew the power a hug held, how it had a way of making the world right, even if only for the moments in the embrace. She had watched Morgan all day, the best she could. Her own heart Jared and Andrew had rushed through the kitchen, not saying a word.

Sara had talked with Jared through out the day, so she had been kept in the loop, she had hoped for an opportunity to let Morgan know, but there just hadn't been the time. Even now wasn't the time. So, she would just hold on till Morgan was ready.

Jared walked in the front door, he moved quietly through the house. He spotted the sisters in the kitchen and not wanting to ruin that moment he just went to sit in the study. It was by far his favorite room in the house, with its light gold walls, chocolate leather chairs, and couch. It had dark stained wood floors and matching bookshelves. He could see men gathering, smoking cigars, and playing poker in the room.

"Jared?" Morgan said sounding surprised to see him, Sara was standing next to her smiling.

"Hey, how's it going?" Jared looked over both girls, he could see the day had taken its toll on Morgan. Sara was her strong self; he could however see the worry under it.

"It's going fine, we were just going to go up to talk about the nursery," Sara said moving to the desk she kept, retrieving a notebook and pencil.

"That sounds like a lot of fun." Jared didn't bother to keep the light sarcasm out of his voice. Sara just laughed and shook her head.

"Yes, I can tell you seem so excited about it." Sara walked over to the bookshelf, grabbed a remote, and pushed back two panels to reveal a large flat screen TV. She walked back to find Jared smiling.

"Perhaps you better rest, don't want you to get too excited with baby talk." She said as Jared turned the TV on, after surfing he noticed they had the sports package.

"Kadie" Sara said watching him "She has a hidden passion for sports, she loves to watch the drama of it all." Sara bent down and kissed his head. "See you later." Smiling both sisters headed up to the nursery.

Jared had a newfound respect for the Mathews women. The things they worked with were the best and they worked to keep it in good condition. They extended that love and respect to their hobbies. Jared found a game, sat back, and enjoyed it.

Sara and Morgan walked into the nursery; Sara flipped on the lights. Morgan was taken by surprise at the bareness of the rooms. Abby's room had been the smallest of the four on the second floor as she had thrown fit after fit claiming she needed her own room. When their grandmother had passed away, they had put a pair of French doors in that would connect the sitting room and Abby's room. She had lived with them till about 6 months before the wedding.

"She took it all?" Morgan asked as she walked through the small room to the sitting room, another set of French doors led to the hallway.

"We talked about it, I decided that I didn't want to keep it the soft rose and cream. I hadn't figured out what to do with it exactly, but I knew I didn't want to keep it the same color and all her stuff matched." Sara said it with a shrug walked in behind Morgan.

"So, what did you have in mind for the colors," Morgan asked, thinking about what could be done with the space.

"I was thinking a gray-blue, with white trim-"

"Black furniture" Morgan finished for her. "I like it. I'm having boys so the blue gray would work, I could see if I could find dark blue bedding sets. Oh, I'm getting excited, when can I start shopping?" Morgan asked turned to Sara.

"Soon, that brings up another thing we need to talk about; a baby shower." Sara put her hands up to stop Morgan. "I know you don't want to be the center of attention like that but sweetie you're having twins and there are going to be aunts, cousins, and friends who are going to be expecting some kind of party," Sara said watching Morgan try to wrap her head around the idea of a party.

"How are they even going to know? I thought I could just be oh look I have children." Morgan put her hands to her eyes. Sara felt bad she hadn't meant to push; she didn't know that Morgan was that close to the edge still.

"Ok, never mind, I'm sorry that I brought it up," Sara said rubbing Morgan's arms.

"No, it's fine, I'm just really over today. I'm going to go take a hot shower and go to bed." Morgan said whipping her eyes.

"Sounds good" Sara brought Morgan into her arms again.

"SARA!!!!" Kadie yelled from downstairs.

"God, she can still do that," Morgan said pulling away from Sara.

"Yes, she can, go take that shower I'll see you tomorrow. It's Sunday we get to sleep in" Sara said smiling at Morgan then went to help Kadie.

"WHAT?" Sara said coming down into the kitchen then swinging into the living room. She found both Jared and Andrew standing with their arms crossed, blocking the door. She couldn't help the smile. "Oh"

"Make them get out of my way." Kadie sounded younger than she was. Kadie was all dolled up with her hair spiky, and makeup dark. She was wearing a well fitted top, paired with a short skirt, and converse to pull it all together. Sara stepped in front of her to face Andrew and Jared.

"She is going to the club with friends, she has cab money, and will call if she needs to." Sara gave both men the look.

"But look at what she's wearing," Andrew said looking at Jared for backup. Jared nodded and stood firm.

"She has shorts on underneath," Sara said waiting for the next thing they were going to complain about.

"Does it even matter that I'm almost 23?" Kadie said from behind Sara.

"No," Both Jared and Andrew said.

Sara turned to Kadie, and pulled her into a hug.

"Go, have fun, love you."

"Thank you," Kadie said, she kissed Sara on the cheek and danced around the guys and out the front door.

"Had to be done," Jared said when Sara locked eyes with him.

"Um," Andrew said clearing his throat "Where is Morgan?" Sara turned her attention to him.

"She's taking a shower and going to bed, her emotions were

intent today, back and forth. One minute she's close to tears, the next she is so excited, then back to tears." Andrew nodded his head then headed upstairs.

"Is he ok?" Sara asked turning into Jared who had stepped up to her to bring her in his arms.

"He will be as soon as he sees Morgan, and she'll be better when she sees him." Jared started to kiss her neck.

"How do you know?" Sara asked closing her eyes.

"Lucky guess." He said pulling her to the study.

Morgan stood under the hot water, relaxing in the way it moved down her body. Her mind ran over the day, as much as she tried to not let it. It seemed that's just what you did in the shower go over everything. She hadn't heard him till the last minute, Andrew was standing behind her. He put his hands on her shoulders, slowly moving them down her back, massaging as he went. Finally, he settled on her lower back that had already started hurting.

"I was mad at you today," Morgan said turning around to look at him, they danced around so that Andrew could stand under the water. He didn't move his hands off her hips.

"I know." He said moving to the side so that they could both stand in the water.

"Why didn't you stop and talk to me, look at me, anything?" Morgan asked looking at him. She wasn't sure if she wanted him to know just how much she needed him. As she was just realizing it herself, she couldn't find her ground in it.

"Baby I couldn't, if I had I wouldn't have been able to do my job. If I had looked at you, I would have wanted to hold you for the rest of the day and all the night." Andrew said then looked away for a moment as he was hit with the fresh memory of his whole world coming to a standstill when he received her text.

Scared didn't come close to how he felt. He had almost left Jared at the stations he lit out of there so fast. He looked back at her, taking her in. She looked so tired, so worn out.

"I was asked if I could stay objected before you and your sisters let me know what was going on, that is what I did today." He said, not hurt, or irritated, just stating facts

"I know, and when you say it, I know that's what we asked of you," Morgan said frowning, her mind was working against her. Andrew reached down and turned the water off.

"Let's get you to bed." He said, getting out first he wrapped a towel around his waist, then held his hand out to help Morgan out, wrapped her in one as she got her footing.

Dried they donned pajama pants and t-shirts. Andrew had packed extra as Morgan had started wearing his. Finding his more comfortable than her own with her growing belly.

"I need to go shopping, none of my clothes fit," Morgan said as she slid into bed. She smiled as Andrew settled in with her. "Sara and I talked about the nursery tonight." She was cut off by a yawn, that kept her eyes close.

"How was that?" Andrew asked knowing it was only a matter of minutes before she fell asleep.

"We're going to paint and have black furniture." She said dreamily

"You're not going to paint; I'll take your place. Bad for the boys" he added as she frowned

"Andrew?" she said softly

"Yeah baby," he said looking down at her.

"You're important." Morgan sighed and drifted off to sleep. Andrew kissed her head, grabbed a few books from his place, picked one up from the nightstand, and settled into one. Holding her as she slept, feeling more content than he ever thought he could. He had waited all day to end up right where he was, he was a bit taken aback by how easy they were together. He a man who never thought he would settle down, felt content settling with Morgan.

20

———

Morgan had decided that she didn't want to know about anything regarding Mark. Jared, Andrew, and Eddie kept Sara in the loop. Mark had called his dad as soon as he could. Jake Brown had shown up the following Monday, and thanks to Andrew making a call, Eddie was able to meet with Jake.

In that meeting, Eddie was able to lay out what his client, Ms. Mathews indented to do, and that he, Mr. Brown should advise his client to sign the termination of rights agreement when they received it. Eddie also informed Mr. Brown that Morgan would sign the denial of payment in exchange for the termination of rights.

"He got mad when I mentioned how Morgan was not going to take the money, as it was the trade for Mark signing his right way," Eddie said standing next to Andrew and Jared's desk.

"Why would he care? He was the one who wrote that stupid prenup, you would think he would be all for the idea of not having to pay Morgan" Andrew said leaning back in his chair.

"Morgan gave me a copy of the agreement when we came over for dinner last night. They pinned her down pretty good, it wouldn't seem bad if it had all worked out." Eddie shook his head

"What do you mean? And please remember we don't speak lawyer." Jared said.

"As a first language." Eddie joked. "They had it set up in the event Mark wanted out all he would have to do is say so. Whereas Morgan would have to prove she wanted out. If he hit her, cheated, ectara." Eddie said shaking his head.

"Explains why her first thought after finding him was to get a camera," Andrew said thoughtfully.

"She what?" Eddie asked.

"The day she found out she was pregnant, she went home early and found him on the kitchen table with someone else the first thing she did was find a camera and take pictures." Andrew had admiration in his voice.

"Remind me never to piss her off," Jared said shaking his head.

"I love them all, and I wouldn't want to piss any of them off. Kadie is the least sneaky about it of the bunch, I have often wondered if being a lawyer tipped things in my favor." Eddie said looking over just in time to see Mr. Brown walk his son out.

"That makes me feel all warm and fuzzy inside," Eddie said after they were in the elevator.

"That's the coffee," Jared said seeing that Eddie had grabbed his by mistake.

"What?" Eddie asked then looked down, realized it wasn't his cup. "Sorry, where did you get that?" Eddie asked.

"Mathew's café." Jared smiled and watched Eddie put it together.

"I'll have to ask Abby to make it," Eddie said setting the coffee down.

"No, go ahead." Jared waved his hand at Eddie, in a go-ahead gestor. "A thank you for coming down so fast," Jared said

"Anything for family," Eddie said, picking the cup back up. "I'll see you around." Then he headed out.

Jared and Andrew got a call moments later calling them out. Grabbing their stuff they headed to the new case and a full day's work.

"So how was the doctor's appointment?" Sara asked taking a drink break as Abby and Morgan walked into the back door of the bakery. The doctor had decided he would see Morgan every two weeks from her first appointment with him. They had been able to enlist Abby to take Morgan to her appointment. So far Morgan had been able to increase the fluid around the boys, and the three of them seem to be gaining good weight.

"It was fine," Morgan said as she walked in and set her bag down, she began to shift and readjust her shirt. "Alright, that's it we have to go today." She had started fighting with all her clothes. "I can't wear yoga pants every day, it makes me look like I couldn't be bothered to get dressed, and nothing fits anymore."

"But you couldn't," Kadie said from her corner, leaning ever a set of cupcakes.

"Very funny," Morgan said sending her an annoyed look. "I'm serious I need to go shopping," Morgan said walking to the front of the bakery.

"I'm sorry," Abby said looking at Sara "Did I hear the hand-me-down queen just say she needed to go shopping?" Abby questioned.

"Yep, she doesn't fit in any of her clothes anymore, and she would wear yoga pants, but they are getting too small. Andrew and I talked about it this morning." Sara said pouring cake batter into pans.

"You better hope she doesn't find out you're talking about her behind her back," Kadie said looking up.

"Agreed," Abby said as she moved to the rack of cupcakes that needed frosting.

"I know, but it helps to avoid the mine field." Sara started the mixer on the next batch of cake batter needed for a large six tear cake needed that weekend. When she knew it was done, she turned it off.

"Want to join us?" Sara asked looking over at Abby.

"Can't it's no phone night," Abby said with her head down, focused on what she was doing.

"Oh, what's that," Kadie said teasingly.

"We turn our phones off the moment we get home and don't turn them back on till the morning," Abby said head still down the sisters didn't miss the smile she had.

"I like that." Sara said, "Just your time together, that's good."

They stopped talking as they spent the rest of the day working on what was needed. Sara found it funny how before she and Abby couldn't handle working in the same space for very long. One of the reasons Abby didn't put in the kind of hours the rest of them did. Sara smiled to herself; she wasn't going to look a gift horse in the mouth.

Sara climbed into bed early, Saturdays were turning out to be the killer day of the week. They had been able to hold Morgan off on the shopping till Sunday. They hadn't left the bakery till after six, with it being so late they decided dinner and bed were better than hours more at the store.

She pulled a desert book to her, opened and started making notes. She hadn't seen Jared since the day before, they had talked but the case he was working on had consumed both him and Andrew. She was hoping they would see each other tomorrow. Sara put her book down, turned her light out, and was asleep before she could even try.

The alarm was going off, she didn't want it to be so. Before she could swing an arm out to shut it off it stopped. Opening her eyes, she saw Kadie's spiky hair. She wrapped her arm around her sister.

"You're too hot," Kadie mumbled.

"I know," Sara said, she took another moment then hoped up and headed to the shower. She was dressed in her usual when she walked into the kitchen and stopped short. Jared was sitting at the kitchen counter with a cup of coffee in front of him.

"We had Morgan let us in." Jared stood and walked to her.

"You look very tired; did you sleep last night?" Sara said wrapping her arms around his neck.

"No, I was hoping to catch you in bed for a few minutes, but no luck." Jared rested his forehead on hers.

"Well, it should still be warm, why don't you go up and sleep for a little bit? Then come to the bakery for lunch. If you get up by then." Sara said closing her eyes, breathing him in.

"I'll get up by then," Jared said, kissing her till Kadie came down.

"Hey Jared, sorry," Kadie said going to fill her to go cup.

"Are you ready?" Sara asked.

"Yes," Kadie said drinking her coffee. Moving to sit at the counter to wait for Morgan to join them, which wasn't long.

"Alright, I'll see you later," Sara said to Jared, giving him one more kiss then heading out the door.

Sara was wiping her counter down; Kadie was doing the same. The shop was quiet, they could hear the thunder of the summer storm that had moved in. She had plans to work in her yard, but the storm changed them.

"Are you alright?" Kadie asked pulling Sara out of the dream like state she was in.

"Yep, why?" She asked looking at Kadie.

"You just don't seem here."

"I was planning on working in the yard, now I'll need to wait." Sara finished and looked at the clock. They were closed, and they were going to get out of there on time. It was a great way to start the weekend.

"There's something else," Kadie said walking over to Sara's area.

"No, there isn't," Sara said looking over at Kadie.

"Lunch?" Kadie said raising an eyebrow.

"He had to go back to work. He was lucky to get the few hours he did." Sara said in defense.

"It isn't that big a deal, it's going to happen." Sara tried to move away from Kadie.

"Alright, if that's how you want to play this. Just know I'm here if you need me." Kadie said giving her a soft smile.

"Yeah, I know," Sara said recognizing Kadie wanting to help. "Are you going out tonight?" Sara asked changing the subject.

"Yep, I have a diner date," Kadie said almost bouncing with joy.

"Wow, same guy?" Sara asked happy Kadie had moved on.

"Yep, Kyle," Kadie said with a smile.

"Are we going to meet him anytime soon, we have a tradition now." Sara teased.

"A tradition about what?" Morgan asked coming back with a bank bag and handful of receipts.

"I have a date tonight and Sara is asking when I'm going to bring him around." Kadie didn't take her eyes off Sara as she answered Morgan.

"Oh well, that would only be fair." Morgan pointed out.

"We'll see how tonight goes and I'll let you know." Kadie said with an eyeroll.

"Good," Sara said then turned to Morgan "Ready?"

"Yep"

They walked in the warm rain, laughing as they went. Sara went upstairs to change and when she came back to the kitchen to start dinner, Kadie was putting on her shoes.

"Hey, have a good dinner tonight," Sara said pulling items from the fridge.

"I will, call if you need anything." Kadie blew a kiss and walked out the door.

Sara and Morgan enjoyed the chicken fettuccine, they laughed and talked. They moved to the study to watch a movie; Morgan hadn't lasted through half of it. Sara helped her to bed then made her way to bed as well. She realized she was trying not to be mad. One side of her was thinking it was stupid to get mad it was his job, the other part of her, the one that had gotten used to having him in bed with her every night just about had steam bellowing from her ears. There was another side, one that she absolutely refused to allow get a hold of her. She needed him; she was falling in love with him. He had become such a calm, safe place to be. She couldn't think about it, she wouldn't.

Walking back to bed she shook her head, climbed in, and shut the light off. It was silly to think that that would shut off her mind, she rolled over and drifted into a restless sleep.

When she woke the room was light, weak but light. Looking at the clock she noted it was after eight.

"Holy shit," she said, then felt the bed shift next to her.

"What?" Jared's voice was alert, as he sat up. Sara rolled over.

"What, how?" Then she relaxed, he was safe, he was here. Without saying another word, she grabbed him and brought him down to her. He went willingly, let her kiss his neck, his face then finally his lips. His hands moved up her, she pulled at the shirt he wore, he moved her shorts down to find her warm, wet heat. They worked together for the common goal of coming together. It wasn't slow but it was sweet, demanding, but not hard. It was exactly what they needed.

Sara rolled them so that she could sit on him, and take from him. Her hips moved; his hands guided. The heat built, and when she started to come Jared sat up taking her mouth, taking her screams. He bought her with him as they lay on the bed spent.

"I'm picking the lock again if it is accompanied by morning sex." Jared rubbed her back, hoping the motion would keep him awake long enough for a shower and coffee.

"You picked the locks?" Sara smiled, thinking she should ask her sister if he could have a key.

"We need to shower," Jared said kissing her head.

"Yes, we do." Sara said moving, "It's after eight. Well, almost nine now." Sara couldn't help the smile that came over her.

They showered, and when they walked back into the room Jared went for the bag, he had on the window seat.

"You can put them in here if you want," Sara said walking to her tall dresser.

"What?" He asked.

"Your clothes, the top two are yours." Sara walked to her closet to pull on an old, well broken in pair of jeans and a t-shirt. When she turned around, she found Jared looking at the drawers. "What's wrong?"

"I have drawers." He looked at her smiling.

"And closet space." Sara teased.

"What?" Jared couldn't help teasing her back, she walked over to him. He bent down and kissed her; he kept his hands to himself sad that she had already dressed.

"Get dressed I need coffee," Sara said pulling away. Sara walked out of the room and closed the door behind her. She bounced down the stairs and found Morgan and Kadie in the kitchen sitting at the bar.

"Hey girls, how's it going?" Sara asked walking to the coffee pot.

"Well, looks like someone had a good night." Kadie teased

"Good morning," she said unable to hold back the smile. "How was your night?" Sara asked moving to lean on the counter across from them.

"Well, I got kicked out," Kadie said more proudly than she should have been.

"Honey that isn't a good thing," Morgan said shifting as one of the boys stretched.

"Oh, but it was so worth it." Kadie stopped to take a sip of coffee. "All right, so I went to dinner last night with Kyle it was going well. I told him that I wanted him to come and meet my sisters. I didn't mention Andrew and Jared because-." Kadie paused

"You're mean," Sara added.

"Anyways, he seems to handle it fine. We finished dinner then went to club 89 to catch up with some friends. After one of my trips back from the bathroom, I'm walking back to our table and notice a couple doing some serious making out. Like they are almost doing it at the table. I almost just walked away but then they shifted, and I saw it was Kyle, and his 'friend'" Kadie sipped her coffee.

"You got kicked out." Sara was nodding her head, "Now it makes sense."

"What did you do?" Morgan asked smiling.

"I moved to the DJ, as it was Lia a good friend of mine. Really the only reason I go to 89. I pointed them out to her, she talked to her light guy. We got it all worked out and fast as they still thought I hadn't caught on. Lia turned on a good beat and I pulled her off him by her hair. We were spotlighted, it was wonderful, he slipped out of the booth and started to yell at me, how I'm just the hired help. How I only have a job because I work for my big sisters. Once you find out I don't have talent you'll move someone else in. At that point, I didn't even care that I caught him making out with another woman. I brought my knee up to meet his nuts, and as he bent over, I had the pleasure of telling him that I own the business, that I don't work for anyone but me." Kadie smiled so proud of himself.

"He fell on the ground about the time security came and walked me out. The stupid bitch got up and told on me."

"You make me proud to know you," Morgan said getting up to find something to eat.

"Ditto," Sara said sipping her coffee. Then turned to see Jared coming downstairs.

"Hey, Kadie, how was your night?" Jared gave her a small smile as he made his way over to the coffee pot.

"Fine thank you." She smiled and then raised an eyebrow in question.

"Good" Then he winked at her.

"Stop, what do you know?" Sara turned to him.

"Nothing that you don't, I just took care of the after," Jared said drinking his coffee.

"What after, there was no after," Kadie said taking a bite of the fruit bowl Morgan was eating.

"Then I did my job. Kadie I would like to tell you to be careful who you hurt, but I know better." Jared smiled then plucked a piece of fruit from the bowl and ate it. Just then Andrew came in.

"Hey Kadie, how's the knee?" Andrew walked over to kiss Morgan, then moved to the coffee pot. Taking the last of it, he looked to Sara. "Teach me your ways so that I may not leave an empty pot." Sara waved him away to start another pot.

"Thank you, both of you," Kadie said with her brightest smile.

They sank into the morning, Jared made eggs, Sara another pot of coffee. They were sitting around the table talking and teasing when Jared looked over at Sara.

"What are you doing next Friday night?" He asked her.

"I don't know, why?" She said taken off guard.

"It's my father's birthday party. Will you be my date?" He asked smiling at her.

"Well, I'm already your girlfriend I thought being your date just went with it." Sara smiled; her eyes bright. Andrew grabbed Morgan's hand.

"I said no, it would be too awkward." Morgan sat back to give the boys room.

"What if I could make it less awkward?" Andrew asked.

"How could you do that, look at me. I can't exactly hide." Morgan stated as she waved a hand in front of her growing belly.

"Not hide, never hide. Morgan, you know that I want to be with you, I have made no secret of it." Andrew was looking at her, just her. The table became quiet, Jared reached out and took Sara's hand under the table. Knowing what was coming next.

"I want everyone to know that we're together, I know you want and need time. I will wait for you, that too is no secret. Can you, will you promise to be with us for the rest of our lives?" Andrew opened his hand in front of her, it held a beautiful ring, it was gold with curves, had small diamonds curving into the center from each side that housed three larger diamonds. It took Morgan's breath away; it wasn't big and showy it was quiet and stunning.

Morgan looked at Andrew; she knew if she said no, he wouldn't leave he would just wait for her. Her heart filled; happiness overcame her. She had found her safe place, the place she could be herself. He had and would love her no matter what. The room waited on bated breath.

"Yes, I can," Morgan said looking into Andrew's eyes. He smiled brightly, slid the ring on that fit perfectly. Grabbed her face to kiss her, he kept it short and sweet. He gave her a look, a promise for later.

"Damn that's sweet, and I'll go get that," Kadie said wiping the tears from her eyes as she stood up to go answer the doorbell.

"Agree," Sara said wiping her eyes too. She rested her head

on Jared's shoulder. The world was right. She was suddenly overcome with the feeling of missing her mom. She always felt it most when happiness soaked the air. She turned her face into Jared's shoulder, and let a few tears fall for their mom.

Jared wrapped his arms around her and just held on. He didn't say a word, he didn't have to. Sara snapped out of it when Kadie came back to the table.

"Morgan it's for you." Kadie looked down, something she did when something was wrong.

"Who is it?" Sara said standing up.

"Jake Brown," Kadie said looking at Sara then they both looked at Morgan. Morgan giggled and looked at Andrew.

"I'll go with you." He stood and held a handout for her, Morgan took it nervously. Standing she took a deep breath and walked into the living room. Jake was standing by the door waiting.

"Jake, please come in." Morgan motioned with her hand for him to have a seat. She noticed his eyes went right to her growing belly. He sat in a chair, she sat on the couch across from him. Andrew stood behind her, his arms crossed. "What can I do for you?" Morgan asked and watched Jake take a breath.

"I came for a few reasons. I'll start with this." He opened his briefcase and took out a large manila envelope. He reached out and set it on the coffee table in front of Morgan. She scooted to the edge of the couch and reached for it. Jake remained quiet as she opened it to find several sets of papers. Her divorce papers were the first set she read. It was final. She was a free woman, free to be with Andrew. She smiled then turned to look at him.

Going back to the papers the second set was the termination agreement. Mark had signed his rights away. He had no claim to the boys, they were hers. She reached behind her to give them to Andrew. That was when she saw the third set. It was the pre-nuptial argument, with it came the four checks. All made out to her. Morgan looked up and met Jakes's eyes.

"I know I could never apologize for what he did." Jake took a breath. "I can only apologize for not raising a better man." He stood then. "I'll let myself out, congratulations." Morgan tried to stand but couldn't with her belly. Andrew came around to help her, he kept a hand on her back, and she shook Jake's hand.

"Thank you, Jake. I'm sorry that it had to be like this." Morgan said solemnly.

"So am I" He looked at Andrew. "Best of luck." They nodded at each other. Then Jake turned and left.

Andrew and Morgan stood there for a moment, then he spun her around and kissed her. Kadie cheered from the kitchen, the three of them had been eavesdropping. Coming into the living room Andrew released Morgan so she could hug Sara. Morgan moved from Sara to Jared, going up on her toes to kiss his cheek, and did a little dance when she met with Kadie.

Andrew came around the table to catch her. "How do you want to celebrate?"

"I have no idea." Morgan smiled up at him. The only thing planned was shopping for Morgan, Sara kept that to herself. "let's just hang out, do nothing." Morgan smiled at the people around her, her people.

"We can do that, hey isn't there a game on today?" Jared said as his arm wrapped around Sara's waist.

"Hell, yes there is," Kadie said with renewed excitement. Sara watched as Andrew, Jared, and Kadie moved to the study to watch the game, Morgan grabbed one of the baby books she was reading and joined Andrew on the couch. Sara happily looked at her family, then she went to the kitchen.

She cleaned up the breakfast, then pulled out what she needed for her popcorn. Putting music on low she settled into making an extra-large batch. She had reached a stopping point, breaking for a moment to get fruits, veggies, crackers, cheese, and a pitcher of lemonade. She timed it just right to set it down for them when a commercial was on the TV.

"Thank you, sister," Kadie said reaching for crackers and cheese.

"What are you doing?" Jared asked her.

"Stuff." She smiled as she sat on the arm rest next to him and watched the silly commercial.

"Popcorn, leave her be," Morgan said not looking up from her book.

"Deal," Andrew said, then Sara left when the game came back on.

She worked the caramel, she had spread the popcorn on flat cookie sheets, so she could drizzle the caramel over the popcorn.

Jared walked into the kitchen later to find every surface covered with sheet pans. Counters, stools, the table, and chairs, and no Sara. He looked out back and found her on her knees digging in the dirt. His heart stopped, she looked so beautiful it knocked him stupid. He remembered talking to his father about the party. He wanted to make sure that his mother had let go of the Meg thing. Jared wanted Sara to meet his dad, he wanted her by his side.

"Pretty isn't she," Kadie said as she came up behind him. "Morgan and Andrew started making out." She added when he looked over at her.

"Pretty is putting it lightly," Jared said looking back at Sara. "And here she comes."

"Hey, what's up?" She asked when she saw Jared and Kadie standing in the kitchen.

"Morgan and Andrew started making out. Do you need help?" Kadie pointed to the pans.

"Yes, please. There is a box of tins above the garage. Can

you go get them?" Sara watched as Kadie left. "How was the game?" Sara asked moving into Jared's arms.

"Good, want to go out for dinner?" He wasn't sure why he had asked her so quickly, but the slightly surprised look on her face told him he needed to do it more often.

"Sure," Sara said smiling up at him.

Kadie brought the box in and together they worked on putting the popcorn away. Kadie took a tin to the living room. She was happy to see that Andrew and Morgan had left, so she settled into a movie. When Jared and Sara went to dinner, she made herself a sandwich and went up to her room. Kadie was deep into a book when her phone went off telling her she had received a text message.

"Have I waited long enough to see how you are?"

Kadie smile when she saw who it was from, Graham Peterson. They had gone to school together, he had been in the same grade as Morgan. They had met through Morgan, though the two never dated never anything but friendship between them. Kadie had always thought of him as a good guy, he had tried to be there for the sisters when they had lost their mom. That had been a hard time for all of them. Kadie had sometimes wondered if she would or should ever try to be more than friends with him. It always seemed like the wrong time, when he was single, she was not, and vice versa. They still stayed friends and even now it was something in the back of her mind, what if?

"Yes, and I'm fine. Tell me how did Jared and Andrew find out about last night?"

Kadie wondered how long she would have to wait for his response and was happy not to have to wait long.

"I was asked to keep an eye out for you, so I did."

"You have always kept an eye out; I'll ask you again why did you have to bring them into it?"

After the thing with your car, Jared got in touch. He asked

me to look out for you. I told him I always did. He asked me to do it for him too. Abbot is just an extension of that.

She had to think about that for a moment. Jared and Andrew had her back. She wasn't used to having so many people looking out for her. It almost made her feel like they didn't trust her not to get into trouble. Before last night she would have had a leg to stand on,

"Thank you, be safe tonight."

"Always."

Kadie went back to her book, and it wasn't until after she knew Jared and Sara were home did, she drift off to sleep.

21

Jared's alarm was going off, after he stopped it, he rolled over to put his arm around Sara and found she had grown twice as big. His hand landed on Kadie's lower ribs, he patted her and moved his hand. He had learned early that if Kadie was in bed with them the night had not been kind to her. One morning he asked her what the nightmares were about. She couldn't really describe them just the feeling that came over her, alone, dark, scared, she couldn't find her way back to her family.

Jared knew almost at once that it was tied to the people that she had lost. He didn't bat an eye on the mornings he found her in bed with them, it would most certainly make it worst if he denied her that and end his relationship with Sara. He rolled out of bed and headed to the shower. Sara wrapped an arm around Kadie.

"You're hot," Kadie said half awake.

"I know" Sara smiled; she loved her sister.

"Your boyfriend was feeling me up."

"No, he wasn't," Sara said with a smile in her tone

"I know" Kadie snuggled in for another minute. "I'm going to go; you can go jump your man for some shower sex. It would be a nice way for him to start his week." Kadie flipped the blanket back and started to get up.

"Kadence," Sara said.

"Wow, the big guns." She turned around to look at her sister.

"Would it be ok to give him a key?" Sara asked, and Kadie watched that this was her decision. If she wasn't comfortable with Jared living with them, she could say no, then she thought about what Graham had said.

"Yes, I'm surprised it took you this long." Kadie smiled then left. Sara got out of bed did a little dance then went to start Jared's week with a boost.

"I have to give you something," Sara said when she and Jared were standing in the kitchen alone.

"This sounds promising, first the shower now a gift. I just don't know what to say." He smiled at her, it was turning out to be one hell of a Monday, and he wasn't stupid enough to say it out loud. He watched as Sara opened a drawer and pull out a key. She slid it over to him and watched him.

He couldn't catch his breath; it was a key to the house. He had earned their well-guarded trust. He had taken the time to get to know them. It struck him this wouldn't just be Sara's decision it would be a family matter. He was being trusted, a gift he was overcome with.

"I'm speechless," Jared said just stared at the key.

"If it's too much-" Sara started.

"No, it isn't that. This is very humbling. You girls don't let anyone in, family included. The four of you are a set, how long did it take Eddie? I don't mean to say that you're rushing this, I'm saying I get that this is big." Jared looked at Sara.

"That plays in your favor." She smiled then leaned in to kiss him. They were interrupted when Kadie came down.

"Jesus wasn't the shower enough." She skirted them wide to

get to the coffee. She was taken by surprise when she was taken up into Jared's arms.

"Thank you" He whispered, he set her back down. Kadie just nodded her head and went for her coffee. Andrew and Morgan came down. Shared in the good news, Andrew got his key and he too thanked Kadie. It was different for Andrew to get a key; he and Morgan would move out eventually. It felt the same as when they gave Eddie a key. Kadie sat on the stool and watched her sisters as the coffee worked its magic.

After a good breakfast and bidding the guys goodbye the ladies went out shopping. It had turned out to be much harder and easier than Sara was ready for. They started with paint for the room, moving to get new clothes for Morgan. Morgan had been happy with the new comfortable clothes; she even wore some out of the store. She was good with the belly band, new pillow, and even the clothes that she could grow into. The hard part was when they were in the car, and she was hit with buyer's remorse. It took Sara pulling over, and both Kadie and Sara talking to her for her to calm down.

Sara decided it was time for lunch and headed for food as soon as they got Morgan ok. With the emotional roller coaster, and a full belly Morgan had fallen asleep in the back seat on the way home. Kadie had lugged in all of Morgan's new clothes to her sister's room while Sara worked on getting Morgan in the house and to the couch.

Sara and Kadie attacked the house. They had routines; they had slipped some over the last weeks, so they dove into it. They started in the attic, scrubbing the bathroom, vacuuming rugs, mopping, dusting, and changing bedding. Mondays were the day the washer never stopped. They moved to the second floor and did the same, they moved together. Starting in the sitting room they mopped, washed windows, and dusted the built-in shelves. Moving into the bedroom, swinging through the bathroom, going through Morgan's room. Crossing the hall, they dove into Sara's master bedroom and bathroom. They mopped the hall and moved down to the study and dipped into the little bedroom and bathroom. Morgan was still sleeping on the couch, so they held off on vacuuming the first floor.

Sara walked to the fridge and pulled two beers out, they sat at the kitchen table. They kept the kitchen clean all week, so it didn't need the Monday treatment.

"Boys have moved into our house," Kadie said setting her feet on the chair next to her, taking a sip of her beer.

"Yes, they have, they do seem to try to be clean though," Sara said doing the same. She looked at the clock thinking dinner would need to be started soon. "Three hours not bad sister." She toasted Kadie.

"I have an important yet inappropriate question." Kadie looked at Sara.

"Shoot," Sara said as she lifted her beer up to take a drink.

"I noticed the condoms aren't in the garbage anymore. What are you guys doing?" Kadie asked not questioning their senses but their method.

"I started the pill; I had an appointment after one of Morgan's appointments," Sara answered calmly, she knew Kadie was just worrying. It was just what Kadie did. "So, changing the subject. When do you want to do the baby shower?"

"Does she even want to have one?" Kadie asked.

"Well, I'm worried that if we don't do something someone else will, and that would end so badly. She shook her head "We also need to ready ourselves for Andrew's mother." Sara said taking a drink.

"I totally didn't think about that," Kadie said taking another drink of her beer. Andrew and Eddie's mothers were sisters, not close unless it benefited them.

"A little early to start drinking don't you think?" Morgan

said in a short tone as she came walking into the kitchen, went right to the sink for water.

"When you clean the house top to bottom in three hours you earn a beer anytime you want," Kadie said a little snappy, her lack of sleep topped with shopping, topped with cleaning had left her tired and grouchy.

"Alright I'm sorry, thank you for cleaning," Morgan said using a tone that was anything but apologetic, sitting down, and glaring at Kadie.

"I'm going to stop both of you right there. Both of you are cranky, so I'll give you the following options. You can either, sit here and fight it out, end up making each other cry then make up. Or you go your separate ways and do an even bigger blow up in a day or two. The third and final option is to stand up both of you right now, tell each other why you're cranky, and give each other hugs." Sara stood up to go change the laundry and let them figure it out. When she came back, they were standing, and hugging each other.

"Good, so I need to go to the study to pay bills and figure out what to do for dinner. Any requests?" Sara asked as the sisters stepped apart.

"Tacos," Morgan said. "I'll do them since I slept through the cleaning."

"Alright, that's settled." Sara set off to the study. They both followed her in and settled in front of the TV.

Morgan got up after a few shows and moved to the kitchen to start dinner. Sara took the planner book, and her notebook and followed Morgan.

"I've been thinking." Sara started as she walked into the kitchen.

"Not a surprise, what's up," Morgan said pulling items out of the fridge to start cutting up.

"I think we should work on painting the nursery this weekend and move you downstairs. There are a few reasons, the big one being and let me say first I love you and you are growing those babies like a boss. I don't want you to fall."

Morgan looked up from her cutting to give her sister a look that translated to a sassy thanks. Sara continued as if she didn't notice it. "Secondly I don't think it would be wise for you to sleep in a room heavy with paint fumes. Even with windows open and doors closed I don't want to change it." Sara let all that settle in.

"All that makes sense, and I know it would make Andrew feel better he is more worried than you are." Morgan put all the cut lettuce in a bowl, moving on tomatoes.

"The next thing is the baby shower. Before you say anything, you need to know that if we don't do one, someone else will. I have some wonderful ideas that will make this more bearable." Again, Sara just waited for Morgan to work it over in her head.

"Ok, do you think we could include Andrew?" Morgan asked when she had taken a minute.

"Yes, I have an idea. We'll talk about it when they get home." Sara said making notes. Then as if on cue Jared and Andrew came walking in.

"Speak of the men," Sara said not looking up but smiling as she felt Jared come up behind her.

"Holy F- what happened to you?" Morgan said, Sara's head snapped up, and turned to look at Jared. He had a split lip.

"I got slapped today." Then he turned to Sara "We need to talk, later if you can wait." Sara just nodded.

"I hope you'll be able to eat dinner, it's tacos do you want me to make something else for you?" Morgan asked as Andrew held her from behind. He rubbed his hands over her huge belly, she laughed when one of the boys started to move. "Every time," she said smiling.

"No, it should be fine," Jared said, then looked at the notes Sara was writing. "What are you working on babe?"

"The baby shower, and stuff. I need to talk to you." She turned her attention to Andrew.

"Alright," He looked questioningly.

"How many guy friends do you have?" Sara looked at Andrew to Jared who was looking at each other. "Ok if you were to have a party how many guys would show up?" Sara tried asking a different way.

"When we have had a get together, smallest 20, largest 30." Andrew smiled. "Good times"

"What are you thinking?" Jared asked.

"Do they get rowdy, break things, pee in the house plants," Sara asked taking more notes.

"No, well there is always that one guy, but we could just keep an eye on him," Andrew said watching Sara take notes. "Sara, what is this all about?" Andrew moved to the fridge pulled a soda, held it up to Jared who nodded. He walked back and stood next to Morgan.

"Ok, we are going to have a baby shower for Morgan and the boys, she would feel better if you could be included somehow. So, I was thinking about a diaper party, we get a keg, you invite all your guy friends, tell them they can come to get their drink on only if they bring a pack of diapers." Sara watched as all three of them mulled it over. Then she decided to give them all her plans.

"You could have the driveway, garage, and the space above the garage. I'm thinking corn-hole in the driveway, beer pong in the garage, bring your big TV and your nice couch put a game on upstairs."

"That sounds amazing," Morgan said looking at Jared and Andrew

"Where will you be?" Jared asked.

"Inside with women and baby games and presents," Sara said, she watched Morgan's face fall.

"What?" Andrew asked moving to rub a hand down her back.

"I don't want everyone to touch my belly, I know how many women would come, I don't want to spend all the party telling them not to touch me. These babies are like a beacon, I'm glad I have a counter between me and the customers, though that doesn't stop some." Morgan looked down at her belly.

"Put it on the invitation, a warning," Andrew turned Morgan, tilting her chin up so that she had to look at him. "They are not allowed to touch your belly. If they can't respect that, then they deserve to get their head bitten off." Andrew smiled as he was given one of Morgan's bright smiles.

"When do you want to do this?" Jared asked Sara.

"She is at 25 weeks now, and we'll be lucky if she makes it to 37, I think we should have everything set up by 35 weeks just in case, so" Sara looked at the calendar "week 30? That's five weeks from now, it will give us the time to get the guest list, register at a baby shop, get the invites out, get the room painted, move your furniture over if that's what you want." Sara looked at Jared. Then went back to writing a to do list. "We can put the rule on a big board at the door as a friendly reminder."

"What are you talking about?" Kadie asked coming from upstairs.

"The baby shower," Sara said writing things down.

"Oh, good Lord you got her planning," Kadie said walking over to sit next to Jared. "So how was your day?"

"Not bad." He said with a shrug.

"Your lip would disagree." Kadie looked at it then at Jared.

"Yep, how was your day?" Jared asked to change the subject.

"Cleaned the house and had a beer. Just got done drawing up some new designs." Kadie said then got up to get a glass of water.

"You drink after cleaning?" Andrew asked.

"Yep, cleaned top to bottom in three hours, it deserved a beer," Kadie said coming back to sit with Jared.

They continued to talk and moved into eating when Morgan finished the tacos. Andrew and Jared cleaned the kitchen. Kadie read in the living room, Morgan and Andrew settled there as well.

"Come with me." Jared led Sara out into the warm summer night. They sat at the table; Jared pulled a chair out for her. He needed to keep it short, she had work tomorrow. Once he was settled, he looked at her. "Meg caught me outside the station today, she isn't allowed up to my office, so she waited. Sara, she isn't taking no for an answer, and it isn't helping that my mother seems to be having the same problem."

"She slapped you today?" Sara asked, and Jared could see her eyes had a glow to them when she got mad.

"No, that was another woman." Jared smiled trying to lighten the mood. It worked for a minute; Sara gave him a small smile. "I told her again that I was with someone and wasn't interested, but I have a feeling that isn't going to be the end of it as it hasn't put a stop to it yet."

"You're worried about something. Tell me that part of it." Sara sat back.

"I'm worried my mother and or Meg are going to try to pull something at the Birthday party." Jared looked at Sara he was worried that this could be what ended it. He knew his mother was a piece of work, but she was taking it to a whole new level."

"Ok," Sara said looking out at her yard, thinking about how she had laid out the options for Morgan and Kadie. "These are the options I see, one I go with you, meet them, prove that we are together. Two I stay here you go without me, or three we say to hell with the whole thing, and I meet your dad another time." Sara looked back at Jared, waiting for him to make the final decision.

"You are with me; I want everyone to know about it. I want

you at my side at my dad's birthday, I want to introduce you as mine because that's what you are. Not to be hidden away just because my mother has gone off some deep end." Jared smiled; Sara melted as he said just the right thing.

"Alright then, I'm going. Now we need to have a plan if they do try to pull something." Sara said, and together they talked and planned what they would do if or when something went wrong.

They moved up to bed when Sara started yawning. They readied for bed, and once they settled in Jared turned to her.

"I'm in this all the way Sara. I have never wanted anything more than to wake up with you, go to bed with you, you are my everything." Jared waited for Sara to say something, but when he listened for her, he heard her breathing was even, she was sleeping. He smiled to himself and drifted to sleep.

22

———

THE WEEK WENT by faster than Sara realized, before she knew it she was getting out of a shower Friday after work. The four sisters had gone shopping Wednesday to find dresses for Morgan and Sara. Morgan had found a semi formal dress that was a dark blue, making the green in her eyes pop. It was loose and went down to her knees, her favorite part had been the high neckline. Sara's dress was black, it had two layers, the first was a silk strapless the second an organza overlay with straps. It hit her just above the knee, both Sara and Morgan decided to wear Converse. The secret joke was just in case they needed to make a quick escape they couldn't do it in heels.

Sara dried her hair straight, put light make up on, put her dress on, then her all black shoes. She bounced down the stairs, stopping short when she found Jared and Andrew standing in the kitchen. Jared was in black dress pants, white dress shirt, and black vest. He too was wearing all black Converse. He had the top bottom of his shirt undone and his tie loose.

"Why hello," she said smiling making her way over to him. She stepped into his arms easily.

"You look amazing," Jared said looking into her bright eyes

"Thank you," Sara looked at the clock. "We need to go. Morgan?"

"Right here." They all turned to see her coming down in a flow of dark blue dress. "All right let's do this," Morgan said walking to Andrew, she slipped under his arm with ease.

They decided to take Jared's truck, Sara sat in the front seat holding Jared's hand when she could. She knew that tonight was going to be a big night. She just didn't know how. They pulled up to a very large Mansion house, Sara counted the windows three stories plus an attic. The green grass went on for what seemed like miles, it was met with either a tall hedge or light gravel that made up the driveway and walkways. The house was light tan with dark shutters, it was big, grand, and breathtaking.

"This is where you grew up?" Sara looked a Jared.

"Yep, I mostly stayed on the third floor." Jared seemed to become stiffer the closer they got to the house. Jared parked off to the side where all the other cars had parked, Sara had a brief thought it would be easy to make a quick escape parked the way he had.

Jared got out and walked around to open the door and Sara carefully slid out. He looked down at her. She came up on her toes the same time she wrapped her arms around his neck. She kissed him, lightly at first, then she didn't care that Andrew and Morgan were near she deepened it taking Jared with her. He pushed her into the seat of the truck, his hand gripping her hips to keep the ground under him.

Sara broke the kiss and looked into his eyes. She felt if she would ever say it, now would be the best time. Jared bent his forehead to hers.

"I love you." She whispered for only him. Jared smiled "I love you too." he pulled back grabbed her hand and lead the four of them into the house.

Sara had seen parties before; this took it to the next level.

There were so many people, Jared kept his hand on her lower back as he led her from room to room introducing Sara as his girlfriend. He was met with a few confused looks, and he could tell his mother had decided not to listen to his request. Sara acted like nothing was happening, like she didn't notice the few looks she got.

Andrew and Morgan were much funnier to watch, here Andrew a man about town, showing up with a woman on his arm, with a large bun in the oven. The ring on her finger flashed, having people talk more about not knowing they got married than how she was pregnant.

Keeping with soda and water, the four made it to the back of the room and found a good chair for Morgan to sit in. The four had joked in hush tones, laughing to settle nerves. Then there was a parade of people who had to stop to say hi, find out what was going on with those boys, the ones that came from money but didn't live like it.

Sara felt Jared move her closer to him just before a stunning blond in a vintage 1960 light pink semi formal dress swept up to them.

"Andrew I was just talking with your mother, and she didn't mention this." Helen Brooks swept a hand down at Morgan.

"We asked her not to say anything, yet. It's nice to know she kept her word." Andrew said. What nobody knew about was the conversation Andrew had with his mother weeks before. He had informed her that he met the love of his life and was going to marry her. Then to make his point clear he told her that if she gossiped or argued about his decision at all then she would have no place in his life or her grandchildren's.

"Mrs. Brooks, Morgan Mathews. Morgan, Mrs. Helen Brooks." Andrew introduced them. Morgan didn't attempt to stand.

"Sorry for not standing, summer and pregnancy have really taken it out of me. It is wonderful to meet you." Morgan said holding her hand out. Jared watched his mother take it weakly. Then she turned to Jared.

"Sweetheart how are you, have you seen your father yet?" Helen greeted her son and refused to acknowledge the woman standing at Jared's side. She was the woman that they had ordered the cakes from and as far as Helen was concerned, she was below them.

"Mother" he said as a greeting. "No, I haven't but I'm sure he'll be around in a bit. Mother, this is Sara Mathews, Sara my mother Helen Brooks." Jared watched his mother, her eyes had frosted over the moment he said Sara's name she continued to refuse Sara 's presence. Just as Jared feared she then turned her ice eyes on Sara.

"Yes, how nice to see you again. Thanks again for making the cakes for the party." Helen didn't want this woman near her son. She would fix this once and for all. "Jared" Helen turned back to Jared "why don't you go find your father? I'm sure Sara won't mind staying with her sister, you and Andrew should make the rounds. Say hi to friends and family." She watched her son willing him to leave the little gold digger with her for just a minute.

"No, thank you. If anyone wants to say hi, they'll make their way to me." Jared said, "I think you should go check on the kitchen."

"Very well." Defeated, for the time being, Helen turned and walked away. Just as she was out of earshot Sara looked down and Morgan, their smiles turned to quiet laughter. Jared relaxed at Sara's laugh, she was handling it, and better than he was, he turned to her.

"You are amazing." He smiled down at her, grateful for her.

"I know." She winked at him.

"Oh no, where is the bathroom? The boys had decided they are in a heavy metal band and are head butting my bladder." Morgan stood up quickly.

"It's just around the corner. I can go with you if you want, for protection." Jared said as he scanned the room.

"Have a little faith, ok?" Sara gave him a look.

"Alright," Jared said then watched as Sara and Morgan made their way to the bathroom.

"You need a drink man, want me to drive us home?" Andrew asked when he watched his friend.

"Maybe, I'll think about it. Let's see if it gets worst, if anything we can have a drink at home." Jared looked at Andrew surprised by what they were called the Mathew's house.

"Ya, I get it. More than half my stuff is there. It's home, it's where they are" Andrew nodded in the direction they had sent the girls. Jared and Andrew were approached by a few of their friends, and time slipped by.

Sara stood by the bathroom and waited for Morgan to come out. While she waited, the people watched some ignored her, some looked over and whisper amongst themselves. When Morgan came out Sara noticed she was moving with caution, and she looked a little pale.

"Are you ok?" Sara asked but before Morgan could answer they were approached by Helen.

"Glad I caught you," Helen said her tone so sweet it made Sara's teeth hurt. "You must come to meet Andrew's mother, Margaret," Helen said starting for the library. Sara took a breath shared a look with Morgan and followed Helen.

"My dear look who I found," Helen said as they walked up to a beautiful woman. Margaret Abbot had gotten the memo and was dressed in a beautiful light blue semi- formal dress that like Helen's was from 60's fashion. Margaret turned around just as Helen said, "This is Sara and Morgan Mathews." Sara noticed the settled way Helen stepped back and her eyes lit up as if she was going to enjoy this little meet and greet.

"Miss May, how are you? I haven't seen you since the

wedding" Sara stepped forward to hug and kiss Margaret's cheek.

"Well, I'm just fine, what are you doing here?" Margaret smiled, she had thrown a few curve balls, and snide remarks at Sara when they were planning the wedding. Margaret and her sister Janet were close enough. Giving Eddie's aunt Margaret a close seat to helping plan the wedding. Sara thought it funny now that she had never mentioned her good friend Helen Brooks, but it did explain how Helen ended up in the shop. Sara had stood tall and hit whatever Margaret had thrown at her right back earning Margaret's good side.

"I'm dating Jared Brooks, and this is my sister Morgan. She hadn't moved home yet when we were planning the wedding." Sara said smiling as she watched Margaret put the pieces together.

"Oh, my goodness, this is Morgan." Margaret reached out and grabbed Morgan's hand "Oh my, it is very nice to meet you. I 'm sorry that we didn't meet at the Wedding, my husband had started to not feel well and we left early. I told him he shouldn't eat so much, but what are you going to do." She shrugged her shoulders. "So, you're the missing sister?"

"Yes, ma'am I am, I had some things to wrap up before I could come home. I was disappointed that I couldn't be here to help" Morgan smiled.

"You are also the love of my son's life, as I've been told," Margaret said then she smiled looking down at Morgan's belly. "I didn't figure he would make me a grandmother so quickly, how are you doing?"

"I'm doing well, they like to fight most of the time, I worry about when they run out of room," Morgan said not realizing she had begun rubbing her belly.

"They?" Margaret asked surprised.

"Yes, two boys, it came as quick a surprise," Morgan said smiling.

"Oh, we have to have a shower, when are you due?" Margaret asked with a smile and light in her eyes.

"We are planning one for her, Kadie, Abby, and myself," Sara said smiling. "We would love for you to have a hand in it."

"Why that is very nice of you. You still have my number, call me with the date and the details as soon as you figure them out. I wouldn't miss it. Two boys, my goodness. You and Andrew are going to have your hands full." she looked at Morgan.

"Andrew talks to them every night and morning. He wants to make sure they know him, that he is a safe place." Morgan said, knowing she was giving something private, and special.

"Andrew's father did that too." Margaret nodded as if she got the answer that she needed. "Here I'll walk you back, I would like to say Hi to my son." Margaret led Morgan out first, before Sara could follow Helen grabbed her attention.

"Sara there is someone I'd like you to meet." Helen began walking away again. Sara thought about just going back to Jared. Then her curiosity got the better of her, and she followed Helen.

Sara noticed her before they stopped before her.

"Meg dear" Meg Emerson turned from who she was talking to, and Sara got a full look at the woman who had been at Jared for weeks. Sara smiled; the girl needed to eat a cheeseburger. "This is Sara Mathews she is the one who made the wonderful deserts, Sara this is Meg Emerson, my son's fiancé," Helen said, she would enjoy watching Sara's heartache.

Sara 's surprise wasn't from the hurt or being blindsided. She was surprised by how far these women were willing to go. It also sunk in why when they walked the room Jared and her were getting weird looks and whispers. Sara told herself she was ready for anything, calming herself she reached out for Meg's hand.

"Meg Emerson? The Meg Emerson?" Sara smiled brightly. "And engaged to Jared, wow." Sara frowned a bit "Don't you think that's kind of sudden, I mean you just met him a month or so ago?" Sara turned at looked at Helen.

"Mrs. Brooks I'm surprised by you. Don't you think they should have had more than one lunch together? Of course, I've never been a fan of prearranged marriage." Sara shrugged her shoulders and waited to see what they could swing at her next. When they didn't say anything, Sara turned her attention to Meg.

"By the way, I'm someone special Jared has been seeing for several months now." Sara watched Meg's eyes light as she put the pieces together.

"Oh, and you're a baker?" Meg smiled 'That's so beneath him. It won't be long before he's done playing with you then he'll come find me." Meg said with confidence. Sara couldn't believe how very little both Helen and Meg knew Jared. Well, not so much Meg, but Helen. It took her a minute to wrap her mind around the kind of Mother Jared had grown up with, and how much he did to be the complete opposite.

"I have found that Jared doesn't believe in levels, he would never make anybody feel like they were beneath him." Sara said more than done with this conversation, she wanted to get back to Jared "If you'll excuse me" Sara turned and walked away. Jared was hers; she was in love with him. She moved through the crowd, smiling as she saw him waiting for her. She felt her whole body being pulled to this man.

"Hi." She said stepping into his arms, she tilted her head up, wanting his lips. She smiled when he bent and kissed her. He kept it light and sweet. "Are you ok?" She asked him.

"I am now" he squeezed her a little tighter. "I was getting ready to send a search party out for you, but Morgan assured me that you were fine," Jared said looking down at his girl. Sara could feel this body relax as she stood in his arms.

"I was fine, I met your fiancé, Meg Emerson." Sara smiled then looked over at Morgan who was looking even more paler.

"Are you ok?" She asked Morgan pulling herself out of Jared's arms.

"Yep, fine," Morgan said too quickly and shut her eyes knowing that it was a lie. Sara moved to Morgan; she tucked her dress as she bent down at the knees.

"Morgan?" Sara questioned, then waited.

"We need to go, now," Morgan whispered opening her eyes staring at Sara.

"Ok, can you stand? Where did Andrew go?" Sara asked in a hushed tone.

"No, his mother wanted him to say hi to someone or something" Morgan looked around the full room

"Ok, we're going to get you out of here." Sara stood and touched Jared. He turned to her smiling, "We need to get out of here, right now. What is the best way to get to your truck?"

"I'll go get it; those French doors lead to the side of the house. What's going on?" He asked with a smile on his face. He noticed her tense tone.

"Morgan can't stand, we need to get her to the hospital, something is wrong," Sara said trying to keep the smile on her face. "We lost Andrew in the somewhere, we don't have time to find him." She added

"Ok you stay here; I'll get the truck and we'll get her to the hospital," Jared said then kissed the top of Sara's head then headed into the crowd. Sara turned back to Morgan.

"Tell me what you're feeling, and I'll call ahead," Sara said bending down again.

"My belly is tight, and I'm wet," Morgan said, Sara could see her sister was worried and very scared.

"Do you think your water broke?" Sara's mind went into overdrive, Morgan was 26 weeks, if she had to deliver would the babies make it? She took a deep breath if she freaked out Morgan would freak out.

"No not that wet," Morgan said as she shut her eyes and started taking deep breaths.

"You aren't cramping are you, just tightness?" Sara asked.

"No cramping, just tightness, and wet." Morgan said then added, "I'm sure that I've ruined this chair." Her eye's watered. Sara took a deep breath.

"It's going to be ok; we are going to go to hospital. They are going to check you out, check on the boys and we'll go from there, ok?" Morgan only nodded back her eyes closed again. Sara stood up not letting go of Morgan's hand as they waited for Jared.

As soon as Jared left the room, he texted Andrew

"911, Morgan."

If he had to, he would leave Andrew at the party. Morgan and those boys were too damn important.

Andrew was standing with his mother and a group of her friends when his phone went off. He dug it out and lost his breath.

"Excuse me." He said then kissed his mother's cheek and left. He rushed back to Morgan, his mind going over all the bad things that could be going wrong. He headed to the last place he left her. He couldn't see either Morgan or Sara. He went to the back corner, making his way through a group of people talking, he found Morgan sitting looking very pale, and Sara bent down talking to her.

"Morgan?" He said squatting down next to Sara to look up at Morgan.

"My belly is tightening, and I may have ruined this chair," Morgan said looking at him, she was too worried to give him a smile.

"Ok, Jared went to get the truck?" Andrew asked looking at Sara

"He said those French doors were the closest he could get," Sara said standing to wait, again. She gave Morgan and Andrew room to talk. Andrew stood pulled his phone out, and walked over to the doors to let Jared in.

"There is no way to get her out without a scene, she can't walk," Andrew said shutting the door and talking to Jared.

"Can you carry her?" Jared asked then stopped when he caught the look on his friend 's face. "Hey, we'll get her to the hospital. Let's just do it." Jared put a hand on Andrew's shoulder.

"Ok, yes I can carry her." Andrew walked back to the girls. "Alright, baby let's get you to the hospital." He scooped one arm under her legs, and one around her back and lifted her. Sara looked at the chair and saw what she feared the most, blood. Sara grabbed Jared's shirt, he turned and then looked at the chair.

"Shit," he said under his breath, he led her out the French doors which he closed behind him. Sara rushed to open the back door of the truck for Andrew, he set Morgan in the back and climbed in next to her. Sara jumped in the front as Andrew shut his door just in time for Jared to take off.

Jared was cursing down the road when he felt his phone go off, he dug it out and tossed it to Andrew. He would have had Sara answer but if it was work, she would have to pass it over anyways.

"Abbot," Andrew answered without taking his eyes off Morgan. "Jared it's you, Dad," he said pulling the phone away from his mouth.

"Tell him happy birthday for me and let him know I'll call him when I can." Jared drove on, trying not to take turns too fast. Andrew tossed the phone back at him. Sara caught it and put it next to Jared.

When they pulled up at the hospital Morgan choose to have Sara go in with her. The ER moved Morgan up to Labor and Delivery. They had Morgan undress and wear a hospital gown. Morgan's doctor and the ultrasound technician came in at the same time. The doctor watched the screen, then told the nurse to start something, Sara didn't understand the doc-talk. She was moved out of the way as a nurse put an IV in Morgan's hand. The tech continued the ultrasound. The same nurse attached three round disks the size of a baseball to Morgan's belly. The room stayed quiet as the doctor watched the tech. The nurse stood back waiting for further instructions.

"Morgan I'm going to put you on pelvic rest." He stood and watched the ultrasound and the monitors. "The boys aren't under any stress. You aren't dilating, which is good, and the contractions are getting further apart." He continued to watch the ultrasound; they are both still head down. We will most likely be able to deliver naturally, we just need to get you there."

"Pelvic Rest?" Sara asked.

"No sex, No orgasms, No heavy lifting. Nothing over a gallon of milk." The doctor said looking at Morgan.

"I'll be able to go home?" Morgan asked.

"In a few hours when you finish that bag and maybe another. I need to check with you to make sure the bleeding has stopped.

"Visitors?" Morgan asked.

"No parties, unless I'm invited. But I don't see a problem with it." He said getting a set of gloves and walking back to Morgan.

"Dinner?" Sara asked moving to stand by Morgan's shoulders.

"If she's up for it." The doctor nodded at the tech who pulled the ultrasound wand off of Morgan's belly and cleaned her up. "Can we get someone for you?" He asked as he moved to the foot of the bed.

"Yes, we left my fiancé and brother-in-law in the ER waiting room," Morgan said laying back.

"I'll send a nurse for them." The doctor did his examination, and Sara held Morgan's hand as they waited for it to be over. "Alright, your bleeding has stopped. Another good sign." The doctor set the blanket to the right and walked away. "Now we just wait and watch. Let me know if you need anything." He nodded at both Sara and Morgan then left the room.

"Well, that's too bad," Morgan said pulling her gown down and the blankets up a bit.

"What?" Sara asked moving to sit at her feet.

"The no sex." Morgan smiled. "It was really good." Sara just looked at her sister, her shy, kept to herself sister. Then they both started laughing.

Jared sat in a chair and watched Andrew pace the room like a caged tiger. Jared didn't know what to do for him, he hoped to see Sara walk through the doors every time they opened to tell them that everything was ok. When the doors opened and the nurse walked through, Jared found he held his breath.

"Mathews?" She asked looking around the room. Then watched Andrew turn and walk up to her.

"Andrew Abbot her fiancé, Jared her brother-in-law," Andrew said he didn't turn but he felt Jared move behind him.

"Follow me please." The nurse turned on her heel and lead them out of the room. She took them to elevators and to the third floor. She walked them down a hall, not far from the nurse's station. She tapped lightly on the door then walked in. She moved aside letting the guys go in.

Andrew walked into the room to find Morgan sitting up, in a hospital gown, an IV in her hand, and Sara at her feet. Both looked relaxed, a good sign, Andrew moved to Morgan.

"Hi," Morgan said smiling, looking up at Andrew as he moved to stand next to the bed.

"Hi, how are you?" He asked as he tucked hair behind her ear.

"We're good, they did an ultrasound, both the boys are fine." Morgan turned to look at the screen that monitored both heartbeats and contractions.

"What did the doctor say?" Andrew asked.

"Pelvic rest and I have to stay to finish the bag," Morgan said holding his hand, smiling as she relaxed even more with him in the room with her.

"Do you get to go home?" Jared asked looking from one sister to another.

"Yep. I really like that part. I also need to drink a lot more water, which is sad because that means more bathroom breaks." Morgan said and shifted in her bed. Andrew was nodding his head, he was still trying to take it all in, Morgan was ok, the boys were ok.

"What is pelvic rest? Do you have to stay home?" Jared asked he stood next to Sara, rubbing her back.

"No sex, No orgasms, and no heavy lifting. The doctor said nothing over a gallon of milk." Morgan said her cheeks showed a hint of pink. Then she turned to Andrew, to find him still. "No," she said reading where his thoughts went. Sara picked up on the moment at once.

"We're going to go call Kadie and Abby, Kadie will most likely come should I have her bring dinner?"

"Sure, that sounds good." Morgan gave her a quick glance. Sara stood took Jared's hand and walked out with him.

"What?" Jared started but was pulled from the room before he could finish asking. Once they were out in the hall Sara turned and looked at him.

"Andrew is blaming himself for Morgan ending up here. I'm sure sex played a part in it, the other part is her not resting enough, and not drinking enough water."

"But Andrew is going to take that on," Jared said nodding. "Alright, so you're going to call Kadie and have her bring your Jeep and dinner. Then after we eat, we'll leave my truck for Morgan and Andrew." Sara smiled at him.

"Yep," Sara said giving him a big smile. Jared smiled back "would you like me to call Abby."

"Yes, please." Sara gave him Abby's number, they made the calls and waited for Andrew and Morgan to have their talk.

"I did this," Andrew said running a hand through his hair.

"No, and yes. Andrew, I've been checking with my doctor, my body is the one that changed the game." Morgan watched as Andrew paced the room. She didn't notice that her heart rate was going up, but the nurses outside did, Morgan's doctor who had been in the station watched it going up, decided to check on it himself.

"Morgan?" He asked when he walked in. He saw a man stop pacing the room the look of stress on his face, and Morgan looked worried. The doctor understood at once. "Hi, I'm Morgan's doctor, Ben Martin." He held his hand out. Andrew closed the space to shake his hand.

"Andrew Abbot."

"The fiancé, very nice to meet you. So, we are going to keep Morgan for a few hours, the bleeding has stopped, and her contractions are slowing with the help of the added fluids. When she finishes the bag, we'll watch to see if the contractions come back. If not, you can take her home. I have put her on pelvic rest, it's a common occurrence." Ben watched as Andrew attempted to take in what the doctor had been saying. "Mr. Abbot, can I have a word? Morgan, do you mind if I steal him for a moment?"

"That's fine," Morgan said taking a deep breath. Andrew followed the doctor out. They stopped a little way down the hall.

"Mr. Abbot."

"Andrew."

"Andrew I'm going to give it to you straight. You didn't do anything wrong; anything could have caused this."

"But it was us being together," Andrew said running his hand through his hair.

"Morgan is going to pick up on that, you have got to keep

your cool. Stress is not what is good for them right now, do you understand? This wasn't your fault." Ben said and watched Andrew look at him.

"Alright, I can do that." Andrew nodded and took a few deep breaths. "Thank you." Andrew held his hand out, the doctor took it. Andrew watched the doctor leave to check on another one of his patients. He started to head back to Morgan, he needed to get it together, he would and could do that for her.

"Hey," he said walking back into the room. Both Sara and Jared were back.

"Kadie is bringing the Jeep and food," Sara said.

"Abby and Eddie are having a no phone night, so I left a message, by the time they get it you'll be home."

"What are you going to do tomorrow?" Morgan asked.

"We'll work it out. We have been able to get a good handle on it over the last month or so." Sara said she had moved to the couch in the room. Andrew moved a chair next to Morgan, he sat down reaching for her hand, she took him with a smile.

"What is she bringing?" Andrew asked.

"Don't know she was a little frantic, I tried to reassure her that everything is fine. So, she might be busting in here any minute." Sara said looking at Morgan and Andrew. Jared was sitting next to her, with his arm across the back of the couch, Sara burrowed back against his body.

"We need to move me downstairs, I know we talked about it, we need to do it," Morgan said looking from at Sara, then to Andrew.

"I can take care of that when I get home," Sara said.

"We can take care of that." Jared corrected her and kissed her head.

"I want to go in tomorrow." Morgan said "I can sit most of the day, Abby could be my runner, you can keep pushing the fluids at me. I won't go in till we open, I'll take it easy." Morgan looked at Sara. As much as Sara wanted to make the call, she knew she was only part of it. Andrew was on the other side of that. Sara looked at Andrew, she could see he was worried, and trying to keep it under wraps.

"Baby you don't know you overdo it till it's too late," Andrew said

"I can't just sit at home and wait for all of you. I can't, I'll go crazier and that is saying something. Please." Morgan realized she needed to talk to Andrew about it, not Sara. Sara could say yes, but if Andrew said no. Andrew just looked at her, she was everything to him.

"I'll take you in, we'll play this day by day. We need to talk to Abby about working every day, I know she has been coming in to help, but this will be different. What about Evie?"

"She quit," Sara said.

"When?" Morgan looked at Sara.

"A few days ago, she called and said she was done." Sara shrugged her shoulder. "She hasn't been in for almost two months, I'm not sure why she waited till now to call." Morgan just frowned, then turned back to Andrew.

"Day by day?" She asked.

"Day by day." Andrew said, "We'll see when you get out of here, and see how you feel tomorrow. Let's hope Abby calls in the morning."

"Ok." Morgan nodded her head.

Kadie walked in a little while later with her arms full of food with Abby and Eddie behind her, Eddie was carrying drinks.

"Look who showed up just as I was trying to figure out how the hell, I was going to get all this up here," Kadie said she set it all down on a small table the went over to Morgan. "She said you were ok, and the boys are ok, but you need to tell me," Kadie said leaning down to hug Morgan.

"I'm fine, they are fine," Morgan reassured Kadie then rubbed her belly when she moved back.

"What happen?" Abby said standing at the foot of the bed.

"I was doing too much and didn't know that I was pushing my body. I also wasn't drinking enough water." Morgan said as she felt Andrew squeeze her hand, she squeezed right back. "I'm hungry, let's eat. Then we can talk about the shop." Morgan smiled at both Abby and Kadie.

They all ate, Abby and Eddie were at the movies and got the message when it ended. It was decided even before dinner was done that Abby would start working for the bakery full time. She would be Morgan's muscle most of all, and when Morgan wasn't there, she would work in the back for Sara.

Jared handed Andrew the keys to the truck, Kadie handed the Jeep keys to Jared. Everyone hugged then headed out. Sara, Kadie, and Abby had to open in the morning. Sara and Andrew had shared a look. They would play it day by day; they didn't expect Morgan the next day.

"Still 5:00?" Abby asked as they rode the elevator down.

"Yep," Kadie couldn't help the small smile that curved her lips.

"Please tell me you'll have coffee." Abby looked at Sara.

"I was going to ask you to make it like that," Eddie said turning to Abby.

"I can't it's a Sara special," Abby said and turned her begging eyes on. "Please a to go cup is all I ask; all I beg for."

"No, it isn't, you try for popcorn too." Sara smiled as they stepped off the elevator.

"Ya, try. I'm not going to give up on the coffee."

"You should sell it at the shop," Jared said offhand as they walked to the Jeep. Sara had tucked her hand into the crook of his arm.

"What?" She asked

"Oh my god yes!" Kadie said almost bouncing.

"No," Sara said flat out when it hit her what he was talking about. Popcorn and coffee would be her life if she wasn't careful.

"How come you have never had her coffee?" Jared asked Eddie when they were standing next to the cars.

"I didn't stay, Abby would stay with me." Eddie shrugged his shoulder. "I also think that she made it different for the Brunch we had the morning after the wedding." The guys turned to Sara.

"I don't know what you're talking about." She smiled. "I'll think about the coffee. Let's get home." She looked over at Kadie who was leaning over, whispering something to Abby. Then Abby looked at her.

"You have been making popcorn?" Abby accused with narrowed eyes.

"Kadie" Sara rolled her eyes. "Yes, I'll bring you a coffee and a tin of popcorn tomorrow. Now can we go, we have to move Morgan's bedroom down, and get to bed." Sara said sternly.

"Holy F-, could you sound anymore like mom." Abby smiled and looked at Kadie

"Yes, she can, don't get her started. I'll see you in the morning." Kadie hugged Abby, then Eddie. She got into the Jeep as Sara and Abby exchanged hugs, and the guys shook hands.

Once home they had to simply change the sheets and bring down Morgan and Andrew's clothes. They had it done in about an hour or so.

"I'm going to bed," Sara said making her way up the stair. "Good night."

She was standing in her room trying to get her dress off when Jared came up behind her.

"Are you ok?" He asked helping with her dress, he couldn't help but kiss her neck. He ran his nose along her neck just to smell her.

"Ya I'm just tired, it was a busy night," Sara said closing her eye's enjoying him.

"Do you want me to go?" Jared asked kissing her again.

"No." She said and turned around to take his mouth. Jared fell into the kiss, into Sara. They were lost in each other. The heat and need became more, overtaking the evening they had had. They found each other and that was all that mattered.

23

Jared sat straight up. The scream had ripped through the house. Because Sara was laying on his shoulder, she was awakened by the movement.

"Kadie." Sara was out of the room and up the stairs faster than he had ever seen her move, he understood why the little lamp always glowed in the bathroom. To make sure she didn't hurt herself when she had to get up like that.

He lay in bed wondering how he could help. He looked over at the clock, they had beat the alarm by minutes. He got up and went down to find the coffee pot ready for him, bless that woman he thought. He made two cups for himself and Sara.

Sara heard the screams and ran out of the room, she took the steps two at a time, she rushed to Kadie's bed. She reached down to touch her, to wake her up.

"Kadie, Kadence," Sara said touching her sister trying to wake her up before she screamed again. Sara let out a breath when Kadie opened her eyes. "Sweetheart, you're home, I'm here so is Morgan the guys stayed the night. Abby and Eddie are home safe." Sara caught Kadie as she sat up and clung to her sister as if Sara was what grounded her.

"Well, I don't think I'm going to need the coffee today. Are you ok?" Sara said after a minute, her heart still racing.

"I'm sorry, I think I'm ok. Is Jared, ok?" Kadie asked, then she was tired all over again. Being scared took a lot out of you. Her alarm started to go off. "Well, that settles that. I'm going to go shower." Kadie slid out of bed. Sara watched her sister move across the room. They had decided a while ago that they didn't need or want to talk about it. It was something that happened and that was that. The last thing Kadie wanted was it to be a big deal, she hated that she still had the nightmares.

"I'll see you down there," Sara said and moved down the stairs to her room, she wanted to kiss Jared before she headed off to the day. She walked into her room to find him sitting up in bed he had two cups of coffee on the bedside table.

"Have the first cup with me?" Jared asked, Sara couldn't help the flip her stomach did or the smile she got on her face.

"I would love to," Sara said then walked over and climbed back into bed, sitting up and settled Jared handed her a cup of coffee. They just sat there talking and drinking their coffee, starting the day together. Sara looked over when she saw Kadie standing in the doorway.

"It's later than I thought." Sara smiled, then climbed out of bed and went to the bathroom for a quick shower. Kadie was turning to go get a cup for herself, it was going to be a rough day with the little sleep she got.

"Kadie" Jared said stopping her. She turned to look at him. "Are you ok?" She could see the concern on his face.

"I'll be ok. I'm sorry I woke you. It's been a while since I had one of those dreams." She said

"I'm not going to take her away, this is where she belongs. I'm just hoping I can become part of it, not take her out of it." Jared watched Kadie think about it. He saw her work it out.

"Ok, thank you." Kadie walked away before he could see

that he had nailed it, again. Sara was her sister, yes, but she was also the one that had held her together when the world fell apart. Kadie didn't want her need for Sara to ruin her relationship with Jared. She was working on stepping back more and more, but it seemed the more she did the worst the nights got. She shook her head as she went down to get her coffee, "too early for this." She whispered to herself.

Sara and Jared came down not too long after Kadie had her coffee, they talked about the day ahead of them. Jared was going to the gym and then to the gun range. He could never get into a solid routine of it, as he was always on this case or that case, and it became even more sporadic when he started dating Sara. It was planned that Andrew would join him but with Morgan, he wasn't sure.

"We need to get the nursery painted; we got the paint last week I just can't seem to get to it." She was talking to Jared as she made a to go cup for Abby.

"Ok, I'll see if I can get to it today. Do you think you're going to get out of there on time today?" Jared took his cup and put it in the washer.

"I'm not sure, I know we always have a full day Saturday." She turned and then walked to the cabinet that housed the popcorn. "Wow, I thought we would be going through this faster." Sara pulled a tin for Abby.

"We want it to last, you really don't like making it, so we are trying to conserve what we have," Kadie said then took the last sip of coffee. She got up and put the cup in the dishwasher. "Ready?"

"Yep, let's do this" Sara turned to Jared. "Have fun today, I'll see you later." Sara kissed him quickly then walked out with Kadie. Sara and Kadie started to talk about the shop on their way in, they worked to keep working at work and home at home. Sometimes it worked sometimes it didn't.

They pulled up into the back parking lot of the bakery, turning the spotlights on. As they always got to work when it was still dark the lights were too bouncy for Kadie's liking. Abby pulled up before they got to the back door and bounced out to greet them.

"Don't give her coffee she doesn't need it," Kadie said walking into the dark kitchen, flipping the lights on, and heading to her station.

"Still not the morning person," Abby said quietly behind her back.

"Nope," Sara said handing Abby her coffee, "Popcorn is in the Jeep, let's get to work." Sara went turned on the radio, then her ovens. Abby moved to the front of the shop to get ready for the day. They worked the morning like they did every day, only Abby was there. She knew enough to run the front, just not as well as Morgan. Abby was making notes, Sara was kneading dough, and Kadie was working on a cake to go to the front when the back door opened. Morgan came walking in, with Andrew behind her.

"Morning. What are you doing here?" Sara asked looking from Morgan to Andrew.

"I have come to work, we open in 10 minutes, I feel fine, and I want to be here." Morgan turned and gave Andrew a kiss then walked over to Abby. Sara and Andrew exchange a glance, and she gave him a small nod.

"Alright ladies, have a good day I'll see you later," Andrew said then left.

"That poor man," Kadie said from her station.

"Poor man, poor me" Morgan said, "It took me twenty minutes to talk him into bringing me in today."

"Morgan you were in the hospital last night, he was worried about you, we all were. But I imagine he was more so." Sara said still working the dough, it was her third batch, and she still had three to go.

"You're taking his side? You're my sister." Morgan pouted, something she didn't do. So, they chucked it up to hormones.

"I've got your back Morgan; I always have your back. Even if taking Andrew's side is how I've got it. Can you even imagine how he felt last night? How scared he would have been, but he kept it together for you?" Sara said noticing she was using the emotions of the last 24 hours to work the dough. The room was quiet as they let that sink in. Morgan just stared at Sara.

"But I said it was ok, I got the ok. I'm fine." Morgan said defensively. Sara let the dough set for a minute and looked at her sister.

"You can think and say that till you are blue in the face, he still feels like it's his fault. Morgan that man would do anything for you, he wouldn't let anything happen to you or the boys. How do think he feels when he was part of the reason you ended up at the hospital." Sara started to put the bead in pans to bring them to rise then bake them. "Think about that while the two of you open," Sara said kicking both Morgan and Abby out of the back. Sara knew just how much to push, and when to do it. Something she learned young, running the family the way, she did.

"A bit harsh," Kadie said when the two were gone.

"You ever see Andrew look the way he did last night?" Sara said moving onto the next batch to knead.

"Hints, when Mark was in the mix." Kadie stopped as if the light bulb went on. Morgan was being threatened by Mark, and Andrew couldn't do anything about it. Last night Morgan and the boys were not ok, and Andrew couldn't do anything, and he was feeling some guilt on top of it. "Got it."

Andrew called Jared to find out where he was when he got back in the car.

"I'm heading into the gym, then the range. You on your way?" Jared asked.

"Yep," Andrew hung up and headed to the gym. They spent

the next few hours running, lifting, and sparing. Andrew felt the tension ease as he worked his body till his muscles burned. He had music blasting in his ears when he ran and lifted, then he heard the guys talk as he spared. He felt loose and ready when he hit the showers.

His world righted even more when he stood at the line, firing his weapon on target. He and Jared had the art in their friendship of silence. They didn't talk again till they stepped back, ready to leave.

"Why don't we do this more often?" Andrew asked as they headed to Jared's truck.

"Work and women," Jared said sliding into his seat. "I say we work harder at taking the time." He looked over at Andrew. "You feel better." It wasn't a question, more an observation.

"Ya, I do." Andrew took a drink from his water. "Bad sign?"

"No, man you have had your plate full for a bit. Last night tipped you, that's all."

"Wouldn't it you? Everything is fine till it wasn't. Now I can't touch her and feel like shit for doing it in the first place." Andrew sat back as they made their way back home.

"It would," Jared said after he thought about it. "So, you up for painting?"

"Sure, you know how they want it done?" Andrew said happy about the subject change

"Yep, found Sara's notes."

"Those notes will save you." Andrew teased.

"Hell, yes they will, I'm lucky she keeps them." Jared pulled up to the house. They both got out and headed in. After stopping for a few sandwiches, they went upstairs to the new nursery. They opened windows and shut the doors to the house. Sara had already gotten everything they would need, she had it in the room for when she had time. Andrew looked around the room, he frowned at the pink and cream. He worried about what the new colors were going to be, after all, they would bring two boys up in the space. He walked over to Jared who had shaken a can and was popping the top, white.

"Good start." Andrew said, "Where is it going?" Jared pulled the paper out of his pocket.

"White chair rail and down, base boards, all frames, and the ceiling." Both looked up. "She already brought the ladders up."

"Does she ever miss a beat?"

"It's rare, she's the one they count on," Jared said looking at the paper. "That means this can is above the chair rail to the ceiling." Jared bent down shook the third can, then opened it. They found a cool blue grey color.

"I like it," Andrew said, happy it wasn't pink.

"All right let's spread the sheets and get the ceiling done." Jared poured the paint and Andrew started to lay out the sheets. Jared took his phone out to play his music, and the guys dove into the project.

Sara and Kadie worked in silence, with Abby making the trips to the back. Sara frosted a few sets of cupcakes when Kadie had fallen behind a bit. She was working on a set of muffins when Abby came back, "Lunch, and Sara there is a man asking for you up front," Abby said carrying a box of sand-wiches to the back. Sara whipped her hand on a towel she kept in her back pocket. She passed Morgan in the hall; Sara was given a smile. All was well.

"Hello," Sara walked around the counter to shake the man's hand "I'm Sara Mathews how can I help?"

"Sara, it's nice to meet you." He said shaking her hand. "I'm sorry that we didn't get a chance to meet last night, by the time I made it to the sitting room you had already departed. Ross Brooks."

"Mr. Brooks, yes, it's nice to meet you. I'm sorry about last night, my sister was having a few complications and we had to get her to the hospital. I hope that we didn't cause a scene." Sara said stepping back a bit.

"No, when I asked what had happened, I was told you left for other reasons." He waved his hand. "I came to see if you could join me for lunch," Ross said smiling. She knew that smile, Jared used it on her when he wanted to charm her, mostly for popcorn.

"I'm sorry Mr. Brooks but I'm going to have to pass today, we usually work through our lunch on Saturdays. Do you have plans for dinner on Sunday, tomorrow?" Sara made the offer without thinking that Helen might join him. She watched Ross think about it.

"No, Sunday would be very nice. Please call me Ross."

"Alright," Sara smiled, "Does five work for you? Also is there anything you don't like or allergic to?"

"I haven't run into any allergies, and I'll eat something at least once." Ross said, "I'll let you get back to it." He started to move to the door.

"Ross."

"Yes?" He turned back to Sara. She handed him a card.

"My number and our address." She smiled at him, and he took it with a nod.

"Have a good day." He said then turned to leave.

"You as well." Sara watched him go. "Well, that was interesting." She said to herself as she locked the door and walked to the back. She walked over and put the muffins into the ovens. It would be the last set of the day and the final set of the blue berry banana special of the week. Morgan, Abby, and Kadie sat at the end of Sara's workspace eating their sandwiches.

"So, who was that?" Kadie asked.

"Jared's dad," Sara said moving down the table, not sitting she reached for her sandwich. "I invited him over for dinner tomorrow, I figured it would be a nice way to make up for ditching his birthday early," Sara said taking a bit.

"I'm the one who should have offered to make him dinner as I'm the one who made us all leave," Morgan said, shrugging her shoulder. She wasn't doing the poor me thing anymore, just stating facts.

"You can help me decide what to make," Sara said when she finished her bite.

"I can do that." Morgan nodded her head.

"You two are welcome of course." Sara turned to Abby.

"Thank you but we are having dinner with Eddie's parents' tomorrow night," Abby said tossing her wrapper in the garbage, then she was up and started working on cleaning up. The last stretch of Saturday seemed to be the go time; they would be busy from the time they opened the doors to the time they locked them up for their weekend.

Sara watched Morgan pull her phone from her pocket, and text a message back. Sara wanted to ask how that was but knowing she had pushed earlier stopped her. They may be ok but that didn't give Sara the right to know about every text or word that passed between Morgan and Andrew.

Kadie was the next to get up and get back to work. Sara left her sandwich to get the muffins out of the oven, she didn't use timers, she knew by smell and heat when something was done. A thing that her grandmother or mother never knew how she did.

They settled into the work again as Abby and Morgan moved to the front again. Sara only knew about the flow of people by the bell on the door and how often they saw Abby. Kadie was done before Sara was, a rarity. Kadie went up front and started wrapping things for the weekend.

"What's that?" Andrew asked when Jared's phone alarm went off.

"The shop is closed." Jared stepped away from the window, he was doing the touch up on the frames.

"Got it bad man," Andrew said stepping back from the chair rail on the other side of the room.

"How many times have you text Morgan?" Jared asked.

"Just checking on her."

"Keep telling yourself that," Jared said looking around the room, they were done. He would tell Sara to go through it as she would see what the touch ups were. "Let's get this cleaned up, they might get home on time." Jared and Andrew did just that, closing the paints and folding the sheets, the ladders had been put in the hall. Jared took the paint brushes down to the laundry room sink, Andrew shut the door and went to the kitchen for two beers.

A little after six thirty Kadie, Abby, and Morgan walked to the back, Sara had it all wiped clean and getting the mop ready.

"Morgan, are you going home with us or is Andrew coming to get you?" Sara asked as she started mopping.

"With you, he'll bring me then I'll go home with you unless I call him and say I need to go home sooner. I have a feeling if he is unavailable, I might be taken home by a fellow cop or something like that." She said moving to the back door, avoiding the wet floors.

"Alright, do you have anything to put away Kadie?" Sara didn't look up, she worked on the floors.

"Not really, we have a small little bit I was thinking of having Andrew and Jared take it to work with them on Monday." Kadie started walking to the door to wait with Morgan. Abby got her stuff as Sara made the last swipes with the mop. They all went out as Sara set the alarm and locked the door. Morgan called shot gun. She sat in the front seat and closed her eyes. The sisters exchanged a look.

"How did she do today?" Sara started.

"She sat on that stool all day. I think we should get her one with a cushion and a high back on it. She was trying not to be bossy, but it didn't last. I was able to get after her too. I think it went good; we'll see how it goes from here." Abby said then moved to her car.

"Abby" Kadie got her attention and held up the tin of popcorn.

"Oh god, I almost forgot it, thank you." Abby walked back. "Good job wearing her down, you never gave up." Abby smiled.

"I had help, with Morgan backing me up, then Andrew and Jared jumped on the band wagon once they tasted it." Kadie hugged her sister. "See you Tuesday."

"Tuesday," Abby said over her shoulder as she got in her car. Sara watched her go then got into the driver's seat. It felt good to sit, she had sat so little throughout the day. Morgan was lightly snoring next to her.

"She is warring herself out fast," Kadie said from the back seat.

"It's a good thing we have the next couple of days off," Sara said as she drove them home.

"Morgan" Kadie touched her shoulders to wake her up.

"What?" Morgan snapped keeping her eyes closed.

"We're home. If you don't wake up, we're going to have to get Andrew to bring you inside and he'll see you couldn't stay awake on the way home." Kadie said her tone was light and teasing.

"You can be a mean little sister," Morgan said opening one eye to glare at Kadie but found Andrew standing next to her with the door open. "I'm fine," Morgan said quickly. He lent in and kissed her. He meant to keep it light but before he knew it, he was falling, his body responding to her as it had the first time he kissed her, her hands moved up his body, pulling him closer. His hands moved over her, started to move down, and as if on cue one of the babies shifted. Andrew finished the kiss and pulled away.

"Well, that's going to be interesting for the next 18 or so weeks" Andrew looked down at her, heat in both their eyes.

"Yes, it is." Morgan smiled.

"I know you are fine babe, I'm still going to worry about you, so get used to it." Andrew stepped back, to help her out. Morgan looked around, her sisters were already inside.

"How was your day?" She asked as she walked next to him. She could see most of the stress had left him.

"Good, you'll have to see it. You won't be able to hang out for too long but you should see it." Andrew opened the door for her. She walked in to find Jared, Sara, and Kadie in the kitchen. They were talking and stopped when she walked in.

"What?" Morgan said snapping more than she indented. She closed her eyes and took a deep breath. "What are you guys up to?" She asked trying again. Andrew rubbed her back.

"Dinner" Kadie answered "and we were waiting for you. Andrew and Jared have something to show us."

"All right let's go up," Jared said as he slapped his hands and rubbed them together. Morgan led the way with Jared following Sara. They stopped outside the bedroom door. Andrew pushed it open, and Morgan walked in. She couldn't help her quick intake of breath. She walked into the sitting room, turning she was crying. Andrew just took her in his arms, he swayed with her for a minute.

"Hey, let's go eat, then you can take a shower, and watch a movie with me," Andrew said to the top of her head. She gave him a small laugh.

"I won't make it through the movie, you may need to stand by during the shower." Morgan looked up at him, he kissed her and lead her out of the room.

"You guys did a great job," Kadie said looking around the room with her hands on her hips, then her phone signaled.

"Are you staying to eat?" Sara asked as she walked the room slowly

"Yep, see you down there." Kadie bounced out of the room.

"What do you think?" Jared asked watching Sara carefully.

"You do great work; I don't see any need for touch ups." She walked over to him, wrapped her arms around him, and looked up. "Thank you" Jared rested his hands on her lower back bringing her body against his.

"You're welcome." He kissed her. "Let's go eat, we have later." He let her go to take her hand.

Dinner had been quick and easy, Morgan went to take her shower, Kadie went to get ready, and Jared lead Sara out to the back deck after they finished cleaning the kitchen.

In the end, Andrew got in the shower with Morgan, and they kept it short. They both dressed for bed and headed to the study. Andrew brought a book, he knew Morgan was going to fall asleep on his lap, and he would be stuck on the couch. He was more than happy to be there. As predicted Morgan fell asleep minutes into the move.

Andrew was sitting on the couch, one hand resting on the moving boys and the other holding his book. He put down to see Kadie coming down the stairs, dressed to the nine. Andrew thought about it being Saturday night. He remembered how he would have been dressed up ready to go out for a night on the town too. Now he stayed in, reading a book on pregnancy with the love of his life sleeping on his lap. He wouldn't trade it for anything.

"Have fun tonight." He said as she stepped into the doorway.

"Did she make it past the previews?" Kadie teased.

"Only because we started to movie right away." Andrew smiled.

"Jared and Sara?" she asked.

"Last I saw them they were dancing on the deck," Andrew said sincerely.

"Good for them, I'm happy they found each other," Kadie said pulling her phone out

"Call if you need to." He said going back to his book.

"I will," she said and walked out the front door.

Andrew settled back into his book, and a few hours later he got both Morgan and himself to bed. He went to the kitchen for water and could hear Jared and Sara laughing. He went back to bed happy for his friend. Crawling into bed next to Morgan he fell asleep to the boys kicking his hand, he was happy too.

24

JARED'S PHONE WAS RINGING, it was one of those times he wanted to throw it across the room.

"Brooks."

"Sir, this is officer Peterson." Jared was trying to place the name as he woke up, then it hit him.

"Peterson, is she ok?" Jared asked waking up.

"No, sir. I need back up, sir" Graham said sounding a little nervous

"Where?" He asked.

"Club 89" Graham said.

"10 minutes," Jared said reassuring.

"Yes Sir," Graham said sounding relieved.

Jared ended the call, he looked over at Sara who thankfully was still sleeping. He dressed quickly then went downstairs. He walked into Morgan's new room. He wasn't surprised a light was on in the bathroom, a lot of trips in the night could end badly if she couldn't find her way. He walked to Andrew, and put a hand on his shoulder. Andrew's eyes shot open.

"Peterson called, Kadie's in trouble." Jared stepped back giving Andrew room to move. Once he knew his friend was up, he walked out of the room, straight through the kitchen door to his truck, Andrew hoped in minutes later.

"What do you know?" Andrew asked, he had checked his gun as Jared pulled out of the driveway.

"Not much, she's at Club 89, she isn't ok, and the kid needs back-up." Jared took the corners fast, the straightaways faster.

"The kid knows what he's doing, proved it too many times, if he needs back up, he needs back up." Andrew pulled his phone out, a text from Peterson.

Peterson: "When you come in be cool."

Andrew: "I always am."

Peterson: "No flashing your shield."

Abbot: "Are they checking for weapons?"

Peterson: "No."

"This could be interesting, he said not to flash our baggage at the door, and they aren't checking for weapons," Andrew said then thinking of the floor plan and the fact it was a Saturday night he sent another text to Graham.

Andrew: "Where are you?"

Peterson: "The bar, grey/green hoodie, jeans."

Andrew: "You got your pretty shoes on."

Peterson: "You know it."

Andrew relayed the last bit to Jared as they approached the club. Jared parked, and together they made their way in. Jared stopped once he was inside, the place was packed. The music was the heartbeat of the dance floor. Jared looked over when Andrew touched his shoulder when he spotted Peterson. They made their way over shook hands, and talked lightly or so it seemed from the outside.

"She went to the bathroom 15 minutes ago and tripped on her way in. I would go in and get her but if she was slipped something the guy might be waiting for her, and there wouldn't be a way I could get him and get her out at the same time."

"Where is your car?" Andrew asked.

"Deep in the parking lot, yours?" Graham said.

"Not" Jared said smiling. "So go in and get her, get to my truck, call it in if it ends up as bad as you think it is, we got your back." Jared pulled his keys and dropped them in Graham's hand. "Don't leave us." Graham smiled then walked off to the bathrooms.

"This could be bad," Andrew said looking around the bar.

"Yep, or this could be fun." Jared smiled then he set off towards the dance floor moving to flank Grahams right, Andrew moved to flank his left.

Graham came out carrying an unconscious Kadie, He started to watch for moving shadows and saw four. Jared thought the kid knew what he was doing. He wouldn't have been able to get her out without them. They moved slowly; nobody would notice the three were working together. Graham saw two of the four first and weaved in and around the crowd, he was going to get Kadie out. He saw two coming at his left, so he moved back to the right, swinging left at the last minute he went out the front door. Jared looked at Andrew as they watched four guys follow Graham out, moving quickly they left the club.

Graham got Kadie into the truck and got the truck locked by the time the four men made it to him.

"Where do you think you're going with our girl?" One guy asked and moved forward. Graham didn't say anything, he just waited. The guy pulled a knife, then froze as he felt the barrel of a gun pressed to the back of his head.

"I wouldn't do that if I were you," Jared said Andrew was a bit further back. Graham took the moment that they all looked at Jared to draw his gun as well.

"Walker P.D." Graham said, "Everyone put your hands on the truck bed, and spread them." Andrew kept them covered as Jared and Graham did a quick search of the four men.

By the time the uniforms showed up, they could hand over

the drugs and weapons, and the four men. Graham had to go to the station to file his report.

"Get her to hospital, make sure they do blood and urine, I watched that door the whole time no guys went in. When she wakes, she'll be oh it's my fault, don't let her do it." Graham looked at both Jared and Andrew.

"Come by when you're done, stay till she wakes up. I'll let you know when we get her home." Jared said then they headed to the hospital.

Jared unlocked the door to the kitchen; he went in followed by Graham carrying a sleeping Kadie and Andrew shut the door. The light in the kitchen flicked on, Jared and Andrew both drew their weapon and aimed them at Sara. They dropped them instantly.

"What the hell happened?" Sara said sounding very mad.

"I'll explain, this is Graham Peterson," Jared said.

"I know who Graham is." Sara shot daggers at Jared.

"Sara, take him up to Kadie's room and get Kadie changed. Graham will stay with her then come to your room and I'll explain." Jared shot a few daggers back; it was almost two in the morning he was tired.

Andrew patted Jared's shoulder, nodded to Graham, and headed to bed.

"Follow me please, I hope you're strong. You drop her and I'll toss you down the stairs." Sara snapped she too was tired, also scared, and mad.

"I got her ma'am," Graham said nodding his head.

"No, call me Sara," she said then headed upstairs.

After she had Kadie changed, and Graham set up with a blanket and pillow for the overstuffed chair Kadie had she went to get the story from Jared. She found him sitting on the end of the bed waiting for her.

"Jared" Sara looked at him.

"Come sit down," He waited till she did. "After Kadie had

her tires slashed, I found out who wrote the report, it was Graham, I called, and we talked. I asked him to keep an eye out for her, only when she went out." Jared saw something move into her eyes and didn't like it. "He was the one who had security just walk her out of the club the night she got into it with her date. He also talked both the guy and girl out of pressing charges. He was there tonight, he saw that she had gone to the bathroom, tripping on her way. We both know that Kadie is smart about her intake, things didn't add up for him, so he called me." Jared was watching Sara then continued.

"Andrew and I went to give him the backup he needed. We got her out of the club and locked up the four guys who were after her. She was drugged tonight; she was in the bathroom when it hit her. Graham called and we got her out, the four men are in custody, and we took Kadie to the hospital. Get blood and urine for testing and evidence, she wasn't touched. I invited Graham here because I could see he was genuinely worried about her." Jared had watched Sara go from mad, to pale, to worried, she was working her way back to mad. He just didn't know who it was going to be, but he was ready to take anything she threw at him.

Sara's mind was racing, going around and around. She felt anger being the top emotion, but she wasn't angry at Jared.

"So let me get this right." She stood up to walk around the room. "You have a guy watch out for my sister because you were worried. You leave in the middle of the night to have his back while the three of you work to get Kadie safely home. You spend what? A few hours at the hospital? Then you bring her home and ask the guy who saved her to stay with her, which he does happily." Sara looked at Jared, he was sitting on her bed waiting for something. "What?" Sara felt the angry spike, she knew her eyes flashed.

"Nothing, I just told you about something really bad and I'm waiting for you," Jared said standing up.

"This is my family, I'm the one that takes care of them. I'm the one who makes sure they're ok, the one that fixes the problems. I'm the one they all come to, for everything. I kept the bakery from going under, I got Kadie through high school, I got Morgan through college, and through that shit marriage. Abby, we won't even start on all the crap I've done for Abby. This is my family." Sara had yelled, she had her hands going every which way. Sara felt it and Jared watched as the anger faded and her eyes filled.

Jared knew what she had taken on when she decided not to go back to school when their mom died. He couldn't understand it, it was one of those things that you had to live it to get it. She carried the weight of her world; he had wanted to help.

"Sara I'm just trying to help," Jared said looking at Sara.

"Yes, you are, but if you help, and I get used to you helping, taking care of things. When you decide or figure out this isn't working, or you get hurt on the job" She stopped and looked away. Jared stepped to her and tilted her face up to him.

"Sweetheart, that's a chance you're going to have to take." Jared stared into her eyes "Am I worth it, are we, what we have worth chancing it?" He had passed the ball back so smoothly. "Sara, I want you for the rest, my days and my nights. I want to share my life with you, just you. I'm not going to wake up in a week or month or year, hell 50 years, and decide that this isn't working for me."

Sara's mind went over everything in flashes, him saving Kadie, him painting the room, taking care of a dozen little things, how the days were better when she knew he was waiting at the end of them. Her days started in his arms. She closed her eyes, if she lost this, she wasn't sure she would make it through. She heard her mother say, *now Sara what if?* Her mother always said that when Sara was going too far in one direction. Sara opened her eyes, looking at Jared. *What if you lose great love because you were scared?*

"Yes, we're worth it."

Kadie opened her eyes; her curtains had been drawn. She lay there for a moment to evaluate herself. She was tired and weak. She felt hungry but didn't want anything, she tried to remember the last time she ate. As she worked her brain, she became more and more worried, she couldn't remember. Had she even gone out last night? Movement caught her eye, she looked and found someone sitting in her big chair at the foot of her bed.

"Graham?" her voice was weak, and her throat was dry. He stood up, went over to sit on the bed next to her, and held out a glass of water. Kadie moved to sit up; he helped her drink. When she was done, he set the glass on her bedside table.

"What are you doing here?" Kadie asked.

"I needed to make sure you were ok." He just looked at her, watching her.

"Am I?" She asked she could see in his eyes that something wasn't right.

"Yes, we got you out of there, you had a drink with the wrong kind of guy. I called Jared and Andrew; they came. We got you out of the club, we made four arrests, and they took you to the hospital. I met them here, Jared and Sara let me stay with you." He watched as all of what he said sank in. Her eyes started to fill. "No, don't do that. I can handle anything but that."

Kadie didn't have it in her to stop the tears that flowed from her eyes. She had gotten into trouble last night and her guys came for her, protected her. She didn't fight it when Graham put his arms around her, she helped when he moved her body from the bed into his lap. They stayed that way till she finally stopped crying.

"Coffee, food?" He asked not letting her go.

"Coffee, nice strong coffee." She stood and went to the bathroom. When she came back, he set the book aside and stood. "Have you slept?" she asked.

"A little, I like your collection." He pointed to her bookshelf.

"You should see Morgan's" Kadie smiled then headed to the kitchen.

She found the four of them, Sara, Morgan, Jared, and Andrew sitting at the kitchen table. The kitchen smelled of food and had Kadie's stomach churning. She walked wordlessly to the coffee maker, happy to find it was hot and ready. After she had her cup full and ready the way she liked it, she reached for an empty one and handed it to Graham as she walked by him to the table. She stood next to Jared, set her cup down, and waited for him to stand. When he did, thinking she wanted him to move, she wrapped her arms around him.

"Thank you." She whispered to him, then she moved to Andrew, who stood as well. She whispered her thanks. She took her cup, touching Morgan's shoulder she sat next to her sister. Morgan didn't say anything about Kadie's night, in fact, she picked up the conversation they were having when Kadie and Graham came down. Graham sat down next to her, as Sara put a plate of food in front of him. Before she moved away Sara ran a hand down the back of Kadie's head.

"Thank you," Graham said and dug in. Kadie sat back and enjoyed the flow of the morning. It ended when Graham's phone went off, he stood grabbing his phone at the same time.

"Peterson," he said.

The table continued to talk; the girls had become familiar with the interruptions that a cop could have. Kadie watched as he came back to the table, and took his plate to the sink.

"Thank you for breakfast and coffee," Graham said to the room, he nodded to Kadie then left.

Kadie was grateful that her family didn't talk about that night.

"So, I need to know what your dad's favorite meal is?" Sara asked looking at Jared.

"My dad's, why my dad?" Jared asked looking at Sara.

"He came into the shop yesterday and asked me to lunch, but because it was Saturday, I told him that I couldn't, so I invited him here for dinner tonight." Sara sat back and watched to see how Jared would react. She was almost disappointed by his total calmness about it.

"Well, he tries everything once." He said with a smile.

"That is not helpful." Sara looked around the table for some help, nobody said anything, "What is this?"

"You invited him you can figure out what to make for dinner," Kadie said. She stood up and put her cup in the sink. "I'm going to go take a shower." She started for the stairs "I'm fine" she could feel Sara wanting to ask her.

"I thought that was a mom thing to have eyes in the back of your head," Andrew said sitting back with his coffee.

"You aren't going to help me out in the slightest?" Sara looked at Jared.

"Sweetheart he is a man, who will be coming for dinner without his wife for that matter. Meat and potatoes." Jared said grabbing her hand to reassure her.

"Do you know how to grill?" Sara asked him.

"Yes, I do, I could bring mine over if you want." Then he stopped hadn't he lent it to a buddy? "Maybe."

"Check out the one I have first, then if you need to, get yours back from whoever you lent it to." Sara smiled and stood up. Jared followed her out the back door to the deck. He had spent time out here, but it was mostly to talk or just to hang out. He had never really explored. He followed her to what looked like a closet outside. When she opened it, he found a shiny new grill. As he looked at it, he noticed that it was the Cadillac of grills.

'When did you get this?" Jared looked at Sara.

"A few years back Kadie and I wanted to grill and so we went and got one, then we never really used it." Jared looked inside, it looked like it had never been used.

"What classifies as a few times because this beauty looks like it's never seen heat let alone meat," Jared said looking at the grill.

"Twice." Sara smiled. "It's a pain to clean.

"Sweetheart you don't clean it back to store bought." Jared put his arm around her. Sara looked up at him and he took her lips. "I'll cook, let's go make a list."

"You know me so well" She smiled at him.

25

———————

Sara took a deep breath; you would think that making dinner was the last thing she was ever going to do in her life. She felt pressure and didn't like it.

"What was I thinking?" She said to herself as she put the finishing touches to the potato salad. She turned to put it in the fridge and found Jared in the doorway, just watching her. "What?"

"You were thinking of doing something nice, I think you are being cute. You weren't this nervous when we went to the birthday party, and it was way worse than tonight will be." Jared walked to her after she put the Salad in the fridge.

"I think it has something to do with home turf." Sara signed as he hugged her. "It will be fine. Everything will be fine." Sara pulled away to look at the clock. "Oh, crap he is going to be here any minute, where the hell is Kadie." On cue, Kadie walked through the back door with a white box in her hand.

"You need to calm down, or you are going to end up doing something stupid." Kadie set the box on the counter.

"What did you grab?" Sara walked over to open the lid, then froze. "Pie?"

"Yep, pie. I felt it would go well with the theme." Kadie carefully pulled it out and set it on the counter.

"We didn't have any pies. Where did you get this?" Sara lends in and smelled it, warm apple and cinnamon hit her senses. "You made great grandma's Apple pie?"

"Yep, we are going to start running it as a special in a few weeks, so I thought why not. I also thought it would go great with the BBQ chicken that Jared is going to make. Where is Morgan?"

"I think she is watching TV with Andrew," Sara said moving the pie to the glass dome stand she had. Then she froze. The doorbell rang.

"I'll go get it," Jared said kissing the top of Sara's head. "Hey, Kadie can you get Sara a drink, she needs it to take the edge off." Then he left the room.

"Did he just say that?" Sara watched him go then continued to stare at the doorway.

"Yep, and he is right." Kadie went to the fridge "Three choices, wine, beer, or a shot?" Kadie watched her sister. Then Kadie made the decision for her, she reached up and grabbed the tequila from the cabinet above the fridge.

She moved quickly, as she could hear Jared stalling. "Here just take a pull from the bottle."

"I will not." Sara said baffled.

"Do it now or I will make tonight hell." Kadie gave Sara a wicked grin and the light in her eye's told Sara that she wasn't bluffing.

"Oh, alright fine." Sara grabbed the bottle and took a quick pull, she coughed a bit from the burn, handing the bottle back to Kadie who lidded it and put it back in the cabinet.

"See all better, I'm going out there now I can hear Morgan, let that work in and we'll see you in a sec." Kadie smiled and walked out. "Jared I can see where you get your handsome looks from."

Sara smiled, took a few more deep breaths, she took a few sips of her lemonade to take the smell off her breath. Then she walked out to get to know the father of the man she loved.

Ross sat on the back patio, leaned back, and took a puff from his cigar. He was smiling as he watched his son with Sara. He had never seen Jared so happy; he was grateful for the opportunity to share in it. He had enjoyed the whole evening, starting with meeting Sara's sisters. He understood that he still hadn't met the oldest sister Abby, but he knew that if she was anything like the three he had in front of him, he would like her too. They were laid back, there was a quick fire about the way they talked that always kept him in the loop as well as showing him the girls were close.

He was able to find out how Morgan was and the reason for their quick departure from the birthday party. He also made a mental note to make Helen back off, with this Meg girl. Sara to his mind was well grounded, she was the head of the family. He wondered about that, what with her being the second oldest.

"Sara?" He had caught the attention of the table. "May I ask you a question?"

"Sure, anything" She smiled but she could feel her stomach do a flip.

"How did you become head of the family?" He watched as the sisters exchanged looks.

"To be honest with you I'm not too sure, I just know that I've done it for as long as I could remember.

'She was just always there." Kadie said looking at Ross. "She made sure we got home from school, made sure we ate and helped with the homework. She made sure that just because mom was busy, and dad was gone that we didn't act like we didn't have responsibilities."

"Not that mom was crazy and didn't take care of us." Morgan sat back with her hands resting on her belly. "She was just busy. First, it was to help grams, then it was to run the bakery. By the time life should have slowed down even a little, mom was sick." Morgan looked at Sara. They shared a moment that everyone noticed.

"I was a freshman in college," Sara started "I was studying for winter finales. Abby and I were going to go home for winter break. So, I knew that as soon as I finished my finales we would be on our way." Sara took a sip of her drink. "I almost didn't answer the phone when she called, here I was cramming like I had never before. I was going to be home in a few days and my mom is calling. I thought it was something to do with Kadie or Morgan. When I answered the phone, I was short with her. Told her I needed to call her later and that it wasn't a good time."

"Everything stopped when I heard her voice. She said Sweetheart I need you to come home. Still to this day, I can't tell you what it was, maybe her tone I don't know but I froze. I told her that I would be on the next train. I called Abby and told her that I was going to go home early. She didn't ask much, didn't get on me about skipping finales, nothing she just said travel safe and see you at home. She too had been cramming and was in her second year at the same school." Sara took a breath.

"I check the trains and found out I had 30 mins to catch the next. I dump my books for my clothes and bathroom stuff and ran most of the way. I bought a ticket and make the last call. When I get home Morgan is waiting for me, she has no idea what's going on Mom just told her she had to come pick me up after she got off work. It was our quietest ride home that we have ever had."

"We get home and mom is sitting at the kitchen table with Kadie. I walk over to her and when I hug her, she feels so small to me. I knew what she was going to say, so I just held her for a long time. Kadie didn't even say anything she just let me have that moment. We sit down and she tells us that she has stage 4 uterine cancer, and it's everywhere. They can't do anything but make her comfortable."

"After many questions, lots and lots of tears. It comes out that she had been sick, not feeling well for a while. She made my sister's promise not to tell me, she knew that if I knew she was sick I wouldn't have gone off to school. She had gone to the doctor that day to get the results of the tests. She had finally gone in to find out why she wasn't feeling right. She told me that I could go with her to the doctor's appointments and get all the information I needed from them, and in the meantime start taking over the bakery. She was gone three months later."

Sara took a deep breath; she didn't tell that story often if ever. It always took a lot out of her, she looked to Morgan who had tears running down her cheeks. Andrew was holding her hand, handing her a napkin. Kadie was looking out over the lawn, no tears, but sadness in her eyes.

"You were what eighteen, nineteen?" Ross asked.

"I turned 19 a month before she died. It was one of the best birthdays I'll ever have." Sara smiled.

"You became guardian over your two younger sisters and the sole owner of a bakery?" Ross looked at Sara in a whole new light.

"Guardian yes, sole owner no. My mother left it to the four of us, Morgan and Kadie didn't get theirs till they turned 18." Sara nodded

"But you ran it solo, Abby was off at college, Morgan and Kadie were still in high school. How did you make it work?" Ross noticed that his tone had changed slightly, but he was genially curious. Sara just smiled at him.

"Would you believe me if I told you I don't know?" She gave him a small smile.

"No" Ross smiled back at her.

"My mother had a great crew, over the months that she was

getting weaker and weaker they were running more and more of it. In the months before her death, I worked with them, I took business classes at night. Kadie had started making plans to graduate early and go to pastry school. As that was her passion. Morgan was heading off to get her accountant degree. In the last few months before mom left, we planned out what would be our life plan."

"And Abby?

"Abby came home when she could, but she had started her life. She couldn't deal with mom's death, so she stayed away. We talked and I made sure that she had made peace with it, and she had. After she finished school, she went to work her dream job, she only worked in the bakery once in a while. She decided that she wanted to take a break from her job after the wedding. I wasn't behind the idea, but it seems to be the best as she is needed every day at the bakery now."

"What happened to the wonderful crew? It's just the four of you now." Andrew asked looking at Morgan.

"A few different things, they slowly left one by one. One was caught stealing, one quilt when Kadie started working and could do a cake better and fast than her. Let's see Mary quilt when she found out that she didn't get any part of the business when mom left it to us. That almost got ugly." Morgan took a drink of water and shifted so the boys had more room.

"How was it almost ugly?" Jared asked.

"She threaten to take us to court, so we hired a lawyer. He did a background check, turned out she wasn't who she said she was. The cops came and removed her from the bakery. One she had no grounds to go after us and two she was on the run. She went to jail for robbery and attempted murder." Kadie said with a little smile

"Wait, that was seven years ago?" Jared asked.

"a little less, why?" Sara asked looking at him, trying to read his face.

"Andrew, do you remember when they brought in that whack job, she was yelling how she had a successful business, she was going to sue all of us. Take us for everything the city had?" Jared said looking at Andrew.

"Oh ya, what was her name?" Andrew shut his eyes in concentration. "Started with a B, damn what was it."

"Mary Barnette." Morgan smiled.

"Yes! Wait what? She worked for you guys?" Andrew said looking around the table.

"Yep, she had fed mom some sob story, thought that she would get a piece of the bakery, live out her life in hiding," Morgan said.

"So, you made it happen." Ross smiled at each one of the girls he sat with.

"It was never an option not to." Sara took a drink. "You came from a long line of hard workers, was there ever a question of whether or not you would put your blood, sweat, and tears into it?"

"Well in my defense yes, I understand that family drive, however, I came along when the business was much more established. I have had my share of hard times, but nothing compared to the bringing up of it." Ross said then looked down at his watch. "Well kids this has been a great night, but I need to get home." He stood, as did everyone else.

"I'll walk you to the door." Sara stepped around.

Ross looked at Kadie and Morgan.

"It was a pleasure to meet you, and I hope we get to do it again soon." He said and watched Kadie walks over and gives him a hug. "Any time," she said, "Andrew, see you around."

They shook hands, and Ross couldn't help but wink at Andrew and look at Morgan. Andrew knowing Ross for so long picked up the approval and smiled back.

Ross then walked with Sara back into the house with Jared following. As they reached the door Sara smiled at Ross

"Thank you so much for coming." She shook his hand. "Thank you for having me." Ross smiled.

"I'll walk you out, dad," Jared said and opened the front door.

"Goodbye, Sara," Ross said smiling.

"Goodbye, Ross," Sara said returning the smile, then shut the door behind the two men making their way down the front walk. It wasn't until they were at Ross' car did either of them speak.

"I stood in the shadows and watched as you and your best friend took the pledge. I've watched the two of you grow up to be fine men. I have to say I am so happy that I don't have to stand in the shadows and watch from afar as you enjoy and grow this relationship, that I get to stand with you and watch you have something real, and special." Ross said looking at Jared.

"I'm happy too." Jared smiled at his dad.

"I can see that." Ross turned to get in his car. "I'll see you soon son."

"Bye dad."

Jared walked back into the house to the sound of women laughing and enjoying the clean up after a nice dinner, the whole house felt relaxed. He had a moment, his mother's house never felt that way. He smiled as he walked in to find Sara and Kadie doing the dishes, Andrew cleaned up and set the back yard to rights and Morgan laughing at the counter as she drank her evening tea.

"Can I help?" He asked as he put his arms around Sara from behind.

"I think Andrew has the back under wraps, but you could check with him." She smiled as he kissed her neck. Then watched over her shoulder as he headed to the back. He stopped mid step as the phone on his hip rang.

"Brooks.... yep, we'll be right there." He turned to her.

"We've got the rest," Sara said with a smile.

"Andrew let's go." Jared had caught him as he brought in the last of the dishes. They kissed their girls goodbye and headed out.

26

***

Time continued to go by, marked by Morgan's growing belling and the summer moving into Fall. Sara was surprised by how her life changed over the weeks. There was a routine of no routine. She had hers, with her sisters and work. Both Jared and Andrew were working a lot, leaving little time to make a routine at all. Before they knew it Sara and Kadie were cleaning for the babies' shower. Morgan had tried not to complain too much, she was grateful her sisters were hosting, and that rules had been laid out for the co-event. Morgan had tried to take deep breaths as the RSVPs came in. Between the family and friends both Morgan and Andrew had, the inside party guest list was up to 45, and the outside gathering didn't have a count as boys didn't believe in RSVPs. From what Andrew and Jared said they expected a large turnout.

Jared was walking from the kitchen to the front, doing a quick once through. Sara and Kadie had moved furniture out and brought tables and chairs in. There were blue and green balloons, streamers, and tablecloths. He was walking to the study when he heard Morgan growl. Knowing Andrew was in the driveway accepting the drink delivery.

They had roped a rookie into watching the "Door" They blocked off the driveway with sawhorses. Sara had given them a table to place diapers on. It was set up by the entry, where the rookie would sit on a stool. The rules were simple, no diapers no entry.

"Morgan?" Jared knocked on the door.

"Come in." Morgan was sitting on her bed; she had changed into a white dress. With wide straps and a V-neck, she had a blue ribbon tied around the top of her belly.

"What's the matter?" Jared asked calmly. The house was treading lightly as Morgan moved through her pregnancy, she had no patients, and as soon as she snapped she would cry and say sorry so many times that the word was starting to lose the meaning.

"I can't tell if my shoes match, and that is irritating because I don't really want to wear any I just want to wear my slippers but they don't match and my sisters are working really hard for me, and the boys and I just don't want to be the center of atten-tion. If I could drink this is when I would just to calm the nerves." Morgan just sat and looked at the floor.

"Ok." Jared walked to the closet found her slippers and walked over to her. He bent down and took the un-matching shoes off. He slid the first slipper on. "First, I don't think anybody would think less of you if you wore your slippers and if you talked to your sisters they would agree. In fact, I think they would wear theirs too. They have worked hard for you, yes, we all have, you are growing two boys. That alone is hard work, and you are going a great job. Lastly, this is one day, just a few hours really when women will gather to celebrate the fact that you are growing tiny humans. It is amazing and wonderful, and you deserve it." Jared watched Morgan sit up straighter, he didn't know if it was her picking her head up or if the babies needed room.

"You're right." She nodded her head in agreement. "Alright

let's do this." Morgan looked at the clock, they had an hour before everything started. She looked at Jared. "Thank you" She kissed his cheek and walked out of the room.

Sara couldn't believe the people all over her house. The kitchen, living room, and den were full of women, some she knew others she didn't. Kadie had overseen the door. Taking gifts, explaining the games. Due to the sheer size of the guest list it had been decided that the gifts wouldn't be opened at the party. The games were limited as well by the number of guests. Abby and Sara had agreed that one or the other would always be near Morgan. It was only needed a few times. One woman had walked right up to Morgan and put both her hands on Morgan's belly. Sara stepped in to lead the woman away before Morgan started crying, as crying was the reaction to everything from happiness to anger, and everything in between. Sara turned the lady to the kitchen just as Margaret stepped in the way.

"Why hello Katharine, how are you?" Margaret asked swooping in to take Katharine away. Margaret proved to be a helpful surprise, she also stayed close to Morgan. She helped detour questions of the upcoming wedding, and what the names were going to be, and helped to keep the advice to a minimum.

After a while, Sara went outside to check on the men. Just like her house, her driveway and garage were overtaken by people. She saw that the table for diapers was overflowing. Smiling she looked around for Jared and saw Andrew first. He was laughing with a group of guys, relaxed and happy. She found Jared in the garage she walked over to him and slipped her arm around his waist. He smiled down at her, tucked her under his shoulder, and continued the conversation. She stayed for a little bit but knew she needed to go back inside.

They should have known that when you had a good party nobody wanted to leave. Not so much for the party inside as it was for the party outside. Andrew and Jared had moved around talking to everyone. They had called cabs for the ones who shouldn't drive and made sure designated drivers were loaded and set. They were quiet as they cleaned up the outside and set it all to right. The rookie had moved the diapers up to the nursery. He headed off taking the last who needed a DD.

The guys made it into the house and saw that the kitchen and living room had been set to rights as well. Their party ended a few hours before the outside one. Andrew was surprised to see his mother still there.

"Mom?"

"Oh, there you are Andrew." Margret smiled up at her son, as she sat with the girls enjoying a glass of water. "I was just decompressing, I stayed to help clean up. Then we sat and started talking. You have found yourself a good group of girls here." She smiled at them. Then she looked at her watch "My goodness where did the time go, I'll be off." She stood.

"I'll take that for you." Kadie waited for the water glass. "Thank you, honey, No, don't you even think about getting up." She said to Morgan as she noticed her trying to lift herself off the couch. Margret walked over and lend down to hug Morgan.

"Thank you for letting me come," Margret said so only Morgan could hear.

"Thank you for all your help," Morgan said with a hitch in her voice.

"You just let me know if you need anything, anything at all," Margret said as she turned to the door. "That goes for all of you."

"I'll walk you out, mom," Andrew said walking to the door.

"Well, that went way better than I thought it would," Kadie said walking back into the room.

"What do you mean?" Jared asked sitting next to Sara.

"To be honest I expected her to be more like your mom, no offense," Kadie said sitting with Morgan.

"No offense taken, she would have but Andrew set her straight, and hard. Andrew has always just kind of gone with the flow when it came to his mom, and she likes to stretch the lines as much as possible. When he told her about you, Morgan, he told her that it was a packaged deal. You were his choice and she could either jump on board the nice way or not bother at all and not have any part in the life he built with you.

"Oh, I love that man, but he shouldn't have been so cut and mean about it," Morgan said sleepily, resting on Kadie's shoulder.

"If he, hadn't you would have dealt with my mom today, and nobody deserves that." Jared looked up when Andrew came walking back into the house. "Everything ok?"

"Ya, she was just having a moment," Andrew said then looked over to find a half-awake Morgan. "Come on baby girl let's get you to bed." he walked over to help Morgan from the couch.

"Thank you, guys, so much, I love you all, good night." She said walking with Andrew.

"Good night," Jared, Kadie, and Sara said in unison.

Jared was at his desk going over a report when his phone rang.

"Brooks."

"You have a visitor here at the front." The line went dead before he could ask who. He stood to go.

"What's up?" Andrew asked.

"I have a visitor," Jared said with a confused look on his face. He let his mind wander over who it could be and started eliminating. His dad was on a business trip. They had made every other Sunday the night Ross joined them for dinner. Jared was enjoying those dinners, though sometimes he was either called away or didn't make it. He was liking how Sara and his dad were getting along. He had him believing that maybe someday his mother would accept Sara too. Sara was working with her sisters; business hadn't slowed down in the slightest for her. Even having Abby in the front of the house, when it was rumored that she killed sales in the past. It was defiantly not the case now. He came down the stairs to his surprise to find his mother waiting for him.

"Hello, mother." He said walking to her.

"Jared I'm glad you could take the time to see me." She said slightly irritated "Since you don't take my calls anymore."

Jared wanted to roll his eyes "I have been very busy. What do you need?"

"I'm having a dinner party tomorrow night and with your father out of town I need you to be there."

"I-"

"Don't say you can't make it I really need you there. This is very important to me." Jared thought she almost sounded desperate. A tone that he wasn't used to.

"I'll be there. What time?" He was hoping it was a later dinner so Sara could join him.

"Four." She said quickly. "Simi-formal."

"I'll be there unless something comes up."

"Jared please"

With a sign, "Ok I'll be there."

"Thank you so much my darling," Helen said with a smile, he could see her relax. "I'll see you tomorrow." She walked away without another word.

Jared went back to his desk, before Andrew could ask who his visitor was, they were called away.

"So, how was your day?" Sara asked half-awake when he crawled into bed next to her later that night. Way later than he had hoped, but that was the job.

"Busy. Yours?" He asked just as he found the sweet spot on the bed with her curled up to him.

"Busy" Was the last words she said and he heard.

When Jared woke the next morning, the bed was empty,

Sara had already gone to work. He lay there thinking about his day and remembered the dinner at his mother's. He hadn't said anything to Sara about it. He gave himself a mental kick for that and promised to tell her before he went. He went downstairs to find Andrew and a very pregnant Morgan.

"Good morning, guys." He made his way to the coffee pot. He looked at the clock. "Morgan, are you staying home today?"

"Yes," Andrew said at the same time Morgan said "No."

"Ok, I'm going to shower. Have a good day either way." When he got out, he had a message from Andrew meet you at work, dropping Morgan off. Jared just smiled to himself. He thought about stopping by to see Sara, but as he drove by the Bakery it was packed and he knew she didn't have time to stop. So, he just headed to work.

"She won again?" He asked as he walked up to his desk.

"Every damn time." Andrew shut his eyes. "I swear any day now I'm going to get the call that she over did it and is going to the hospital." He rubbed his hands over his face.

"You do realize at this point she is a glorified door greeter and doesn't lift a finger. Well, that's not true she is the account for them too. Just to keep her busy." Jared was checking his email when his phone rang.

"Brooks…. Yep." He hung up the phone and stood. "Let's go"

"Good, I need to keep busy too," Andrew said standing.

It was lunch time when Jared looked at his watch.

"Hey, they closed for lunch, want to stop by?"

"Hell yes."

They walked in the back door as they knew the font would be locked with sandwiches from their favorite shop.

"Oh, how did you know?" Kadie said as she looked up from the cake she was decorating.

"I just know my ladies," Jared said with a smile and set the food down as Sara came around her counter. He felt warm all over as she slid up to him, and into his arms.

"You do indeed. How has your day been?" They brought stools around and settled into eating and catching up on the last few days as it seemed to have been that long since they were together like this.

Morgan caught everyone's attention when she stood up with a yelp.

"What" Andrew was on his feet just as fast, his eyes big, with concern.

"They are way running out of room. I can't sit for too long or they make me stand by ramming a foot into my ribs. I'm fine, just need to stretch out a bit." Morgan started to sway and rube her hands on her belly, I have like six weeks left God willing. I'm huge, and they are running out of room."

"You need to keep them in there for another couple of days at least, we haven't even opened up the gifts from the shower yet," Kadie said as she finished her sandwich.

"We should do that tonight," Sara said.

"Do we have to?" Morgan said with a slight whine to her tone.

"Yes, we need to get it done so we can wash and get your bag packed and get the thank you cards sent, and put their nursery together," Sara said losing her composer.

"Fine but I'm doing it my way." Morgan snapped back.

"I expect nothing less," Sara said taking a deep breath.

Jared and Andrew left shortly after they were all done eating, with only the plan to open presents for the night. Jared kicked himself again for not letting Sara know about his dinner. He stopped for a second, he would call her when they get back to the station. No big deal he thought. But he wouldn't make it back to the station. Andrew and Jared were called to another scene. He silently cures the other detectives who were on leave. His workload had tripled all because four people were out at the same time.

His mother sent him a text at 3:30 that took him off guard. Not the reminder but the time. The day had just flown by.

"Shit I got to go." Jared put his phone away.

"Everything ok?" Andrew pulled his phone out just to make sure he hadn't missed anything for Morgan.

"Ya just have dinner at my parent's house," Jared said making sure he had everything.

"I thought your dad was out of town?" Andrew asked watching him

"He is that is why my mother hit me up. It should only be a couple of hours; can you handle this?" Jared asked Andrew almost hoping he would say no.

"Ya, I got this." He said with a nod and watched Jared leave.

27

———————

HE PULLED up to his parent's house at ten to four. He notices a few cars in the drive but that was to be expected. None that he recognized though. As he walked up, he was hit with a bad gut feeling, he went inside hoping and praying he was wrong.

"Jared sweetheart there you are." Helen bounced across the room. Jared was quick though he saw seven people, Meg being one of them. Standing with a woman who looked like her older sister, and an older gentleman with Meg's eyes. He put the two together, as Meg's parents. Before he places the other four people two male two female, older. Grandparent, it clicked for him as his mother ushered him out of the room with the excuse he needed to change. He walked with her till he knew they were far enough away from the group and stopped dead in his tracks.

"You have got to be kidding me." He said with ice in his tone. He was positive this was the maddest he had ever been at his mother's.

"No, I'm not, I am saving you from yourself. You and that bakery girl have no future. She can never be one of us. Meg on the other hand is a well brought up young lady, who would make you a fine wife. The two of you would be the couple of the year I just know it." Helen was standing her ground this was big her moment, to prove she had some say over Jared's life.

He just closed his eyes, took a deep breath, and thought of Sara. Warm, sweet, kind, loving Sara. He moved on, thinking of her sisters, of Andrew, of the laughter coming from the house itself. When his body relaxed Helen thought she had won.

"Now we are going to go back in there, and you are going to make this work. I've done most of the groundwork, and Meg is on board. So, this won't really be that hard for you." Helen waited for Jared to open his eyes. What she took as acceptance, was his resolve. He would leave here tonight, in the next five minutes, and never see or speak to his mother again. He started walking back to the drawing room with her, just as they approached the door, Meg her parents, and grandparents were heading to the door in a bit of a huff.

"Wait what's going on," Helen asked worried. All she got in return was snide, down the nose looks. She swept into the drawing room ready to lay waste to whatever had her guests leaving so abruptly. She came up so short that Jared almost walked into her. Ross stood in the middle of the room his arms crossed his chest. His eyes lit with anger.

Helen readjusted herself "What are you doing here?" she asked her husband.

"I would ask you the same question, but I know how to put two and two together." He said glaring at his wife.

"I am getting Jared's life on the right track or at least I was till you came barging in and wrecked everything. What did you say to them? How bad did you make me look?" Helen was getting angry, mostly because she was embarrassed.

"Helen this is crazy, why would you do this to Jared? He is happy and in love, you need to let him be." Ross said watching his wife.

"What did you say to them?" she asked again.

"I told them that Jared was not engaged to their daughter or granddaughter. That he has never, nor would he ever date Meg, and I apologized for your behavior." Ross said steel in his eyes

"Ross, so help me." Helen through her hands in the air.

"Well, this has been great I'm going to go now," Jared said as he turn to leave.

"I will destroy her. I'll destroy her family, her stupid little business. She will have nothing when I'm done, she will be nothing." Helen said and watched Jared turn back to her. "You choose this minute, us or her."

Jared felt so weird, cold, and shaky, yet so mad he felt like he was on fire. He looked at his mother, then his father. He saw something in his dad's eyes. Almost a sadness that it had come down to this. Ross gave Jared a nod. He knew his son, knew his heart was with Sara. Jared walked over to his mother and kissed her cheek.

"Goodbye, mother." He said softly. He turned and left with her screaming behind him.

When Jared was in his truck he just sat there for a moment, then he started it and left his parents' house with only one destination on his mind. He pulled up to the back of the bakery. He checked the clock they still had an hour to go before they closed. He couldn't wait anymore, he got out and walked through the back door. Sara and Kadie played music in the back loud enough for them but not loud enough to reach the customers. Jared watched as Kadie sang the song as she worked on a very pink cake. He looked over at Sara and found her slightly swaying to the music as she pulled cupcakes from the oven. He just stood there and watched her. She had a smile on her face, she was happy and then she started singing the song. He had never heard her sing and damn she was good. She gave a start when she looked over and saw him standing there, she shot him her most beautiful smile. The one that always melted him.

His whole world just took one hell of a shake, but he couldn't help but smile back at her. He walked closer to her, and she saw the hurt in his eyes. She walked around her counter.

"I'll be right back," Sara said to Kadie, she nodded at the two of them.

"What happened?" Sara asked as they stood outside, the day ends, the fall air crisp with change.

Jared thought for a moment he would tell her, of course. "How much time do you have?" He said with a weak smile.

"As much as you need." She said watching him.

"So yesterday my mother stopped by the station, she said she was having a dinner party and needed me there because dad was out of town. She sounded almost desperate. So, I agreed to go." He shut his eyes as how easy it was for her washed over him.

"She is your mother and she said she needed you," Sara said trying to soothe.

"I was going to tell you last night, but just fell asleep as soon as I was in bed with you, then I was going to tell you when I stopped by for lunch. Then I was going to tell you when we got back to the station, but we never made it." Jared said desperate for her to understand he wasn't trying to hide anything from her.

"Your workload has been really intense lately, but it will get better when you have a full staff again." Sara just nodded her head she understood it. "So, you went to dinner." She looked at her watch "Right?"

"Yes, dinner was at four, I was hoping that it would be later, and you could come with me." Jared shook his head.

"Honey she didn't want me to join you." She said understanding.

"Ya, I get that now. So, I get there and as I walk up to the door, I get this really bad feeling, and sure enough, as soon as I walk into the drawing room, she rushes me out to tell me that." He took a deep breath. "We, me and you won't make it. You would never be one of us. I need to marry Meg so we can be some power couple that everyone is jealous of."

"Sara, I swear to you I have never thought that of you or of us like that. Then it was weird this anger came over me, and I was super calm. I walk back to the drawing room with her, I'm thinking of making this big exit. Make it known that you and I are forever and nothing is going to change that. But as we reach the drawing room Meg, her parents, and grandparents are leaving."

"They look pissed, so Helen charges into the room to find my dad standing there. He came back early, so she rips into him about what is he doing at home, and what did he say that had her guest leaving so quickly. He rips back at her with how she needs to leave me alone, let me be happy with you." Jared takes a breath; Sara just stands there waiting for the rest of the story.

"I'm watching them go at it, with Helen saying she is getting my life on the right track. I figure that was a great time to leave. I say so and turn to go. That's when she said she would destroy you and everything you have, you will have nothing, be nothing when she was done." Jared couldn't look at Sara he was hurt and angry all over again. "She told me to choose, them or you. I looked at my dad then, knowing it was really her or you. As he loves you and wants me to be happy. I kissed her cheek and said goodbye." Jared let out a shaky breath. He would endure whatever Sara said or did next; he could take it because he was straight with her. She looked away taking a few deep breaths of her own. Finally, she looked at him, there was no anger, just compassion.

"Jared I am so sorry that you had to go through that." She wrapped her arms around him and just held on. It was exactly what he needed. When she pulled away after a while. He looked down at her.

"Just what I needed, now your turn." He smiled.

"What do you mean?"

"Free pass to say what you really think about the situation." He just watched her and waited.

Sara stepped back knowing she was going to be waving her hands around.

"Where the hell does she get off hating me so much that she would make her only son choose between us? Am I really that bad that she can't get over the fact that I work and make a damn good living making food for people? I have a wonderful life and I have worked too damn hard to lose it to some lady throwing a fit because she didn't get her way." She took a huge deep breath. "And another thing, did it even cross her mind that she threatened me to a cop?"

"No, I don't think it did, in her mind, she was talking to her son. Not an officer of the law." Jared waited and then signed when she moved back to him. They stood there holding each other for a while. Finally, Jared pulled back but left his arms around her.

"I have to get back to Andrew, I told him a couple of hours, hopefully, we can be out of there before you guys go to bed." Jared said and kissed Sara "I love you."

"I love you too," she smiled and watched him walk to the car and leave.

"What was that all about?" Kadie asked when Sara when walked back in.

"Jared's mother threatened to destroy me if he didn't break it off, me or her. He chose me." Sara said getting back to work.

"Holy shit," Kadie said, "What are you going to do about it?"

"When we get home and make sure we are all caught up with our insurance, get some more cameras. Tomorrow we are going to take all of the super special stuff out of the bakery." Sara sounded determined.

"Why?" Morgan asked from the back seat "Why not take the stuff tonight?"

"Helen will wait, she will do it in her own time. Or she will hire someone to do it for her either way I'm going to be ready." Sara said her mind going over all the possible weak spots she might have.

When Sara got home, she went straight to the study, she would be ready in more ways than one. She worked on moving money, making sure she had all the right paperwork filed. She double checked with the insurance company that insured the bakery, and the house. She didn't look up till Morgan came and told her dinner was ready. They had just sat down when the boys came in.

"So, Jared, I heard you got a new family today?" Kadie just stared at him, then smiled.

"Yes, I did, if they'll have me?" He smiled as he sat down.

"I'm not sure if you've noticed buddy but you've been stuck with us for a while now," Kadie said

"A guy can hope. So how are we going to handle Helen?" Jared looked at Sara.

"Well, I feel like I've gotten to know her over the last few months" sarcasm soaked her tone. "I called the insurance company today, ordered more cameras, and we are taking all of grandma's things out of the shop tomorrow. Also, all the paper work will come home daily." She said sitting back crossing her arms.

"You think she is going to vandalize the bakery," Jared said realizing where all the pre-steps lead.

"I do, and I think she is going to hit the accounts. She thinks money makes a person, so she is going to try to take mine. The bakery is who I am to her, so she will destroy it. Also, this house, if she ever knew this is ours, it's too nice. She would think I didn't earn it, so I don't deserve to keep it."

"You think she would go that far?" Andrew asked.

"Yep, without any hesitation. The only reason she isn't or hasn't yet is because she was hoping her big plan today was going to work. It didn't, it backfired in her face, so she needs to come up with plan B."

"How did you come up with all of that?" Jared asked.

"Because if I made the kind of threats she made today, it's what I would do." Sara shrugged.

"Eddie did say he never wanted to get on their bad side," Andrew said to Jared.

"Ant' that the truth," Jared said back to his friend.

28

OVER THE WEEKS that followed Sara worked night and day securing every bit she could. Pulled money from accounts keeping the bare minimum in them. She put in a security system at the house and increased the one at the bakery. Just as she said they moved all the special things out, told the customs who noticed the changes that they were redecorated, or thinking about it. From the outside, it looked like nothing changed, which is exactly how Sara wanted it. They had Abby and Eddie over for dinner, where they filled Eddie in the best they could. Some things just couldn't be shared with the family lawyer. Sara was as ready as she could be. She felt confident that Helen would make her move, she just wasn't sure when.

"You know the best time would be when Morgan has the babies, or close to that. She would think we were so busy with that we wouldn't think it was her, just chalk it up to another thing to deal with," Kadie said as she sat at the counter drinking her coffee on Sunday morning. Sara stopped cooking the eggs and looked at her sister.

"You know," Sara thought about it. "Your right, but in reality, that would be the best time. Close the bakery for a few weeks, have a little vacation."

"You know that doesn't sound half bad. Then we reopen when we are refreshed." Kadie smiled and drank her coffee. "But I don't really want to go anywhere, don't get me wrong a break sounds great but we would lose our minds after the first week."

"I know," Sara said dumping the eggs on a plate just as Jared came downstairs

"Good morning, ladies." Jared walked over to Sara, he Hollywood dipped her as he kissed her.

"Ugg you guys are so gross sometimes," Kadie said coving her eyes.

Jared finished the kiss and stood Sara up right.

"Good morning to you too." She said with a smile. "Have some food." She said turning back to the stove.

"Thank you." Jared went to the coffee maker made his coffee then met the plate Sara made for him at the counter next to Kadie.

"So, ladies what's on the agenda for today?" He asked before his first bit.

"We're going to..." Sara stopped lost in thought. "I don't know. We have the nursery ready, the thank you cards are all sent. Morgan's bag is packed. We don't need to pull an extra day at work. The only thing on the books is dinner with your dad later." Sara looked at Kadie "Can you think of anything?"

"Not really, we could do the house cleaning today instead of tomorrow. Get it done." Kadie was quiet then as she looked at Sara and Jared. "Do you think we could add one for dinner tonight?"

"Sure," Jared said quickly then went back to his breakfast.

"I don't see why not; Abby and Eddie are joining us tonight. What's one more?" Sara shrugged.

"Great thanks." Kadie stood taking her plate and cup to the sink. "Just let me know when you want to start cleaning." Then she went up to her room.

"You played that very cool," Jared said when he knew Kadie was out of earshot.

"Thank you, so did you. As it's a damn big deal for her to invite anyone to dinner, with us." Sara took a drink from her coffee. "But then again it isn't like Graham hasn't eaten with us before."

"Nailed that one didn't you," Jared said with a smile.

"I'm just glad she is starting to share with us. Lord knows it takes a brave soul to sneak in and out of a house that has two cops here regularly."

"Caught on to that too," Jared said as he stood and took his plate to the sink

"Hard not to. So" She said changing the subject. "Do we need anything for dinner tonight?"

They talked about the menu and all that was needed for dinner that night. Jared had kept his word to his mother. He hadn't seen or spoken to her since that day. He found that he didn't miss her enough to reach out to her. His dad on the other hand had continued to call and come over for their standing Sunday dinners when they could all come together. Tonight, he would ask about her, just to see how she was doing and maybe find out if she was really planning to move on her threat.

By three that afternoon the house had been clean from top to bottom. Morgan had helped to the best of her ability being so big at 35 weeks. She had sat on the couch until Andrew and Jared headed to the gym and shooting range. Then she was up and moving, she did the small stuff behind Kadie and Sara. She liked the movement of it and after she was done, she went to her downstairs room for a nap before dinner.

Morgan lay in bed waiting for sleep to take her over when

her belly tightened ever so slightly. It released as quickly as it had come. She sat up and reached for her large bottle of water never far from her. She drank deep, then knowing it was going to be uncomfortable to lay back down she moved to the rocking chair. They had set up a small nursery in her downstairs room. Just a rocking chair and two bassinets. She liked just sitting there daydreaming about the day she would have her boys.

Kadie went to check on Morgan and found her sleeping in her chair. She went back to the kitchen, grabbed her beer off the counter, and joined Sara out on the back patio.

"To a job well done. Now we have to figure out what to do tomorrow?" Kadie said as she sat down.

"Oh, I'm sure we'll find something to do," Sara said as she looked out over her garden, she could tell the season was changing by the air and how her yard looked.

"It's going to be an interesting Christmas," Sara said.

"I know you like to plan ahead but damn that far, even for you." Kadie looked over at Sara.

"Well, last year it was you and me. Abby and Eddie had come over in the morning, but it was just us. This year..." Sara trailed off.

"I get it, not just the two of us." Kadie waited a beat. "How do you want it to be?"

"Honestly, I want to wake up Christmas morning and have us all here. Like Sunday dinner just in the morning, everybody in their pjs. Coffee and gifts, breakfast, and then just hang out and be together."

"That sounds really good," Kadie said as she took a pull from her beer.

"Are you going to invite your plus one to Christmas?" Sara asked knowing she was poking. She knew Kadie would get around to telling her, however, she also wouldn't be doing her sisterly duties if she didn't poke now and again.

"Do you think that it says something about us that we

would choose men who could leave us at the drop of a hat?" Kadie looked at Sara "Not leave us like walk out but leave us to leave us?"

"I think if anyone knows how precious time is, it's us. Sure, we could cut ourselves off from being with someone, but why? We aren't spending our lives going poor us everyone leaves, and if you think about it not everyone leaves. We still have each other."

"I know, I just think it's stupid to fall for a cop," Kadie added just staring out across the back yard.

"I don't think it's stupid to fall in love with Graham, I think it's the best thing you've ever done." Sara watched as Kadie jerked her head and looked at her.

"How?" Kadie started to ask then stopped, it was Sara she was talking to, and more times than nothing got passed, Sara. "How long have you known?"

"After the night at the club and Jared told me that he wanted to stay with you through the night. You haven't had a bad night since." Sara watched Kadie soak in what she had just said. Hoping it wouldn't scare her into retreat.

"I feel safe with him, and he doesn't stay every night." Kadie said looking at Sara.

"I know." Sara took another drink, they sat together in silence until Morgan came out to join them.

"Hey, sister how was the nap?" Kadie asked as she watched Morgan lower herself into the chair next to her.

"It was fine." Morgan took a breath. "Kadie where is your phone?"

"My back pocket why?" Kadie pulled it out and set it on the table.

"I think you need to pull up that contraction app you down-loaded." Morgan sat back and closed her eyes.

"What?" Sara said and Kadie worked to open that app.

"Ok, we're all set just say when" Kadie watched and waited.

"The code word is going to be "Honey'.""

"Why?" Sara asked.

"Because I don't want to go to the hospital until it's time, and I'm not sure that it is. We all know the minute Andrew finds out I'm having any kind of pain that could be interpreted as a contraction I have to go to the hospital and then they will either keep me or send me home. I would much rather be home for as long as possible- Honey" Morgan started to take slow deep breaths and closed her eyes.

"We need an end code word too," Kadie said as they watched Morgan.

"Baby." Morgan opened her eyes and smiled "Now let's just talk and relax until we know what we know and have to go."

The girls talked about everything; Morgan agreed that Graham would be a good guy for Kadie. Sara watched as Morgan's Honeys were getting further apart and Baby was coming shortly after. By the time they had dinner done, Kadie had put her phone away. Morgan seemed at ease, smiling and laughing when Jared and Andrew came in with Ross behind them.

"Well now, looks like you had a good day." Andrew walked over to Morgan and kissed her forehead.

"I did, I helped clean a bit then took a nap. We sat out back and had a wonderful visit." Morgan said smiling up at him.

"With whom?" Andrew asked looking at Sara and Kadie.

"Each other," Kadie said moving away from Andrew to move plates and silverware to the table.

Abby and Eddie came in next both all smiles. Sara watched as they hugged and moved around the room, they both just glowed. She knew the moment she got a good look at Abby. Having spent so much time in Morgan's company Sara knew an addition was on the way. She shared a look with Abby, the couple was going to wait to share with the family.

"You look so beautiful," she said in her ear when Abby gave her a hug.

"Thank you," Abby said with an even brighter smile. "What can I help with?"

"You can start taking the sides to the table," Sara said then looked to the front of the house when the doorbell chimed. Sara looked at Kadie who was looking at her phone. Kadie shook her head, telling her sister that it wasn't Graham at the door. Sara went to answer the door to find the pleasant surprise from Andrew's mom.

"Miss May, please come in." Sara stepped back.

"Morgan called me earlier and invited me to dinner. By the look on your face, you didn't know about it." Margarette said stepping in.

"I didn't know, but that doesn't mean that you are unwelcome quite the opposite. Please join us we are just about to eat." Sara shut the door and took Margaret's sweater. "How was your day?"

"Very good thank you, it smells amazing." they walked to the kitchen.

"Thank you, it's my mother's lasagna. Add another setting Kadie we have one more." Sara said as they walked into the kitchen.

"Mom what?" Andrew walked over and hugged his mom.

"Morgan invited me," Margaret said looking around the room. "Ross, how are you?"

"Good thank you," Ross said with a nod. They smiled at each other.

"Miss May, can I get you something to drink? Kadie asked putting her phone in her back pocket.

"Wine if you have it." Margaret moved to sit next to Morgan. "How are you feel my dear."

"Done, so done. I want to meet them, hold them in my arms." Morgan leaned back and rubbed her huge belly. "Oh here." Without hesitation, she grabbed Margaret's hand and put it on her belly over the place she felt the hardest kicks. Margaret sat stunned for a minute then quietly whipped a tear away.

"So strong, I can't wait to meet them either," Margaret smiled at Morgan.

29

———————

Sara stood in the kitchen and watched as her sisters talked to the men in their lives and including Ross and Margaret. She was overcome by the change that had taken over her life in the last 6 months. Going from a big house that was quiet too much to having to dig chairs out of the garage to accommodate everyone.

The table was set, Sara and Kadie each bringing a pan of Lasagna to the table just as Graham walked in the back door.

"Just in time Peterson," Jared said from his seat. He caught Kadie's eye and winked at her. She smiled and walked over to Graham.

"Hi," she said.

"Hi," Graham smiled down at her.

"Everyone this is Graham Peterson. I like him so be nice to him." Kadie pulled him to the last empty seat saved just for him. "What can I get you to drink?" She asked resting a hand on his back.

"Just water, please."

"Do you have to go back?" Andrew asked as he added salad to his plate.

"No just want to keep a sharp mind." Graham smiled

"Oh, loosens up, if you have the rest of the night off, relax. No need to wait for something to go wrong" Ross said lifting his whiskey in cheers.

"Alright then a beer please Kadie," Graham said with a smile.

Dinner was wonderful, everyone ate and talked and ate some more. Sara had put a few big bowls of her popcorn on the table getting everyone's endless praise on how wonderful it was. Morgan was next to Kadie, at one point Sara noticed the two in a hushed conversation. She was about to ask what was going on, but her attention was pulled to Ross and a question he had about the bakery. When she turned her attention back to her sisters, they were in a group conversation with Andrew, Graham, and Abby. She grabbed Jared's hand under the table and just watched the room. She rested back on Kadie and Morgan.

Kadie seemed to have her hands on her lap, and it looked like Morgan was holding Kadie's hand. Morgan closed her eyes when Andrew turned to talk to Abby. Sara watched as her sisters were working together. Morgan was squeezing Kadie's hand under the table. Kadie was keeping track of her phone, in her other hand. Abby was distracting Andrew so he wouldn't notice Morgan breathing through the contractions. Sara caught Morgan's eye and smiled; Morgan turned to Kadie who then looked at Sara. Kadie nodded to Sara with a big smile, Sara let her breath out.

"What's going on?" Jared asked.

"What?" Sara looked at Jared. "What do you mean?"

"You just let your breath out, you do that just before you gear yourself up for something." He said smiling at her.

"I need you to distract Andrew for a bit, why don't they guys head out back and enjoy a cigar or something? Light the fire pit, anything." Sara waited for Jared to ask why. He just stared into her eyes and then smiled.

"I can do that." He looked at his dad who had been talking with Margaret. "Hey, dad do you still carry a few extra cigars?"

"I do." He eyed his son "Why"

"I have an inkling for one. Andrew, do you want to join me? Graham, Eddie?"

"Sure, why not" Andrew said. The men all stood and moved to the back yard.

"Ladies let's move to the living room," Sara said as she stood up.

"I think I should be getting on my way," Margaret said as she too stood up.

"No, I think you should stay," Morgan said standing up and moving to the living room. Kadie sat next to Morgan. Abby brought in Morgan's glass of water.

"Honey" Morgan said then shut her eyes and started taking slow deep breaths. Sara watched as Margaret sat on the other side of Morgan and lightly took her hand. "Baby," she said and Kadie tapped her screen. "So, I had this feeling that you needed to be invited to dinner tonight." Morgan smiled at Margaret.

"A woman knows when the time is close. Thank you for the invitation for dinner and stay."

The five continued to talk as Kadie kept track of how far apart the contraction was. After an hour Kadie looked at Sara, Margaret, and Abby. "It's time, Morgan they are five minutes apart."

"I could have told you that," Morgan said snapping at Kadie. She finished her breathing and looked at her sister. "Sorry"

"It's ok you get a pass today. But only for today." Kadie said holding Morgan's hand.

"Where is your bag sweetie?" Abby stood up asking Morgan.

"It's in the closet next to Andrew's bag. When do we tell

him?"

"When do you want to tell him?" Sara asked eyeing her sister. No matter how much her life had changed Morgan was still private. Sara had been surprised that Morgan had let Margaret stay.

"You know what, I think I'm going to go now and meet you at the hospital," Margaret said still holding Morgan's hand. "If that's ok?"

"Yes please," Morgan said smiling.

"Graham and I can meet you there too, Abby and Eddie too." Kadie stood up "I'll go take care of this." She took a few steps then stopped turned and gave the phone to Sara. Just tap the green, and it turns red tap again when it ends." Abby came back in with two bags,

"I'm going to take these with me, ok sweetie?"

"Yep, that's -Honey" Morgan shut her eyes and gripped Margaret's hand.

"Just breath sweetie, you got this," Margaret said soft and soothing. The room stood still until Morgan let out her last breath and said, baby.

"Alright, I'm going to go and see you soon." Margaret stood then last second lend down and kissed Morgan's head. "You got this." She stood and walked straight out the door.

Kadie walked in with Graham, Ross, and Eddie. "So, we're going to go, we'll see you later," Kadie said and Ross stopped and kissed Morgan on the head.

"Let me know when you can and thank you for the wonderful evening." He smiled and walked out.

"Eddie love can you take those bags to the car?" Abby asked then turned to Morgan. "See you in a bit sweetheart."

"I told Jared you were taking care of some things, he said he would check on you soon." Kadie nodded "see you there." Morgan and Sara watched as the four walked out of the house.

"Sara?" Morgan said with a catch in her throat.

"What sweetheart." Sara grabbed her sister's hand.

"I miss mom" Morgan closed her eyes, and a tear ran down her cheek.

"Me too babe, me too. I see her in you, the way you are. Strong, brave, she was fearless at times, and I see the same in you. You are also going to be an amazing mom." Sara whipped the next tear as it ran down Morgan's cheek.

"Do you think she's watching over us?"

"Every day, and especially tonight." Sara took a deep breath "Morgan."

"I know. We need to go." She took a breath. Sara pulled her phone out and texted Jared.

"You guys need to come inside."

"Honey" Morgan kept her eyes close, Sara hit the green tab. They worked together through the contraction. "Baby" Sara tapped the red. When Morgan opened her eyes, Andrew was standing in the doorway.

"I'll go start the truck; do we need to get anything?" Jared asked as he walked to the front door.

"Nope, we have about four minutes to get Morgan to the truck," Sara said. then she noticed that Andrew was still just standing in the doorway. "Andrew.... Andrew?" Andrew snapped out of his daze.

"Ya," he looked at Sara with an almost blank look.

"Are you ok?" Sara asked as she walked over to him.

"Ya," He said just looking at her.

"Ok we have to get Morgan to the truck, we need to take her to have the boys, it's time." Sara kept watching him. She turned to look at Jared as he walked back into the house. "Jared we may have to leave him." She turned back to Andrew hoping he had snapped out of it.

"Go to Morgan and help her to the truck. We will be there in a minute." Jared walked over to Andrew. Sara went back to the couch just as Morgan closed her eyes.

"Honey" She was having a hard time keeping her breathing even.

"You got this sister, just stay with me." Sara sat down next to her, holding her hand, and breathing with Morgan.

"Baby" Morgan said as she exhaled the last breath. "Ok get me to the damn truck." Together Sara and Jared had her on her feet. Jared walked Morgan all the way to the truck.

"Should we leave him?" Jared asked Morgan.

"Yes, he can find his own way. Let's go have these boys." Morgan sat back and Sara moved her hair away from her face.

"Ok," Jared said he shut the door and went to climb into the driver seat. He had the truck in drive and down the street when his phone went off. He passed it to Sara.

"Jared Brook's phone."

"Why did you guys leave me?" Andrew seemed to have snapped out of it.

"We don't have time to wait for you." Sara looked over at Morgan just as she moved into her next contraction. "I got to go" Morgan let out her first scream as Sara hit the end button.

"It's ok baby, just breath." Sara realized that Morgan wasn't breathing. "Morgan, look at me" She yelled at her sister. When Morgan turned to look at her. "Breath you have to breathe for the boys" Morgan nodded her head and started her breathing as the contraction ended.

"Andrew is behind us. For what's it worth." Jared said as he took the last turn to the hospital.

"Ya, that's good, right," Sara said looking at Morgan.

"Ya sure" Morgan had her lend her head back and was resting with her eyes closed.

"Morgan?" Sara watched her sister.

"Not now. Jared are we there yet." Morgan asked.

"Ya babe we are." Just then Jared pulled up to the hospital doors. Kadie had two nurses with a wheelchair waiting for them.

"Oh god bless her," Sara said. Then Kadie opened the door and the nurses moved in to get Morgan out of the truck. "We only have like a minute till the next-" She was cut off as Morgan let out a yell. Sara slid out of the truck and around the nurses who were now holding up a contracting Morgan.

"Morgan, look at me." She waited till Morgan looked at her. "You have to breathe, remember for the boys. Breath with me" Together they worked through the contraction. As soon as she was able to move Morgan was sitting in the wheelchair. The nurses knowing, they didn't have time moved fast. Sara moved just as fast as Morgan. Jared was standing by his truck watching Sara in her element.

"Was your mom like that?" He looked over at Kadie who was standing next to him.

"Yes and no. Mom could make any problem better, but Sara makes the problem not a problem. It's hard to explain." Kadie smiled as Andrew ran up.

"Where is she?" He looked panicked.

"They took her in and up. You better get a fucking grip before you go in there." Jared said looking at his best friend.

"What's your deal." The tone stunned Andrew and shot back temper.

"What's your fucking deal. It's show time and you freeze. Good luck getting in the room." Jared said scowling at Andrew.

"I'm allowed a fucking minute to catch up," Andrew said glaring at Jared.

"Not 10," Jared said adding more anger.

"What would you have done?" Andrew shot back.

"I went and started the truck. I drove them here. I did what I needed to do. I didn't just stand there like an idiot with my thumb up my ass." Jared just watched his best friend. "This is real, they are coming tonight. It's not just playing house anymore. Step up like you said you would or get the fuck out of here."

"I can't believe you, where the hell do you get off? You think because you're with the head of the house you get to call the shots. You are no more a part of their family than I am. I can tell you right now, we're the ones who have been fools." Andrew racked his fingers through his hair.

"When did you talk to him?" Kadie asked in a quiet voice. Jared and Andrew had been so caught up in their fight they forgot Kadie was standing there.

"Who?" Jared looked at Andrew.

"I don't-"

"Lie to me I dare you. You think long and hard about that before you finish that sentence." Kadie's eyes glowed with heat.

"Last week," Andrew said defeated.

"We'll talk about that later. If YOU want to be a part of this family get your ass up there. I guarantee she needs you." Kadie turned to Jared. "Go, park your truck, we'll be on the third floor."

Kadie and Andrew rode up together, not talking. As soon as the doors opened Andrew rushed out. He saw Sara talking to the doctor, he rushed up to them.

"Is she ok?" Andrew asked breathlessly.

"We have her checked in, she is almost 10cm, and everything is looking great for a natural delivery." The doctor nodded, "I'll be by in a bit to check her again."

"Thank you, Dr. Ben," Sara said. She waited till the doctor was out of ear shot. Then she turned back to Andrew with her arms crossed.

"Sara-"

"Save it. She's asking for you. Your mom and Abby are with her. I'll tell you this once, if you don't want to, or you have any doubts. Don't go into that room. This is when you walk the walk." Sara stared at him. He could feel it go right through him.

"I'm going in to be with her Sara." Andrew walked past her and into the room. Kadie walked up to Sara.

"We have a problem"

"Oh, I'm sure we do." Sara looked at her sister. "What?"

"Dad" Kadie let out her breath.

"Oh," Sara said as she looked at the door Andrew had just gone through. "We'll take care of that later. Tonight, we have our nephews to meet." Sara saw Jared in the waiting room with Eddie. "I'll be right back." Sara walked to the waiting room and Jared.

"How is Morgan?" Jared asked as Eddie and Kadie went to sit down.

"She's fine, we have to talk later." Sara looks Jared in the eyes, she loved how they saw her. How she had come to do depend on the strength she found in them.

"I know. I don't know about what." He added quickly as Sara's eyes grew. "Tonight is about Morgan and the boys. We will find time to talk later." Jared pulled Sara into a hug. "Everything is going to be ok." Sara closed her eyes and soaked in the warmth and hoped that he was right.

"Sara," Margaret said from behind Jared. Sara and Jared pulled apart. "I'm sorry, Morgan needs you."

"Ok" Sara looked up at Jared.

"Go, see you later." He kissed her hand before he let her go. He watched as she made her way quickly to Morgan's room. Then he turned to Kadie.

"Sara is going to talk to me later, anything you want to add before she does?" Jared simply waited for her response. Graham came in carrying drinks.

"What's going on?" Graham asked as he set the drinks down on the little table next to Kadie.

"Nothing," she said shaking it off. "If Sara said she's talking to you later then she'll talk to you later." Kadie turned her attention to Graham. "You got my favorite."

Jared knew that Kadie was going to stay tight lipped, so he settled himself to wait.

30

SARA PUSHED the door open to the sounds of Morgan ripping into Andrew.

"I CAN'T BELIEVE YOU WOULD LISTEN TO THAT SON OF A BITCH" Morgan yelled.

"I'm sorry. How many times do I need to say that? I'm sorry." Andrew was standing at the foot of the bed. I didn't realize what was going on till it was too late." He raked his hands through his hair. "Morgan" he walked to the side of the bed. "You are all I have ever wanted. You are who I want for my whole life. You are my life, no matter good or bad. You know that in your heart, you know that."

"I just don't understand why you didn't tell me before," Morgan said with tears running down her face. "Hold that thought." She started to breathe as the contraction took over. She grabbed Andrew's hand when he reached for her. Abby who had stayed quiet was on her other side. Telling her to breathe and that it would be over soon. As Morgan's body relaxed, she looked at Andrew.

"Well?"

"Morgan, do we really need to get into this right now?" He asked in a pleading tone.

"Yes, because I need to know why you didn't tell me that my horrible excuse for a father came to see you." Morgan tossed the blankets off her. She turned to Sara. "Did you know he was in town? You always know." Morgan closed her eyes, she shifted in her bed.

"I didn't know," Sara said then she looked at Abby.

"No, I didn't know either. Morgan, it doesn't matter, he doesn't matter." Abby said being reassuring.

"Yes, it does." Morgan started to say but stopped as the contraction moved over her. She let a few yells out. "Yes, it does" She started when the contraction was over. "He put doubt on us, on Andrew and me."

They all looked over as a nurse came in to check on Morgan.

"How we are doing in here?" She walked over and checked the computers. "I would like to check you." She pulled on gloves as she walked to sit on the other side of the bed. "Just breath for me honey." After a minute she pulled away and was walking to the door.

"Is everything ok?' Sara asked before the nurse walked out.

"I need to get the doctor she's ready." the nurse smiled and sailed out the door,

"Ready? Ready for what?" Morgan asked looking at Sara.

"I'm going to go out on a limb here and say she means you're ready to meet your boys."

"Oh, thank god, It's almost over." Morgan looked over at Andrew "I'm sorry. I should have told you about him. We don't talk to him; we don't see him. He isn't a part of our lives."

"I'll forgive you if you forgive me."

"Deal-" A contraction came swiftly; they were trying to get Morgan to breath when the doctor came in.

"Yep, sounds about time. Morgan are you ready to push?" the doctor asked getting his gown and gloves on.

"No, I need Kadie." She said winded as if she just ran the mile.

"Are you sure honey?" A nurse that had just joined the party gave Morgan a sideways look. "You already have so many in here." Before the Doctor or Sara could say anything Morgan too calmly looked at the nurse.

"I am about to bring two more, so why don't you stop counting and go get my sister." Morgan smiled as she watched the nurse leave.

The room changed around them, nurses were in and out. Morgan's bed was changed to better accommodate the pushing mother. Kadie walked in and fell in line next to Andrew.

"Alright Morgan when you feel the next contraction, I need you to push, we are going to count to 10 you take a breath, and if you still feel the contraction you push for another 10. Are you ready?" Morgan grabbed Sara's hand, then Andrew's she looked at Abby then Kadie.

"Yes, I am."

Jared, Eddie, and Margret were sitting, Graham was pacing the waiting room when they heard feet moving quickly down the hall. They all turned to find the girls' faces bright walking into the room. Jared and Eddie shot up just in time to catch Abby and Sara into big hugs.

"How did she do?" Jared asked.

"She did amazing. The boys are beautiful, so little, and just wonderful." Abby said with a huge smile on her face.

"Margret, they asked for you," Sara said smiling. Margret stood up quickly.

"Really?" She asked in surprise.

"Really, go on in and meet your grandsons." Sara moved to give her a hug.

"I'll be back" Margret moved quickly down the hall.

Morgan was resting in bed holding one of her sons. Tears were silently running down her cheeks, she looked over at Andrew who was holding her other son. She watched Andrew; he was so intent on the little boy in his arms. He too couldn't hold back a few tears. Andrew looked over at her.

"You did amazing, they are both perfect." He reached out and grabbed her hand and gave it a squeeze. "I'm in love with you, and I'm in love with these boys. I am so sorry for earlier."

"I know you are, I'm sorry for earlier too. We need to talk about it." Morgan and Andrew both looked as the door opened and Margret walked in.

"Oh, my god." She said as she took in the room. Andrew stood up.

"Mom," he said as she walked over to him. "We would like you to meet Murphy John Abbot." He passed over the sleeping baby. Margret smiled and held the baby close, she soaked in the little face as she sat down.

"Morgan, you did an amazing job, my dear, he is so beautiful." She looked over at Morgan who was wiping yet another tear.

"Thank you. Andrew wanted his dad to be a part of the new stage of his life, and yours."

"It's perfect," Margret said Andrew went and sat on the foot of Morgan's bed just watching his mom hold this new little man in his life. He looked over at Morgan when he felt her shift in her bed. She was trying to pass him his second son. He reached out and like passing a football he pulled his son to his chest.

"Mom" he waited till she looked up at him. "This is Matthew Cooper Abbot." Margret stood and passed Murphy to Morgan then took up Matthew. Morgan watched as Margret fall in love for the second time in a matter of minutes.

Sara sat with Jared his arm laying across the back of her chair and she leaned into him. Abby, Kadie, and Sara went over the labor and delivery in awe. Sara's life would be forever changed by watching not just one, but two boys come into this world. Oh, how life had changed.

"I'm so glad we don't have to go into the shop tomorrow," Kadie said snuggling into Graham.

"Me too," Abby said playing with Eddie's fingers.

"So, I think we need to have a family meeting," Sara said looking at Abby and Kadie. "As soon as Morgan is home."

'I agree" Kadie said she turned to Graham "you need to be there too."

"Wherever you need me I'll be there." He lent in and kissed her forehead.

"Has the time come?" Eddie asked looking at Abby.

"Ya, it has," she said. Then looked up to see Margret walk into the room.

"Guys they want to see you, I'm going to go home and come back in the morning." Margret walked over to Sara and pulled her into a hug.

"Little did I know when I met you, that we would become family." Margret held tighter for just a moment and whispered "Be watchful"

Margret pulled away and moved to the others in the room before Sara could ask what she had meant by that. Jared watched Sara's face as she watched Margret.

"What's the matter?" He whispered as the rest of them headed to Morgan's room.

"Later" She shook it off "Come meet the babies."

31

———

THEY ALL WALKED into Morgan's room and found only Morgan and Andrew.

"What's going on?" Sara asked as she looked from Morgan to Andrew.

"The nurses came to take the babies for tests and baths," Morgan said looking at Sara. "We all need to talk."

"We are, once you're home," Kadie said with her arms crossed.

"No. now. We always push it to the back burner. We need to deal with it now." Morgan said then looked at Sara.

"Are you sure?" Sara closed her eyes when she got the nod from Morgan. Letting her breath out she began. "Adam Carter is our father. He met our mom when she was young and dumbed her words, and she didn't talk about him much. They had a fast romance and before they knew it Abby was on her way. He moved them into a little house a few states away. He didn't want grandma intruding on their business, and he had better work not here. So, mom stayed home, and he worked. Times were good and rough, then I came. Mom was so happy to have two daughters, but Adam wasn't. Morgan came and things got worst. When Kadie came, he left."

"In the handful of years that mom didn't talk to grandma, he had isolated her to the point she didn't drive anymore. It made his just walking out more than just a slap in the face. Mom had no idea what to do. It took her some time, but she finally called grandma. She came and got all five of us and brought us home. We didn't see him again till grandma died and he came sniffing for money. By then mom had changed our names when she found out that they were never legally married."

"He has tried to see us a few times, blows into town stirs up trouble, and leaves. The last time that I saw him or heard from him was a year after mom died. He was looking for money, and when he doesn't get what he's after he blows up. He says mean horrible things, how we made him leave. We made him feel unwanted, we didn't welcome him into the family." Sara took a deep breath and looked at Andrew.

"I am so sorry about this. What and how did you talk to him?" Sara asked.

"I was walking into the station one day, and this guy had asked how Morgan was. I didn't know him and acted dumb at first. He said he heard that I had moved in with Morgan Matthews into the family home. He asked me how it was working out for me to live in a house run by women." Andrew stood and walked to the window. "He told me that I didn't belong with you guys, that you were using me because that's just what you all do. That you had used him, then kicked him out of your life when you were done with him." He turned and looked at Morgan. "I don't know how or why I let a stranger affect me so much."

"Last week" Morgan looked at him "I knew there was something going on with you, I should have asked. I thought it was the workload or stress from the boys coming. I'm sorry too"

Andrew walked over to her and grabbed her hand, lifting it to his mouth.

"What is he even doing here?" Kadie asked the room.

"I don't know, and I don't know how to find out," Sara said looking at her. Jared sat and thought about it for a moment. He was used to taking pieces of information and putting them together to get the picture.

"Hey Graham, what ever happened to those thugs that tried for Kadie?" Jared asked.

"They're in the county. Why?" Graham looked at him with a frown.

"Just wanted to know." he looked over at Abby "Anything kind of weird or scary happen with you guys lately?

"No," Abby said then looked at Eddie. Eddie looked from Abby to Jared

"What is it?" Jared asked.

"A few weeks ago, I took Abby's car in to get the oil changed, I about ran into the shop I take it to. I asked the guys to check the breaks. They laughed at me because I had gotten the breaks done before the wedding. When I went and picked it up, they said the brake lines had been cut." Eddie looked at Jared "Before you get all huffy, I didn't know how to report it. The car is either at home or at the bakery. I don't know who it could have been. I don't know when it was done."

"Jared, what are you thinking?" Sara asked as Jared pushed out of the chair and walked to the window.

"Something bad is going to happen. Andrew, go check the nursery." Andrew didn't hesitate he was up and out of the room. "Graham calls some guys to go drive by the bakery, the house, and Eddie's place." Jared took a deep breath as Graham walked out of the room. "You three need to stay here with Morgan. Eddie, stay with them."

"What are you going to do?' Sara asked walking up to him.

"When Andrew gets back, I'm heading to the county" He

looked down at her. She saw something in his eyes. She had seen hints of it when he was fresh from the job.

"You think it's all connected," Sara said reading him like an open book.

"I really hope it's not." Jared slid his hand up to cup her face. "I love you"

"I love you too," She reached up and pressed the hand that was on her cheek.

Andrew came walking back in breaking the moment Sara and Jared were having.

"They are both there, I told the nurse that you wanted to feed them so she should be bringing them in," Andrew told Morgan.

"That's fine, I'm not going to let them out of my sight again." Just then two nurses came in with both boys.

"Visiting hours are almost over." One nurse said as she looked around the room.

'Some of us are leaving," Jared said trying to reassure her

"Do you need any help getting started?" The other nurse asked

"No, I'll be fine. Thank you." Morgan said readjusting herself so that she could feed her boys

"Well, I'm going to take a walk," Eddie said. Just then Graham walked back in.

"Alright well, our ride is here," Jared said. "Come on Andrew let's go get you that welcome to fatherhood drink" Jared stopped by Sara and kissed her good-bye. "Stay here and wait for my call" he whispered to her.

By the time he was walking to the door, Andrew and Graham had bid their goodbyes too.

"Why do I feel like we just sent our boys off to war," Kadie said when the room just held the sisters and brothers

"Because we did," Sara said trying to relax as her mind went a million miles an hour.

32

———

THE THREE MEN climbed into Jared's truck. They didn't say anything as they headed to the county. It was a bit late but the guard being a good friend of Andrew and Jared let them in to see the guy who had slipped the drugs to Kadie.

Jared noted the guy walking into the conference area was just a kid. Well old enough to know better. Parker Haste sat down in front of Jared and Andrew.

"You pull me out of bed for chat gentlemen?" Parker said with eye roll.

"Yep, we did, we want to know why you went after that girl. I mean there were so many others in the bar that night." Andrew said with cool confidence.

"She's just a girl, millions like her everywhere," Parker said leaning back in his chair.

"Do you know what you're looking at here, and you being the one who physically put the drugs in her drink?' Jared asked deciding to mirror Parker's laid back, don't care attitude.

"I got a new lawyer coming, suppose to meet him tomorrow so if you guys want to come back tomorrow introduce yourselves," Parker said with a slight grin.

"How did you get a new lawyer? I didn't think you had that kind of money." Andrew said trying to push a button.

"I've got friends in high places what can I say." He threw his hands up in a what the hell jester.

"So, was it this friend that asked you to go after the cute little thing in the bar?" Jared asked then smiled as he saw the slights shift in parkers deminer. "Interesting," Jared said and looked at Andrew

"I have to ask do you know the name of this new hot shot lawyer coming to save you?" Andrew asked.

"Why should I tell you?" Parker asked frowning.

"Come on Parker we just want to know, that way we can prepare ourselves. What you got up you sleeve?" Jared asked. His tone implying Parker would be doing Jared a favor.

"Alright fine. Edison St. Clair." Parker smiled like he just won something. It took all the training Jared and Andrew had to keep from showing any kind of reaction. They didn't even look at each other.

"Never heard of him," Andrew said sitting back for the first time in the meeting crossing his arms over his chest.

"The hell you haven't, He is one of the best. I'll be walking out of here by tomorrow night." Parker said leaning back as well, only his deminer was in confidence.

"So let me get this straight, your friend in high places wants you to drug some girl. Have a good time with her and if you're caught will send the best lawyer money can buy?" Jared asked as he rested his elbows on the table.

"More or less," Parker said with a shrug. With a sigh he continued "I was told the girl could be a party favor, I didn't mean to get my boys busted."

"Do they get the fancy lawyer too?" Andrew asked working like hell to keep it together, knowing Jared was struggling as well.

"Well, yeah we all get to get out of here," Parker said losing some of that confidence he had before.

"Good thing, can you imagine what your boys would do to you if you got out and they didn't?" Jared said then whistled. Both Jared and Andrew enjoyed watching a pale face give way to fear.

"That's not going to happen," Parker said with some anger in his voice.

"You hope it doesn't." Andrew looked at Jared. "You know this friend of his could totally be blowing smoke up his ass."

"Ya, they could be" Jared looked over at Andrew "Let's go, we'll come back in a few days to check on you. Maybe." They stood to leave.

"You'll see, I'll be out by dinner tomorrow." Parker stood as well, mad that he was talking to their backs.

Jared and Andrew didn't say anything till they got back in the truck. Jared just sat there for a moment to collect his thoughts.

"We need to go back to the hospital," Andrew said

"Yeah we do," Jared said as he started the truck.

When Jared and Andrew walked out, they saw Graham on the phone pacing by the truck. He looked up at them as they approached. He disconnected his call.

"What do you know?" Jared asked.

"They did a drive by, all was quiet. I had a few units sit on the house and bakery. I just got off the phone with the guys at the bakery. They noticed a few guys walking up, checking the front door then headed to the back. The other car that was parked back there waited till the crowbar was out and they were trying the door before they walked up on them. One of the dumb shits took a swing at Martin. By then Prince and Waite had moved to the front of the building and caught the guy who was making a run for it. What the hell is going on?" Graham asked looking at Andrew and then Jared.

"Get in we're going back to the hospital," Jared said and moved to the front seat.

"Is Eddie still here?" Andre asked.

When they were back at the hospital the nurse tried to give them a hard time, to which they flashed their badges, and she backed off. They walked into the room as quietly as possible.

"Is it safe to come in?" Andrew asked as he was leading the way.

"Yep, it's ok," Morgan said from her bed. Andrew walked over to her she was holding one of the babies. He looked down at the sweet boy and kissed the top of Morgan's head.

"So, what's going on?" Sara said from the chair next to the bed holding the other baby.

Jared looked the room over; Abby was sitting between Eddie and Kadie. Then he moved his eyes back to Sara.

"This is what we know." Jared looked at Graham who gave him the go ahead with a nod.

"Some guys tried to break into the bakery tonight. As we had put some eyes on the place, they didn't get in. We have a few units sitting on the house tonight as well. As of right now, all seems good there." Jared said and then turned to Eddie.

"You have a new client you're seeing tomorrow?" Jared asked and watched Eddie go still.

"I do, how do you know about it?"

"First tell me what and how you came to know him?" Jared said and watched the room turn in his direction.

"My mother called me and asked me to take it on pro-bono. I haven't read the police report yet, I don't know the details. All she told me was this guy was in the county and didn't belong there. He's a friend of a friend, a good guy." Eddie said not seeing how it connected to what was going on.

"Parker Haste" Andrew began, and Eddie nodded his head in agreement. "Is the guy who drugged Kadie's drink." The room froze.

"What do you mean?" Kadie said standing up her eyes starting to rage.

"The night we went and got you from the bar, four guys followed me out. I got you locked in Jared's truck by the time they were on me. After we got them to the station, they all had something to say, and Haste is the one who confessed to putting the drugs in your cup." Graham said walking over to Kadie and pulled her into him.

"I don't get how Eddie is involved in this?" Abby asked.

"We went and met with Haste tonight, he told us that he would be out by dinner tomorrow night. That the friend in high places, the one who told him who to drug, also got him the lawyer that would get him out." Jared said looking from Eddie to Abby finally resting on Sara.

"So" Sara started her voice so calm it made the hair on Jared's neck stand up "You're telling me that Kadie was attacked on purpose, my father is back in town, Abby's breaks were cut and two guys tried to break into our bakery tonight?" Sara's eyes were locked on Jared.

"Yes," Jared said letting out his breath.

"What do we do, what can we do?" Morgan asked after a moment, noticing something unspoken pass from Sara to Jared.

"You, Andrew, and the boys stay here," Sara said looking at Jared.

"I'll get a few guys to come to sit watch," Graham said moving away from Kadie, heading to the door.

"And Abby's," Sara said, getting a nod before Graham left the room.

"We have to do something tonight," Morgan said looking at everyone.

"Yes, we do, we are going to go home. You and Andrew are going to rest and take care of your boys." Sara said looking at Morgan.

"You can't be serious." Morgan shot back.

"Morgan your main priority is being a mom and getting as much rest as you can so you can be home. I need you to do that." Sara said watching Morgan.

"You-" Morgan started then Sara cut her off.

"Morgan" Sara started then sat on the edge of the bed, still holding a sleeping baby. "What have I always done?" The sisters looked at each other for a moment then Morgan let out her breath.

"Taken care of things," Morgan said letting out a breath.

"Why?"

"It's what you do, for us," Morgan said her eyes beginning to fill.

"That's right, so when I tell you to worry about being a mom, and not about the hot mess around us it's because I know what I'm doing." Sara gave her a reassuring smile.

"And you're going to take care of it," Morgan said and watched Jared move to stand behind Sara.

"We're going to take care of it," Jared said and kissed Sara's head.

The room was quiet for a moment then Graham came back in.

"I have two sitting on Abby and Eddie, they are heading there now. I would like it if you would let them sweep through the house first." Graham said looking at Abby, and Eddie.

"Sounds good, we'll head home," Eddie said standing and holding a hand out for Abby. She made her way over to Sara and Morgan. Giving Morgan a half hug, and then Sara.

"We'll call as soon as we get home," Abby said to Sara before she let go.

"Thank you," Sara said and then watched them leave.

"You called for two to come here, right?" Andrew asked looking at Graham.

"Yes, and they are going to stick with the boys. Anytime they leave the room, the officers are with them. I cleared it with the nursing staff." Graham said holding hands with Kadie.

"Who did you send?" Andrew asked.

"Martin and Willis," Graham said.

"Good men," Jared said He looked down at Sara who was looking a the little baby in her arms. He felt a pull on his heart. Their life right now was so crazy, yet he couldn't wait to see their baby in her arms.

"Ok, guys let's go home," Jared said running a hand down Sara's back. She nodded and Andrew moved in to take the sleeping little boy.

"Should I be worried that after all that the boys didn't wake up?" Morgan said watch Andrew.

"Honey" Andrew started as he settled in the chair. "I would be more worried if they did." Kadie gave a little giggle at that. Sara smiled and looked over to see Morgan smiling too.

"You're right." Sara let out a breath.

"Ok we will see you tomorrow, and hopefully by then the doctors can tell us when you get to go home." Sara leaned over and half hugged Morgan.

"I love you," Morgan said softly.

"I love you too sister." Sara straightened and made her way to stand by the door. Once goodbye was said Jared, Sara, Kadie, and Graham made their way out of the room. The guys stopped briefly to talk to the officers just outside.

"We'll meet you at home" Sara had called after Kadie and Graham when they were outside and heading to their vehicles. Sara and Jared didn't speak till they were moving.

"I knew she was going to make her move; I didn't think she would go as far as she did," Sara said looking out the window.

"I didn't think so either," Jared said and reached for her hand. "I need to know something."

"What?" Sara said looking at him.

"Are we ok? Do you still want to be with me?" Jared would understand if she never wanted to see him again.

"Jared WE are fine, and absolutely I want to be with you. Do you want to be with me?" She asked in return.

"Of course, I do, it's just-" Jared started then stopped

"No, you don't get to do that. Your mother is the one to blame. All because she didn't like me, she didn't want you to be happy with me. She has struck out at every one of my sisters, and Abby is married to one of her friend's nephews. I'm sorry to say but I think she is a little crazy." Sara said not taking her eyes off him, as he navigated them home.

"No, you are absolutely right. We just need to figure out how to handle it," he said resolved.

"Tomorrow," Sara said looking over at Jared.

"What did Margrett say to you before she left the hospital?" Jared asked remembering that he wanted to ask Sara about it later.

"To be watchful," Sara said as she looked over at him.

"Interesting," Jared said as they pulled up into the driveway, Graham and Kadie right behind them. "You girls go inside I want to talk to the officers," Jared said after everyone had gotten out of their vehicles.

"Ok," Sara said as she looped an arm with Kadie and together, they went inside. Stopping just inside the door. Dinner was still everywhere; they had left so quickly. Sara and Kadie looked at each other and smiled. Knowing neither one would be able to settle, it didn't matter how tired the other one was. They couldn't or wouldn't leave it the way it was. They moved to clear the table first, Kadie turned the music on low as she walked by the stereo. By the time the guys came in Kadie was just shutting the dishwasher and turning it on and Sara was rinsing the last backing dish.

"Couldn't wait till morning?" Graham said with a smile as he walked over to Kadie.

"Not if I wanted to get any sleep tonight," Kadie said with a telling smile, Sara rolled her eyes when she caught the look on Graham's face.

"Goodnight you two," Sara said letting her soapy water out. She felt Jared slide up behind her as the feet on the stairs moved away.

"Come on let me take you to bed," Jared said softly and kissed her neck right under her ear. They both knew that was a favorite spot.

"If you insist." Sara let Jared take up the stair, where he made her forget all about the day.

33

———

Sara woke up slowly, she was home, and safe. When she opened her eyes, Jared was lying next to her. He was on his back staring up at the ceiling.

"Penny for your thoughts?" Sara asked softly.

"I have to get her to confess to everything. I need to talk to my dad, and I-"

"We," she said softly cutting him off. He looked over at her. Here was his girl, his strong, independent girl. The love of his life. She had let him into her world, let him help her with the weight she carried. Now she was telling him that he didn't have to carry his weight without her.

"We," he said smiling. "We need to come up with a plan."

"I think I've got one. But first I need a shower and coffee." Sara smiled at him

"I'm in need of the same," Jared said and moved out of bed. "Will you join me?" he asked and had Sara smiling as she did just that.

A few days later Helen was stilling at her desk in her home office when her phone rang. She waited for one of the staff to pick it up. Moments later one of her house keepers told her it was Jared on the phone.

"Hello, Son," she said in a short tone.

"Hi, mom" Jared replied.

"Is everything ok?" She hadn't heard from him in weeks, and she still held some of the anger for how he had acted the last time they saw each other.

"Yes, I just wanted to call and tell you. You were right." Helen brightened at his words. She couldn't help the smile that formed. She had done it.

"Right about what my darling," She asked trying to sound coy.

"Sara. It turns out you were right" Jared said his voice heavy with disappointment.

"I usually am, she was no good for you son. She didn't deserve you. Now tell me what happen?" She said then cut him off her mind coming up with yet another brilliant plan. "No wait, how about we meet for lunch tomorrow, I can see if Meg would like to join us." Helen was all but jumped up and down.

"That sounds good mom, just let me know the details." Jared said, "Look mom I've got to go."

"Absolutely my dear. Talk soon" Helen disconnected and called Meg.

"It worked my dear, our plans worked. He wants to have lunch with us tomorrow. Please say you can make it." Helen held her breath for just a moment. They had worked so hard for so long.

"Oh, I'll be there, I wouldn't miss this for the world," Meg said happily.

"Wonderful see you tomorrow my darling," Helen said then hung up, she thought about calling Ross to join them. She wanted to show him how well Meg and Jared went together. Ross was off on another one of his business trips. He would see the error of his ways when he was back and could see for himself that she had been right. Helen was on cloud nine for the rest of the evening.

When Helen walked into the club the next day, she felt light and happy, she greeted everyone with huge smiles and light kisses. Her world had finally righted itself. She had just sat down when she saw Jared walk in. She hopped up as if her chair was made of a giant spring. She came around the table to greet him.

"How are you mother," He asked leaning down to kiss her cheek.

"Oh, Jared I'm so happy that you saw the error in your ways and have finally come to your senses. Meg is a wonderful girl and the two of you will have a wonderful life together." Helen moved back to her chair.

"Right, well I just hope she can deal with me being a detective," Jared said sitting down and looking at the menu.

"Well, she and I have talked about that. Jared, it isn't fair of you to be working those kinds of hours, you need a simple job that doesn't call you away at all hours day and night. I'm sure we can talk to your father, and he can find something better suited for you." Helen was too busy looking at her menu to see the anger flash into Jared's eyes. He read the menu over and over till he was sure he was in control again.

"I have to ask, what happened with Sara? I want to be sure that you are done with her for good. Meg doesn't deserve the back and forth." Helen said as she grabbed her ice water.

"She started having all these problems, her sisters included." Jared shook his head and reached for his water. He needed to get through this lunch.

"A family like that has lots of problems." She shook her head and rolled her eyes. Jared could see the 'I'm better than them' on his mother's face.

"You wouldn't believe some of their problems," Jared said going back to his menu.

"Try me" Helen smiled.

"Kadie the youngest of the sisters, I don't believe you ever met her. Anyways she is always partying, always going out, coming in at dawn just so irresponsible. Sara would just wave it off like no big deal. Well, one night some girl of one of her ex's slipped her something in her drink. Sara was called in the middle of the night to go her from the bar." Jared shook his head as if in disbelief.

"Sounds like she got what she deserved," Helen said so matter of fact it almost did Jared in. "Didn't I hear that it was a guy and that he got caught?" Helen asked.

"Well, all she remembered when she came too was the ex's girl." Jared was studying his menu, but he could feel his mother's temper rise.

"It wasn't the ex's girl, for crying out loud. If that was the case, then Parker wouldn't have ended up in jail, him and his loudmouth." Jared looked at his mother. She too was reading her menu and from the look of it, she didn't even know she had made such a slip up.

"When is Meg coming?" Jared asked looking at his mother in a whole new light.

"Oh, she'll be here." Helen waved her hand "Tell me what else happened?"

"Their dad came back into town; he had a heart to heart with Andrew. Andrew broke things off with Morgan. So now Sara is mad at me for Andrew doing what he did." He said waving his hand like his mother did.

"Oh yes, I heard about that. Margret called me and filled me in on all that trouble. She's just as relieved her son got out of raising kids that weren't even his." She took another sip of water. As soon as the waiter arrive, she was going to order some Champaign. "What else happened?" She poked.

"You can't really be this interested?" Jared asked.

"Of Couse I am, I want to know all about it." Helen smiled at him.

"Alright, Abby the oldest sister, the one who married Andrew's cousin."

"Edison?"

"Ya, so she was having to work at the bakery for months because Morgan couldn't"

"What kind of family makes their own sister give up her great career to work in the family bakery," She asked cutting him off.

"Well, her tires got slashed and she couldn't go in."

"Oh, I was told it was her break," Helen said with a questioning look on her face.

"Whatever it was, Sara's complaining about this and that. I just thought we were going to have a good time. Then before I know it, we're talking all this family drama and it was just too much." Jared sat back and looked at his mother. For a moment he couldn't believe how ignorant she was. He was a man of the law, and she was confessing all her sins. He knew that is what he wanted; he just couldn't believe she was giving it up so easily.

"She doesn't deserve you. She doesn't deserve that bakery." Helen said then looked around to see if anyone was close enough to overhear them.

"Well, she's got it-" Jared started.

"Not for long," Helen said smiling. Jared had seen that smile before and it had ice running up his spine.

"What do you mean?" He asked looking directly at her.

"I'm helping an old friend get back what he is owed," Helen said picking her menu up.

"Old friend what old friend?" Jared asked, still not liking the direction she was heading in.

"Let's just say the bakery is going to the other side of the family." She said the words so simply it made Jared's stomach flip.

"There is no" Jared stopped for a minute "Their father, how do you know their father?"

"From school way back when. It was before I knew your father. His parents split up and he had to move. I can't tell you how surprised I was when I got that tad bit of information. I called him up and he told me all about how All the Mathew women had done him wrong over the years. Anyways back to the bakery, I'm just waiting on a bit more information, then I'm going to back him as he takes them for everything those silly girls have. I'm so glad that you came to your senses Jared I wouldn't have wanted you to be around when I destroyed them." Helen said then looked around, she wanted that drink.

"I'm here now so you don't have to do what you're planning on doing," Jared said looking at his mother, trying to find the woman he knew and not seeing anything at all.

"Things are already in motion my dear. They won't have a dime by the end of the week" She said so sure of herself, and the plans she had.

"I don't get it?" Jared asked taking another sip of water. He needed a minute to get his mind back on the task at hand. At this point, if he wasn't more careful, he was going to blow the whole thing.

"Well, Meg knows people who know how to check up on money accounts. She just asked one of her old friends to go in and move all their money into an account I set up for myself. Then I'm going to give it all to their father and he is going to take them to court. With no money and no defense, he will win the business and the house." Helen looked around again. She didn't see a waiter in sight.

"Wow, all because I didn't want to be with Meg." Jared sat back in his chair. He didn't care anymore if she had more to say. She had confessed to Kadie, Morgan, Abby, and Sara. Then he remembered the guys at the bakery. "So, he's just going to take over the bakery. They must get their talent from him then."

"Are you kidding me, he doesn't want it. He just doesn't want the girls to have it. No see, he was going to get someone to break into it. They wouldn't be in it, and with his takeover, he would get the insurance pay out. Hell, he might even be able to make it look like the girls did it. Can you please call for a waiter or something I need some wine?" Helen looked at him smiling. "Or maybe Champaign as we're celebrating" That was it, he had gotten all he needed.

"Did it ever occur to you that I was happy?" Jared asked her.

"You could never be happy with a girl like Sara. I know what's best for you, I always have, and I always will." Helen said looking around. She hadn't noticed Jared going still.

"You were going to destroy her just because I wanted to be with her?" Jared asked, feeling so tired suddenly.

"Oh, Jared let it go, you came to your senses just like I knew you would. Now we can move on from this, you and Meg will have the life you deserve, and you'll work for your father. I've allowed you all these years. It's time to take your place in this family." She said it with a matter-of-fact tone.

Jared just sat there for a moment; he took a long look at his mother. "You should have just let me be happy." Jared took a drink from his water; he knew his dad was waiting outside with the team listening to his conversation with Helen. He knew the moment his father walked into the room. He watched his mother's eyes light up.

"You came back early," She started as he walked up to the table. Ross laid a hand on Jared's shoulder while Helen kept talking "Ross it's wonderful. Jared left that horrible girl and is going to marry Meg. Everything worked out just like I planned it would." She smiled at her husband and then her son. It took her a moment to realize they weren't as happy as she was.

"What's the matter?" Helen asked confusion on her face.

"I know what you did, I am embarrassed to know you." Ross started and held up a hand to stop Helen from interrupting him. "We're getting a divorce; I'm selling the house. I never want to see you or hear from you again." With that Ross turned and walked away. Helen sat there completely dumbfounded.

"What?" she said watching her husband walk away.

At that moment four officers came into the room and arrested Helen Brooks. They cuffed her, and read her, her rights. Jared thought he would never forget that moment. The country club all watching as his mother lost her shit being walked out in cuffs. Once they were outside the cop cars with their lights on drew more attention. Helen froze as she saw Meg sitting in one of the cop car's back seats. She refused to look at Helen. Helen began fighting again telling two officers to take their hand off of her. Then she saw Adam in the back of another cop car, he too didn't look at her. Everything in her body went cold. Once she was in the car, she looked out to see who was watching, and there they were. Ross, Jared, and Sara were standing together talking, they didn't give her a second glance as she was driven away.

34

———

Helen didn't know how long she had been in jail; it had felt like forever before one of the guards came to tell her she had a visitor.

"It's about time my lawyer got here," Helen said as she was led to a room. When she walked in, she froze. "I have nothing to say to you." She said turning and tried to walk out the door. The guard however walked her to the chair opposite Sara, making Helen sit down.

"That's fine, but I have some things to say to you. I went back and forth on whether I should press charges or not. I mean, after all, you are the mother of the man I love. That might make family gathering a little awkward. But then I listen to the tape of you telling Jared that my sisters got what they deserved, drugged, dumped, and almost in a car crash. See you could have messed with just me, I expected it. The moment you went for my family and the life that we built, I knew I had to take care of it. I had help of course, and to be honest it was a lot easier than I thought it would be. Jared bugged your house phone, with permission from Ross. That led to how much Meg was involved, also very helpful. Then there was my father, who is singing his head off. Just a heads up both have said it was all your idea." Sara took a minute and watched as all she had said sank in. Helen had whitened by degrees, and now she was working her way red.

"How dare you come in here and accuse me of such-"

"Oh, I'm not," Sara said cutting Helen off "I'm just letting you know after your confections; I have decided to press charges." Sara smiled. "I would say I won, but it was never a competition." Sara rose and walked to the door. After she knocked three times she looked back at Helen "You know, you could have just let him be happy." Helen looked over at Sara just as she walked out of the room.

It was dinner time by the time Sara and Jared were done with all the police business. They were quiet all the way home. Once Jared was in the driveway he looked over at Sara and grabbed her hand.

"Are you ok?" He asked.

"I will be, once everything settles back down." She answered looking over at him.

"Are things ever settled down?" He couldn't help the smile that came across his face. She smiled back at him.

"Well, how about just not this crazy," Sara said then met him as he leaned in for a kiss.

"Let's go see what's for dinner I'm starting," Jared said getting out of the truck. Sara waited as she knew Jared liked opening her door. "So, what is this week's special?" He asked and just like that he had her mind on the bakery. They were talking specials when they walked into the kitchen and found it full of life.

Abby was pulling something out of the oven, Morgan was chopping what looked like salad. Eddie was pulling a beer from the fridge, yelling at Andrew if he wanted one, who yelled back God yes. Kadie came from upstairs with a package of wipes in one hand and new baby clothes in the other. Just as Graham yelled for her to hurry up.

Sara looked up at Jared "You sure you're up for this kind of crazy?" Jared looked down at her and smiled "I am, as long as I'm with you."